LOVE CRAZY
A Family Memoir

Selby Fleming McPhee

Martin Sisters Publishing

In Memory of my brother

Thomas Talbot Fleming

1927-2008

Above, Tommy and Selby

DEDICATION

For my grandsons

Jackson Holmberg Meyers
Soren Holmberg Meyers
Alexander Owen Skinner
Theodore Elias Skinner

Jack and Peggy

ACKNOWLEDGEMENTS

Grateful thanks go to my cousins John Fleming Polk, Jocelyn Fleming Gutchess, Philip Fleming, Susan Gutchess, Jean Talbot, Harry Talbot, Elizabeth Blunt Wainwright, and Mary Blunt Henson, and to Phyllys Betts Fleming for sharing their memories and providing valuable information about the Fleming and Talbot families. I appreciate the help of Thomas Jackal at UGI Utilities in providing archived copies of the company newsletter, the UGI Circle. I thank Judy Gemmel, archivist at Moravian Academy, and Rose Simon, librarian at Salem Academy, for researching my mother's records on my behalf. I thank John Holmberg for braving brambles, broom sticks and the research section of the Burlington Public Library to do Fleming research on my behalf. I am grateful to Melissa Newman for guiding me through the publishing process. I am forever indebted to my writing companions Cynthia Snyder, Carole Metzger, Stasha Seaton, Jen Hackler, Margaret Smith, Molly Reilly, Diana Parsell, Snigdha Prakash, Mollie Foster, Patsy Morgenstern, Kay Neer, Ann Cale, and most especially Sara Mansfield Taber, for their careful reading and thoughtful critiques of this book in progress. For their constant love and encouragement, I want to thank my daughters Katrina Winsor Holmberg and Erika Fleming Holmberg, and my husband Henry Roemer McPhee, who gives me courage every single day.

1943

Selby

SEVENTY-SIXTH U.S. NAVAL CONST. BATTALION
C/O FLEET POST OFFICE
SAN FRANCISCO, CALIFORNIA
17 December 1943

My Darling Selby Anne:

   I feel a little like a new member of a Lonely Hearts club, writing to a girl I've never seen, but with whose pictures and descriptions I have fallen in love. Pretty, plump and fun loving – who could resist you? I'm a little dubious about offering my qualifications as a father, but it's only fair that you should know the facts, so here goes: In what is hopefully called my early forties, my hair is gray and painfully sparse on top. My chest still leads my tummy by some six inches (put that way, it sounds better) and my height and weight are above average. Beyond that, I seem to have two of everything in good condition, including teeth. I believe I have you there...

By nature a peace-loving person, I find myself, at the moment, in the uniform of a Naval Officer, because our country is engaged in a war against ruthless enemies. If it should seem strange to you that a man of my age should go off and leave his family, of his own free will – please understand that an inner compulsion made him do it, because he felt he could contribute something, because he wanted to feel the pride that goes with so serving, and because he couldn't be happy with himself if he hadn't. And because, for once in his life, he wanted to feel the equal of any man – with a sense of accomplishment, respected, and reasonably confident. This he has achieved – but it does not lessen any the longing he has to be <u>home</u>, with his wife, his son, and his daughter, whom he loves so very much. Now do you understand a little better, Selby?

You already know what a swell mother you have – but you won't know for many years that it wasn't easy for her to have you, and that this war business, with all the trouble and worry that it entails at home, was made many times harder for her by my being away. But you have made her very happy, and I know that you more than compensate for all the sacrifices she has made – and continues to make. You and that wonderful big brother of yours – I can almost see your eyes lighting up and following him around when he is near you. You already know that he is strong and friendly and good. But I can tell you some other things about Tommy – qualities that you are too little to perceive. That he is honest and loyal, and that he is sensitive, imaginative and determined. These qualities he got largely from Peggy (with some of her temper, too) and I can tell you, with these two on your side you have the best friends anybody in the world could have.

Maybe it won't be too long before we are all together as a family again. I can't even try to tell you how badly I want that time to come. In the meantime, I'll just have to be satisfied with pictures and a lock of hair. I'd send you a lock (well – strand) of mine if I thought it would help – but I'm afraid when you first see me I'll be just another strange man. But that strangeness won't be for long, will it?

It's time now, Selby for your father to say good night, and Merry Christmas, and here's a kiss, and God bless you.

~ With all my love, Jack   Lt. J .J. Fleming, Jr. USNR

2011
Letters

I think of the scene, my father sitting down at a jerry-rigged desk, perhaps a teak slab on boxes, in his bachelor quarters, up the hill overlooking the Navy Seabees construction site on Oahu in the Territory of Hawaii. Perhaps there was a warm tropical breeze riffling through the palms outside, lifting the corner of his airmail stationery as he wrote this first letter to me, his unseen baby daughter. I imagine that he might have been looking at a photo of me, an infant, that my mother, Peggy, or my brother, Tommy, might have sent him and he, hopeless romantic and helpless charmer that he was, used the words of a suitor to introduce himself to me. Clearly he thought of my mother, who would read the letter, still angry that he had left her and *volunteered* of all things to go to war when he was, at forty-two, not even really eligible, and he hoped his words would woo her once again, and she would begin to forgive him.

I see my mother opening the letter at home in Philadelphia, with winter coming and the storm windows still in the garage, unhung, thinking of him in that tropical paradise where the air was heavy with the scent of ti flowers and plumeria and hibiscus, and tossing it away, weeping with rage. How *could* he make himself sound like such a hero, such a *patriot*, when he had left her at home with all the work on the house that was never finished? How could he leave her with the endless mountain of bills, and a baby she may have wanted, but who cried for her, who needed to be fed and clothed and bathed and comforted? The fact that she had a baby nurse to do all of those things would not have mitigated her outrage. Maybe Tommy, home from school at the end of the day, picked up the letter and felt for his father, trying so hard as usual.

I first read this, my first letter from my father, when I was 41 years old. I remember feeling moved and thrilled, and then disappointed, hurt, resentful that so much of it was written to placate my mother, whose disappointment cast a shadow over our lives, whose needs would, and did, always come first. Such was my level of animus toward my mother then – my mother, the drama queen, always the center of attention.

I thought it was so predictable that she would not have shown me this letter, this lovely, winning welcome to my world, before. My mother knew the letter was written to her, but I know that it was also written to me. That she was evidently going to have to share my father's flirtatious charm with me must have come as a shock.

I found my father's first letter to me among hundreds of others, in 1984, in a box in an upstairs closet of my parents' house, just as we were moving them into a retirement community. Some letters, in my mother's or father's handwriting, were bundled with old rubber bands and scraps of identifying information (in my mother's hand) – "Jack's war letters," for example. Tommy's letters home and my own, from camp and college, were tucked loosely into the box. On the top of the box was written, in my father's brisk all-caps engineer's print, *"PERSONAL LETTERS OF*

MR. AND MRS. J.J. FLEMING, JR. – TO BE DESTROYED UNOPENED" – an invitation if there ever was one.

Instead of hiding a dark story, my parents' letters introduced a couple I never knew, besotted with each other and with life, adventurous, energetic, hopeful, playful. They tell a story of an instant attraction, physical, emotional, and intense, that addicted each to the other. In them, I met my young father, a handsome, popular college boy, a tennis player who could sing like a dream, an engineer in training who wrote poetry, a boy who wanted to be taken seriously, but whose eyes wandered to coonskin coats and handsome shoes, who couldn't manage his money to save his life. And I met my young mother, a pretty, coy, coquettish, vivacious, and popular brown-eyed girl with a dollop of bad girl energy and an appetite for a life of romantic encounter, a poor student who longed to be smart, perhaps even to be seen as an intellectual, who longed for money and culture, the life of a sort of *grande dame*.

The letters tell of an ardent young couple, persistently naïve, hungry for social status, for a life that reflected their glamorous times, who met and secretly married in 1923 when they hardly knew each other, and then blundered (and sometimes danced) their way through financial hardships and false starts with more naïve courage than anyone ever gave them credit for. I feel this because I followed their patterns, as offspring do, stumbling through marital and financial difficulties of my own with the same blind instinct to get up and try again another day. I like to think there is a kind of courage to it.

My parents' stories are told in the idiom of the early 20th century that casually, incidentally, paint a textured picture of daily life in their times. They tell of books and movies and great events, of the new jazz music and vaudeville, of bathtub gin and speakeasies and wireless radios and Ford motorcars and presidential elections and Lindbergh's solo flight.

Reading their letters, I see my father in his description of himself, moonstruck, writing from college of balling his hands into a fist so that his fingernails cut into his palms, such was the agony of his yearning for my mother. And my mother writing back soothing letters, almost maternal in her tenderness for him. Then I think of him, thirty-some years later, finding peace in the living room reading Dorothy Sayers with a cigarette and a scotch, while my mother sat in her bedroom bunker, fresh from some outburst, some perceived wound, wondering why he wouldn't come to bed.

When I was born, my parents had already been married twenty years, and my brother was in his last year of secondary school. Middle aged, fatigued, discouraged, and chronically at a standoff, they teetered, and our lives teetered, between my mother's hungry need for attention and my father's defeated response, his resignation, knowing that he could never satisfy her need but not strong enough to forgive himself. It was then that my mother created the dramas that punctuated our daily lives and brought her to center stage, retreating behind a locked bedroom door shouting weeping accusations that my father was cruel, unloving, disloyal, irresponsible, and weak, a failure, and my father, bowing under the weight of her condemnation, begged for forgiveness that never came.

That was when my mother's unhappiness – or was it more? – plunged her into nocturnal terrors from which she awoke – and woke us up – with that strange relentless moan that was part of her nightmares, an escalating, oscillating tone that ended in a piercing scream, with my father pleading "Peggy, Peggy, wake up, you're dreaming!" and all of us lying in our beds afterwards, urging our lurching heartbeats back into rhythm.

Were these dramas under her control, did she deliberately stage them or was she suffering from some imbalance, some condition that held her in its grip? Now I'm tempted to name her behavior.

From books I've read, I would say that she had a borderline personality disorder. But I'm not a therapist.

And why did my father never fight back? We kept asking ourselves that. What made him so vulnerable, when someone else – my brother, for instance – could stand up to her demands without even raising his voice – when a mere "cut it out, Peggy" from him could stop her in her tracks.

Was Jack weak, or was he just weak with love?

Amazingly, I was given an opportunity to get to the bottom of my parents' story. I could try to give it, if not a happy ending, at least a broader focus. Seeing the whole picture, I might be able to fix the story for myself.

What happened? That's what I wanted to know. Was it history, hardship, *life* that changed their relationship? Or was their meeting the onset of a perfect storm of need between a beautiful and charming boy and a beautiful and emotional girl, each with outsized ambitions and matching fragile egos?

I didn't know what I would find in that box of letters, but I did know what interested me – not my own letters, or even my brother Tommy's, but letters that would bring alive the past, like a scratchy newsreel of the twentieth century, maybe even some of the nineteenth, with my mother and father and their parents in the starring roles. I also wanted to know how those people whose genes I carry wove themselves into American life in their times.

Incredibly, with the letters, I could turn back the years. My family's history is accessible, made tangible and intimate by maternal historians. My father's mother, Mary Fleming, preserved his letters all her life, from his childhood and school years all the way through the hard slogging years of the Depression. Did my father, the adored baby of his family, learn at home to be so timid, so submissive as a man? Did he learn at home that the best he had to offer the world was a winning charm? Did he never learn that he was strong and smart, too?

My mother's mother, Frances (Fanny) Talbot, saved letters from her husband, Harry Talbot, a dominating character in Talbot family dramas, and from her mother-in- law, Jennie Talbot, who wrote chirpy news from the western prairie of Canada, where she was a homesteader. Fanny saved my mother's most defiant letters from school, presumably as evidence for Harry of the burden she bore in trying to raise this angry, rebellious child who would become my mother. Were the seeds of my mother's fiery need there, in her childhood, in her genetic history, finding fallow ground in the dysfunction of an earlier generation?

My family's story is about an era in American life, and about an exhausting, blindingly intense, volatile, and passionate relationship. It is also, inevitably, a story of class in America – the class into which each of my parents, both children of professional men, was born, the class they aspired to – their dreams of an elegant life, and the impenetrable class they found themselves just outside of in that most famous fortress of the American aristocracy, Philadelphia. Class fascinated both of them, drove their ambitions, and caused their most bitter disappointments.

My parents' fascination with each other and their times led them to save each others' letters, as if to preserve the evidence for a later dramatic or literary retelling.

That's where I come in.

The letters narrate the life of my father, John Joseph Fleming, Jr. – Jack – born in 1901 in Burlington, Iowa, and my mother, Margaret Alexander Talbot Fleming – Peggy – born in 1903 in Buffalo, New York; my brother John Joseph Fleming III, born in 1925 in Chicago, a robust baby who died from septicemia after one week of life; my brother Thomas Talbot Fleming – Tommy – born in 1927 in Chicago, and me, the caboose, born in Philadelphia in 1943.

My father grew up in a household of unpublished poets, and he in particular had a gift, perhaps an Irish gift, for storytelling, scene setting, deft caricatures, vivid details. In this retelling I draw on his gift to set their story in context. And I have my own need. Born into a family that had already completed the trajectory of half a life, with its habits and history, I worried that I might be left out. In 1950, when the census taker came to the house, I, at seven, wanted to be sure that I was counted in the census, that my parents not forget to tell him that there was a new member of the household – me.

I have always had a yearning to be included in the party, never quite satisfied. I attribute this to my placement in my family, but perhaps it also has to do with the sadness and distraction that existed in the household of my childhood. My mother's emotional needs were supreme and I think I was, like other children in fragile families, to some extent displaced by the presence, the supremacy of that need, the center stage she occupied.

I don't know why the box had that provocative "To be destroyed..." instruction. I believe my mother stored these letters away so that she could one day write about her life, a suspicion confirmed by a note in the box, in her handwriting, hinting at a story outline, listing "the twenties, the Depression, the war..." I believe my father was the author of the warning on the box top, wishing to preserve a little privacy, his heart's center, which was his deep love and need for her.

Have I invaded their privacy? Yes, certainly I have, but it's my story, too. I did ask my father for permission to read the letters, and he gave it, but I have to confess I caught him in a distracted moment, on a day when we were dismantling his house, striking the set to move him to a retirement community.

To tell their story, I refer to my parents by their names, Jack and Peggy. For so much of their story, they are characters who were not yet my parents that it seems right to refer to them that way. What forces made my parents who they were, and what on earth was all the intensity about? In the battlefield that was their marriage, what kept them together? Was it love, or were they both crazy? Or is that what love is?

They are all gone now, even Tommy. I have the letters to help me make sense of it all. They are my invitation to the party.

1923

Spring
Jack and Peggy

Ithaca, April 17, Jack to his mother

Dearest Mother,

I know you will be surprised to learn that I just returned from Philadelphia this morning, where I have been for over a week visiting Skip Gibney and then Rod – and as a consequence I did not get your letters until just now, the Catholic Club having forwarded them here. Needless to say I had a perfectly glorious time – you know I must have, or I wouldn't have been three days late getting back. I hope you won't worry about the lateness, tho, mother, because I can make up the work, and I am sure it will be all right. But I must tell you everything I did...

I left for New York a week ago Wednesday, arriving there that night expecting to see Lib, only to find that she wasn't well and couldn't see anyone that night. I settled myself at the Catholic

Club and called up everyone I knew that I could think of, to no avail. So I had to retire early, and start the holidays with a dead evening, and there is nothing more lonesome than to be alone in New York. Thursday afternoon Lib and I had tea at the Ambassador and that was the one and only time I saw her. Libby, by the way, is sick of Who's Whosing and has reverted to cooking lessons and social service – and even contemplates taking bookkeeping. That night Chad Head, who drove down in his Ford, and I went to the Intercollegiate Dance at Delmonico's, where it was sort of a combined Cornell-Dartmouth Junior Week party, and we knew lots of people, and had an awfully good time. There I met Reggie Solomon, a graduate whom I used to know pretty well here, and he asked me to come stay at his apartment the following night. So Friday I moved to his place on West 70th Street.

Friday evening Reggie and Phil Nichols and his girl and I went to another Intercollegiate affair at the Aston, which was practically a repetition of the Delmonico dance. Then Saturday noon I took the train to Philadelphia, and at four o'clock Skip and I met at the Bellevue... We went to a dance at the West Chester Country Club that night, which was a lot of fun...

Well, Monday morning Rod came out for me, and we drove into his place. Then I met Peggy Talbot, who lives in Glenside – and there is the high point of the vacation...

This is where it all started. My parents met on a blind date. They always told me that it was my mother's car that brought them together. Rod, my father's roommate at the time in the Delta Upsilon fraternity house at Cornell, vaguely knew Peggy. Though Rod had access to a car, the fact that Peggy also did made her particularly appealing as an extra girl on their travels.

Jack continued his letter to his mother with an enthusiastic candor:

...Thereafter I saw Peggy daily, sometimes with Rod and another girl and sometimes not. Tuesday we drove to Atlantic City

24

in Peggy's car, and liked rolling up and down the boardwalk so well, we went again Wednesday in Rod's car. After that, the financial supply was exhausted, and we spent the rest of the week going to the movies, window shopping, and occasionally riding about in Rod's car – while I practically boarded at the Talbots, who were very nice to me. And I know I needn't tell you that Peggy is a peach. So much for the vacation and needless to say, Philadelphia is now the Promised Land.

I love to imagine my father, Jack Fleming, foxtrotting off the pages of a Scott Fitzgerald novel, who's whosing in New York, meeting a girl for tea at the Ambassador, going to intercollegiate dances at the Delmonico and the Aston with friends whose names are Reggie and Chad. Libby, the girl he went to see in New York was a new graduate of Spence School whom Jack had been seeing for a year or so. I'd like to know how Jack met her, a wealthy New York girl who would not have crossed his path easily. And it's interesting that Jack's mother, back in Burlington, Iowa, knew about Libby, and not only that, she also approved of her. A year earlier, in the spring of 1922, my grandmother had sent Jack a check so that he could go to New York for the weekend to see Lib – a weekend Jack described in a May 1922 letter:

...Your letter with the check enclosed came a week ago yesterday, just in time for me to telegraph Libby and leave for New York – and I certainly had a wonderful weekend. Erskine Douglas called for us and we all drove out to the Douglas' in Tarrytown. It was a beautiful place – way up on a hill overlooking the Hudson – and of course we all had a marvelous time. Saturday night we went to dances at the new Westchester-Biltmore Country Club – which looks like the Edgewater Beach Hotel – and the American Yacht Club at Rye. Then Sunday we just played around – had tea at the Manursing Island Club at Rye – on the Sound – and then, of course, I had to start back to Ithaca. It certainly was sweet of you to want me to go – and let me – and I appreciate it a lot. I certainly

would hate to have missed it. Lib had just graduated from Spence - she was quite thrilled about being all through school for life.

Jack sounds completely comfortable running with this well-heeled crowd, the kind of people his mother approved of. A year later, in April 1923, he was finishing what should have been his last year at Cornell University, where he was studying for an undergraduate degree in civil engineering.

That same year, my mother, Peggy Talbot, had just graduated from Salem Academy, a Moravian girls' boarding school in North Carolina. In the spring of 1923, she was living at home in Glenside, Pennsylvania, going to movies, playing bridge with her childhood friends Lottie and Mary, attending dances at Lafayette College and Princeton University with boys she knew, and wandering, bored, around the house. Her father, Harry, who worked in New York City and supervised the family from afar, indulged Peggy with a fur coat and the use of the family Ford, while her mother, who disapproved of Peggy's cavalier behavior, tried to rein in her social activities. When she met Jack, Peggy was a month shy of her twentieth birthday. Jack was twenty-two.

Jack and Peggy had known each other for a mere six days when they wrote these first letters to each other:

Jack to Peggy, Ithaca, April 17, 1923
Peggy darling,

I love to write that, but if you only knew how much I wish I could be saying it to you now. I didn't know I could miss anyone so much – honestly, Peggy, I have never felt like this before towards anyone. I've been wandering about all day in a sort of blue daze...

The trip back to Ithaca was just about as pleasant as I expected. I conversed intermittently with your friend Ambler, who is a darn good egg by the way, as far as Bethlehem, where I whiled away the time between trains by munching soggy lunch counter sandwiches in the palatial station. Ambler was all for loaning me money for a berth, but I felt that I had enough people on the cuff as it was, and besides, I was in such a frame of mind that I didn't care where I slept. ... It was the cold gray dawn when I hit this hole, and two hours more sleep didn't help much, except that I dreamt constantly of you, dearest, which made more depressing than ever the waking realization that instead of a short trip to you, I had the same old dull grind of classes ahead of me, and they never sounded so dry and uninteresting as this morning, whenever I snapped out of it and heard what was going on. The amount of work I have to do is discouraging.

I am enclosing an old snap, the only one I have, and I'll send you one of the big ones tomorrow. I have yours cut out and in the back of my watch now, and the more I look at it, which is most of the time, the better I like it.

O Peggy sweetheart, I love you so awfully much and I miss you so terribly. Saying goodbye to you last night was the hardest thing I ever had to do in my life. I know I don't need to tell you how wonderful it was being with you those six days. I'll always remember everything we did together... and I'll always love you.

~ Jack

Peggy to Jack, Glenside, April 17, 1923
I love you!!!!

It seems so strange and awful to know that you're in Ithaca today, and not just about at City Line on the way to Glenside – ouch!! It's hard not to feel all funny again!!

I could have choked Rod and Johnny last night. I wanted to stay so badly – and put you on the train ALONE. They were such an unsympathetic mob. And then after you left, Rod had to encourage me by telling me what a vile correspondent you were. But I'm not specially worried 'cause I believe you and you said you'd write.

Jack, I never had such a darlin' time in my whole life as I had while you were here – that's the truth.

27

I'm going to keep every one of MY promises – so please study hard dear and try to come down for the Penn relays – if not, it's only about two months 'til commencement. That's long – but we're always optimistic, aren't we?

~ *Just, Peggy*

My parents were buffaloed, dazed, bamboozled, felled by love. And when they fell, they found a beautiful world that sparkled like diamonds after rain, one that glowed blue on a beautiful spring day and incandescent on a moonlit night. *Of course, it's a blue Monday without having you near,* Jack wrote, *but it's a delicate, sky-blue, one that's quite bearable, because I can feel so very close to you. It seems as if I never appreciated spring before, never noticed sunsets, and moonlight, too.*

The rhythms of their lives were redefined by the schedules of the U.S. Postal Service. In a few days, they had each discovered in the other someone they could believe in, someone they felt they could trust with their most intimate thoughts and hopes, someone for whom they wanted to take responsibility. And before they parted, they had confessed their affection for each other, using that magic word "love" to light up each other's world.

In those six days, Jack must have confided in Peggy that he was worried about his grades and the likelihood that he would not graduate in June as expected. Peggy was already invested in Jack's success and she took on the responsibility to help him in that effort. It takes a little piecing together of the evidence, but it would seem that Jack had been fighting an uphill battle to stay in college for at least the two previous years.

In July 1921, at the end of his sophomore year at Cornell, Jack had written a letter to his father apologizing for failing to earn sufficient marks to stay in (or as he says, keep from "busting out of") college:

...Now about busting out. It was my fault. I should not have tried to carry too much outside activity and I should have worked harder because I can when I try. I feel badly about it of itself, but I feel a hundred times worse on account of you and mother. I guess you haven't much faith left in me. It is not looked upon as a disgrace here, but I wish I could express what I mean, Dad. It's your feelings and what you and mother think that counts, and I want you to know I realize that. Of course, camping here with the C.E. (civil engineering) *professors, I've gotten to know them intimately, and they all speak matter of factly of my returning in February, or going to summer school and being readmitted in the fall – but of course that is out of the question. I won't have you make any more useless sacrifices for me. It's going to be pretty much of a wrench for me to leave Cornell for good, and I could never be satisfied at Notre Dame or any other place, but I guess there's no alternative, and I don't think work will kill me. Things look pretty black for me right now, but what hurts most is the thought of you and mother, and how inconsiderate I've been to you both...*

A "reinstatement fee" was paid to the college in February 1922, indicating that Jack stayed home for the first semester of his junior year before being allowed to re-enroll at Cornell in January 1922. He must have been trying to make up a lot of course credits in his last year and a half at Cornell. It was against that troubling academic history that Jack threw himself into his new romance. *Cy Siegfried and I have been working on Bill Belden who is the proud possessor of a little red Buick – to persuade him that he really should see the Penn Relays and, incidentally, take us along. If I ever get there, I don't care if I never see a track meet. I got "Morning Will Come" for the house piano pounder. He plays it and I just wander off by myself and close my eyes and think. Naturally, I don't get away with that sort of stuff unnoticed, and I've been in for a lot of kidding of late...*

29

Jack was referring to what must have become *their* song during that first week together in Philadelphia. It was Al Jolson's 1923 hit song "Morning will Come," whose refrain, sung in slow foxtrot time, was:

"Don't mind the darkness, morning will come
Shadows are bound to go by
And when they fly
Rosy dawn will kiss the sky
So don't mind your troubles
We all have some
Watch for the star of the dawn and keep saying
Morning will come."

A class history in the 1923 yearbook, the *Cornellian*, describes the sober state of the campus when Jack's class, the first post-World War I class, arrived in Ithaca for their freshman year in the fall of 1919. Though the "Great War" had ended in November 1918, troops were still coming home and casualties were still being reported from Europe.

"There was an emptiness about the Campus which even the day-old freshman could not fail to notice," the class history reports. *"On every hand, Upper-classmen were lamenting friends and classmates who...would never more tread the Campus. On every hand, there were those who expressed doubt as to ever seeing Cornell again as it was before the war, of ever being able to catch up the threads where they had been severed."*

Historians report that college enrollment grew exponentially after the war, and this new generation of pleasure-seeking youth, sick of other people's wars, viewed college as their own playground. Jack certainly did his part, and that was a part of his difficulty. The 1923 yearbook shows that he was a member of the Delta Upsilon fraternity at Cornell, where he lived, a member of Pyramid, the civil engineering society, and one of 19 members of a social club called Majura, which he described in a 1922 letter to

30

his mother: *...Dad asked about the Majura Society. Election to it is in recognition of doing something, or at least trying to do something, in outside activities on the hill, besides – I wouldn't say it to anyone but you – being well liked. Nearly everybody (myself excluded) is "somebody" on the hill – athletes, managers, and so forth. Its purpose is mainly to bring about a better friendship between the best men of your own class, the ones you most want to know now, and afterwards, after college. So now you know, and I hope you're glad I made it.*

A tall, truly handsome boy with brown hair parted toward the middle and slicked back into a pomaded wave, Jack performed in the 1923 Masque revue "Ulysses of Ithaka," which received such thunderous appreciation during Junior Week they added an extra – sold out – performance. As if that were not enough, he was also manager of a Cornell rowing team. Cornell sits at the end of Lake Cayuga, one of New York's Finger Lakes, Lake Beebe, and Fall Creek, which bisects the campus with dramatic gorges and romantic foot bridges, offering an environment of abundant natural beauty. Any trip on campus, to the post office, to class or to dinner involves an energetic trek up or downhill.

What he didn't do was pay enough attention to his studies, ever, but most particularly in the spring semester of 1923, after he met Peggy. Though she had exacted promises from him to study hard, it was too late. Moonstruck, he read novels – he was an addictive reader all his life – and wrote poetry for Peggy, waited for the mail to come in at the campus post office, and badgered fraternity brothers with cars, hoping to talk them into a weekend trip to Philadelphia.

One of his poems will suffice to communicate his besotted state: *Sweetest, I feel sheepish and embarrassed as the devil when I picture you reading this – it sounds as banal as a popular song, but you know what I mean to convey...*

I love the laugh in your brave brown eyes

I love the lilt in your voice –
What else can I do but love you, Peg?
I have no choice!
I love the light in your soft brown hair
The touch of your slender hand
But I love you most because I know
You understand.
I can't forget the thrill of your kiss
And the pang when I had to go
I miss you, Peggy dear, because
I love you so.

Meanwhile, Jack's mother was decidedly unhappy about his exuberant report of his spring vacation. She must have been disappointed that Libby was disappearing from the picture, and that Jack seemed so taken with a girl she knew nothing about, who, of all appalling things, was allowed to drive a car to Atlantic City. Though her letter is gone, Jack's response tells the tale:

Ithaca, April 22
Dearest Mother –

Your letter came yesterday, and I was awfully glad to get it. You do not seem harsh at all, mother, and I think it is wonderful to have you so concerned with what I do. I know you want what is best for me, and I value your opinions more than anyone's in the world – and for that reason your letter did make me feel badly, because what I did has upset you. I realize, too, that I acted wrongly in staying over, and I'm sorry I did it. It was entirely my own (foolish) idea, and no one influenced or persuaded me in the least – not directly anyway. I was, in fact, advised against it. As for Libby, we're darn good friends, and I hope always will be – frankly, not as intimate as a year ago. And she was mighty sweet to me, and I saw her in New York as much as her engagements would permit until the following week. Naturally I did not crave

32

wandering about New York alone for three days until I could see Lib again. As for leaving the Catholic Club, I thought that would be a means of lowering expenses, and much as I like being there, it is a lonely place for me. Visiting Skip Gibney was the most innocuous – however pleasant – weekend imaginable. And much as there is undesirable about Rod, he is a good boy, and welcomed me, and offered me companionship. As for Peggy, she is not a particular friend of Rod's – a rather new acquaintance in fact – and she was not allowed to drive to Atlantic City – which I suppose makes it all the worse. But mother, I like her very, very much. Give me credit for some judgment; and whatever was wrong, I was in the main blameworthy. Give me credit for some initiative. The fact remains that I was discontented in New York, and in Philadelphia I distinctly wasn't.

Mother dearest, I think you misinterpreted my letter. If I needed comfort, you know I would come to you first for it. I am so sorry I made you feel badly, mother. I wish I could have come home – that would have been better than anything. But I did come back here happy, and your letter did make me blue. What you say means so much to me.

~ Your loving son, Jack

At home, no one gave Jack any credit for having reliable judgment and by now, that must have hurt. He knew how to sweet talk his mother, too, and though he surely didn't think going home would have been "better than anything," he was very attached to her. Neither of my parents would have seriously considered walking away from their parents' authority to define their own rules. Nevertheless, Jack and Peggy were coming of age in a generation that would remake American culture for the rest of the 20th century. More than a million American doughboys came home to a less sophisticated America having seen Paris *and* the horrors of battle. The war taught them that life is short.

33

My parents' generation was a disillusioned age cohort that felt it had been handed a badly injured world, where the young had died in battle against a remote enemy for causes they didn't care that much about – in Woodrow Wilson's words, "to make the world safe for democracy." And if they were going to die, they were going to live first, and with a vengeance, and with all the new toys at their disposal – motor cars, crystal radio sets with new possibilities for connection to the larger world through broadcasting programs, moving pictures and, thanks to Sigmund Freud, a new candor about sex. And though prohibition against the consumption of alcohol had already been made law by an amendment to the Constitution, liquor was clearly freely available and the young were more than willing to break the law to get it.

By 1923, Fitzgerald had already published his first two novels, *This Side of Paradise,* in 1920, and *The Beautiful and the Damned,* in 1922. His books defined the age, the Roaring Twenties, dominated by a war weary, madcap, cynical younger generation hell bent on breaking all the old rules of the culture.

Peggy was the beneficiary of a new era of freedom for women in America. A mere three years before these letters were written, women had finally earned the right to vote in elections. War had left them more independent, more interested in a college education and a job, on a more equal footing in relationships, from sex to marriage. And yet, in the following letter, coy and cute as I think it is intended to be, Peggy betrays her frustration with the constraints she has felt growing up a girl in a post-Victorian age, and especially, I would learn, in the emotional landscape of her family.

Peggy to Jack, early May

Oh, it's the most precious day. You know, cool, but you can just see the little buds coming out. A make believe day, when you want to be a freckle faced, red headed bad little boy, so you could play "hooky" and go runnin' or fishin' or sumpin'. Why aren't you free so you could help make believe too. Found a penny yesterday – do you s'pose that means you're really coming for the Penn relays!! Try.

If I wasn't a darned old girl, we could be "roomies" at college now, and buy a Ford and spend our vacations together, and then keep bachelor apartments. I always wanted to be a man and have a buddy just like you. But then if I were a man, you'd have to fall in love someday – and I'd be mad again. So I guess it's as broad as it is long.

All seriousness now. I love you terribly, Jack. And it's specially lonesome without you – cause it is so nice.

Did Peggy really want Jack to be her "buddy?" Did she really have a secret persona, a freckle faced red headed bad boy, or were her feelings about being a woman reflective of the times? My mother told me many times that she hated women (which didn't make me feel particularly good), but there was nothing ambiguous about Peggy's female-ness. In fact, she made the most of a kind of dependent feminine frailty – she even asked Jack to broach the subject to her parents for her when he invited her, soon after this, to come to Cornell Senior Week in June.

In 1923, girls scandalized the older generation by driving cars, wearing clothes that exposed their legs and bobbing their hair in a style identified with Bohemians and Bolsheviks, and smoking cigarettes and drinking alcohol – in public! Peggy was decidedly not Bohemian, though she might have liked to think of herself that way, nor was she a Bolshevik or even political. In fact, there was a cultural divide between the feminists who brought about women's right to vote and the flappers, so called, who were disdainful of politics but reveled in newfound personal freedoms for women.

I would say that Peggy was neither, exactly. Though she didn't go to college or work or, so far as I know, have any interest in voting, she would nevertheless have been recognized as a

35

participant in the *zeitgeist* of her era. She had a car and knew how to drive. Despite her inadequacies as a student and her fear in the presence of people she considered more literate or intellectual than she was, she knew how to resist authority. She dressed and cropped her hair in the new flapper style. And though I feel quite sure she was not sexually experienced, she and Jack were obviously both interested in, and conversant with, Freud – and sex.

Ithaca, May 10, Jack to Peggy
Darling –

You don't know how glad I was to get your letter – cheered me up so. I was certainly low – no chide, I was at sea level...

How well I do remember how we sat and talked in the Bellevue – about religion and such things, and I held your hand and we were looking at each other, and therefore I thought lots more about you than what we were talking about! When one loves a person – Oh! so very much – and one is looking at said person – you know it's hard to concentrate on some abstract theory. And that same holds right here – even when said sweet person is three hundred miles away. Speaking of concentration, darling, remember how we "distracted" each other while driving, en route to Atlantic City?... Peggy, I know I have loved you since that very first day. I can remember every incident so plainly – when you came for us – the ride down – the boardwalk – ah, just everything. And when we had that last puncture, and you kissed my dirty hands ...

Jack's mother would have been distressed to learn how much time and energy he devoted to schemes that would take him back to Philadelphia or bring Peggy to Cornell. A train trip from Ithaca to Philadelphia involved an overnight ride along the Lehigh Valley branch of the Reading Railroad through western New York and northwestern Pennsylvania to Bethlehem, where Jack would wait in the cavernous Reading station for a train connection to Philadelphia. The trip involved a significant expenditure of time he could not afford away from his school work and of money that Jack, always out of pocket, would have to borrow from one of his friends.

Peggy didn't know it yet, but money, and Jack's inability to hold on to it, was a serious issue and another source of shame in his life. Back in July 1921, Jack had been forced to write the following to his father:

I won't try to tell you how I feel about everything because, as you infer, that won't do any good now – and my being sorry doesn't help matters any, does it? It hurts quite a bit to realize what a poor opinion of me you have, but of course I deserve it. I won't try to crawl out of anything. First of all, I am enclosing bills amounting to about $240 – for clothing and shoes which I thought I needed, and bought during the year, without the consent of you or mother, and without thinking what a sacrifice it meant to you. I wish I could undo what I did, but I can't, and the bills have to be paid. I am enclosing receipts for the $300 which you sent me, mostly house bills as you can see, which I should have paid before. I always thought I was sparing with the monthly checks you sent me. I never had money to spend, but when the end of the month came around, I was always behind – and kept getting behind more and more. I wish I could give you a satisfactory explanation, Dad. I'd give anything if I only could, but I can only say that, although it would seem that way, I never deliberately squandered or wasted your money...

A year later, in 1922, Jack was back in the same boat. Though he had promised to turn over a new leaf with regard to his finances, his eyes had wandered to a snappy Norfolk tweed suit and some handmade English shoes that he had hoped to be able to pay for with the income from a summer job. But it was never enough:

This letter is for dad as well as you, of course, so I might as well include the expenses I must pay before I leave. There is an extra house assessment for work to be done on the house this summer – and I can't tell you how much I hate to say it – I've gotten behind my regular house and board bills to the amount of $75. I thought I was doing better this year – but I guess I'm not. I have hated to write it. I know how hard it is for Dad. But the fact remains that I must pay these, and then my ticket home besides...

Back to spring 1923, Peggy had been begging Jack to come back to Philadelphia for the Penn Relays, a track meet at the University of Pennsylvania, and studies and expenses be damned, Jack couldn't resist the opportunity to spend two precious days with her.

An automobile trip along the Lackawanna Trail in an open roadster, for most cars were open to the air in 1923, was cheaper than a train trip, assuming that Jack could talk a friend with a car into the trip, and pack in enough other boys to lower the shared costs. But long distance car trips were not only cold rides. With routine tire punctures, smoking gear boxes and chattering brakes, the automobiles were hazards in themselves. In this letter, Jack describes his trip back from that stolen weekend – a trip that calls to mind a Keystone Kops movie from the era, with a car zigzagging down the road out of control, careening through busy intersections, and all the passengers holding their hats.

Ithaca, May 1

Darling –

...Peggy, you know what a perfect time I had. When we left, and you were standing there in the doorway, it was as if the bottom dropped out of everything that counted – and I felt that crying impulse, too. That's the only way to describe the feeling.

And the boys were in such an irritating good humor. But that didn't last long, because before we left Glenside we had our first

38

puncture – the ominous beginning of the worst trip I can hope to have. To begin with, neither footbrake nor emergency worked at all. Then in Bethlehem, the reverse pedal broke, leaving low gear and a handy curb the only means of slowing the thing down. If you want a new sensation try driving a Ford without any brakes. Another puncture near the Water Gap helped matters – then a blowout in the most deserted part of the Poconos after dark, with the pump broken, frazzled the nerves a little more. At Scranton we thought we got things fixed up. It was midnight when we left, and I drove from there to Binghamton with three sleeping youths, a full moon, and a sharp wind for companionship. We got to Binghamton without mishap – luckily – for my thoughts were much nearer Roberts Avenue (Peggy's address) *than the Lackawanna Trail...then later, just as I was about to doze off in the back seat after leaving Binghamton, we were cursed with a burned oil bearing – you know the old familiar clank. But we wouldn't stop there, and we literally crawled on towards Ithaca in the cold light of early morning – such a pleasant feeling. Then – the last straw – coming down the long hill into Ithaca, low gear burned out in a cloud of smoke, leaving us coasting gaily down the hill with no means of slowing up. A quick turn into a side road stopped us, however, and we got out and left the damn thing, and trudged, dirty and sleepy, with bags and blankets, to the car line and thence to the house, arriving here about six-thirty this morning – four wrecks. It really was an awfully funny trip, but we found it hard to appreciate the humor of it.*

As the month of May went on, Jack's letters show he had increasing trouble focusing on Mechanics and Hydraulics, Bridge Building, Sewers, and the other dry courses required for a civil engineering degree. His academic problems were reaching a crisis point, but still he dreamt and schemed about ways to see Peggy:

Ithaca, May 24

Peggy sweetest –

... I am sorely tempted to come to Philadelphia this weekend, with favorable conditions (meaning of studies and transportation) and with the slightest encouragement, I am liable to come tearing down. Honestly, dearest, I think if I saw you, it would give me inspiration to finish out the year right. That sounds like a flimsy excuse just to see you – am I kidding myself, or letting love get the better of good judgment? Sometimes, though, often, I feel like saying to hell with good judgment, to hell with such trivial things as consequences – see Peggy and be happy. You know Freud says that it is bad to suppress desires, so if you get sudden news of my being awfully sick, you'll know what it is – I've been suppressing 'em too long.

~ Jack

Western Union telegram, May 25

Freud was right, but no finances. Guess I'll have to bear it till Senior Week. Truly disappointed, Jack

Peggy was now aware that Jack's mother didn't approve of her, (he had written her how unhappy he was about his mother's letter), and she was afraid she would be blamed if he failed to graduate from college on time. Though she was counting the days until Senior Week, she was not encouraging Jack to make any more road trips to Philadelphia:

May 12, Peggy to Jack

...Phil Nichols told me that you weren't studying very hard. Jack when you know I'd be responsible if you didn't pass – and how badly I'd feel I think you might. I'm not going to say any more about it, cause I don't want to be a dirty old nagger – and what I say doesn't seem to have any effect anyway.

Peggy's best efforts to be a good influence were not enough. By June Jack was preparing to face the inevitable disappointment of his parents. He was about to flunk out of college again in his senior year. He wrote this, demonstrating what was becoming a familiar pattern of self indulgence followed by self recrimination. The money problem again...

Ithaca, June 4, Jack to Peggy

Peggy darling –

Lord, what a hectic time this is – with my first final at eight in the morning – and, darling, I confess I'm worried sick – and am in a terribly depressed and nervous state. I feel sure that I'm going to bust out – and if I do, I'll have no one but my worthless self to blame. My family will be hurt and disappointed in me – and, dearest, I know you will feel it, too. Oh – if only I had this term to do over again – If I only hadn't said "tomorrow" so often – if I only had worried when I should have worried – and not used my love of reading as a cloak for pure laziness.

Besides, I have carelessly let myself run up a ridiculously large amount of bills – that, among other things, will displease my father greatly – and make me seem a terribly ungrateful sort of a son – which I don't mean to be at all. Oh – I'm disgusted with myself – for being a lazy, careless fool – and I'm afraid you will be too, as I know the family will. Sweetheart, this isn't a very cheerful letter to write you, but I feel so low. You'll believe in me won't you? If it weren't for our love now, I don't know what I would do.

~ Jack

Jack had one last stupid idea to defeat himself at the close of the year:

Ithaca, June 7, 1923

Sweetheart –

... I may see you within a few days! Phil Nichols has suggested that we start Saturday morning and bum in the direction of New York and Philadelphia – and the idea intrigues me greatly. It is just possible that we may do it, and if so, of course I'll let you know all the details.

I want to come down so badly, as I may not be able to after Senior Week, due to the family's lack of enthusiasm. Five precious days! Dearest, five days will help, but I won't be satisfied till it's always. I love you so very, very much.

Jack

"Always" was exactly what my love crazy parents had in mind, and by June, after a total of 13 days together (six days at spring vacation, two in early May, and another five during Senior Week), they were on a fast train to Always. Instead of sending Peggy home on a train and packing for a summer in Burlington, as dictated by his parents, Jack went back to Philadelphia with her and, in a fit of temporary insanity, they secretly married within the week.

It was a shaky, inauspicious beginning to a marriage of two people who hardly knew each other – a marriage that created the architecture of my life. Who were these two people? I go back to the early letters I found in the box, the letters that tell the stories of my parents when they were little children living a thousand miles from each other - letters saved by the mothers – to start their stories nearer the beginning of their lives.

First, Jack...

1910

Jacksonia Flamingo, the Great Pianist

May 5, 1910, Burlington, Iowa

Dear Mother,

I have been awfully lonesome for you, and I got a hundred in arithmetic at school but I don't know how much I got in my other studies. I will give you this as a present (a drawing of a hundred dollar bill) but be sure you spend it well (you may pay me back when you come home from Europe). I am going to the High School class play and we are going to have three seats from the front and I am going to smile at Polly and make her laugh. I met Father Mullally and I thought he was very nice. When you come home from Europe be sure and bring me a piece of Irish sod and I will sing you the song called "Has Anybody Here Seen Kelly?" which you heard Gilbert Wells sing. Cheer up, old girl!

Your sweetheart yet (even if you are away)

Jacksonia Flamingo

THE GREAT PIANIST

43

P.S. I will pray that you and Papa have a safe journey and please give half of my love to Papa and you can keep the other half yourself.

Jack was the last of six children born into a comfortable Catholic family in Burlington, Iowa, at the beginning of a new century, a beloved baby boy named for his father. His mother, Mary Bracken Fleming, was forty years old when Jack was born. His father, John Fleming, a banker, was fifty. When Jack wrote this letter, he was nine years old, writing to his parents who were on a trip to Ireland and Europe. Jack was at home with some of his sisters, the family servant, Minnie, and his maternal grandmother, Esther Bracken, who lived with the family.

An exuberant, irrepressible, busy boy, and with his grandparents, both born in Ireland, only recently gone, Jack understood well his provenance as a son of Erin.

May 10, Jack to his parents

I hope you crossed the ocean without getting seasick or having any bad storms. Grandma won the pink and white quilt when it was raffled off at a coffee last Wednesday. Dick Murray was here last Sunday and after he went home he sent Esther a five-lb. box of candy. He is going to send us a French bulldog after he has it trained well so it will have good manners in the house. Be sure you bring the piece of Irish sod when you come.

Jack lived in a universe mostly populated by women – his sisters, "Gran" Bracken, and his mother and father. He had one older brother, Philip (who was away at West Point in 1910), and four older sisters, Esther and Agnes, (both graduated from school), and Polly and Mary, who attended school in Burlington. The Fleming sisters were beautiful, cultured, strong willed, and much courted by Burlington boys – one of whom famously complained that the sign at the city limits should read "Burlington, City of 15,000 Friendly People … and the Fleming Girls." They lived in a house on South Hill, a house so fondly remembered that decades later, Jack and his siblings (and succeeding generations) made pilgrimages to see it on visits to Burlington.

Fifty years later, on such a pilgrimage, his sister Polly wrote of remembering the large oak paneled rooms with French doors, large fireplaces and deep windowsills *"where a child could curl up and read"* – a place that could accommodate *"Esther at the piano, surrounded by singers on a Sunday afternoon, Mary in the kitchen, surrounded too, and making tea and cinnamon toast, and how father slammed all the French doors, locking them, when he thought it was time for callers to leave at night."*

The house, a large Victorian in the Alpine Swiss Revival style, occupied (and still does) an entire city block, in the manner of Victorian properties, visible from four corners, with a *porte cochère* in front for arriving carriages, though it would soon accommodate a Ford motorcar, and an expansive lawn in back where Jack's sister Agnes, a poet, would write of watching her younger sisters dancing through the grass, then flopping onto a stone bench in the garden. This was the gracious, cushioned environment in which Jack grew up.

When my father was born, Burlington, though itself only a bit more than sixty years old, was an important Mississippi River city, populated by displaced Easterners who mail ordered their suits from Brooks Brothers, and who had social circles extending to Kansas City and Chicago. During the 19th century, the city had grown from a regional fur trading post with muddy streets and wooden boardwalks that led down to the piers on the river, to a thriving commercial river port, railroad center, and way station for pioneers on their way to homesteads in the West.

Though now past its glory years, Burlington was an important *someplace* in 1900. The city stood at the center of the great American migration. In the middle years of the 19th century, it was host to a steady parade of Easterners migrating west, who were

45

ferried by boat across the Mississippi. In Burlington, they could stop for the abundant supplies of produce from the rich surrounding prairies, hogs brought to Burlington slaughterhouses from neighboring farms, and for the rich stores of molasses, sugar, rice, and coffee that arrived in port daily from side-wheelers and sternwheelers steaming north from New Orleans. Eventually, the town was also home to no less than nine railroads, ferrying freight and passengers to and from Chicago, St. Louis, Kansas City, Peoria, Keokuk and parts west. During Jack's childhood, riverboats carrying travelling troupes of entertainers still occasionally made Burlington a port of call, and on the fourth of July, there were boat races in the river and picnics along the cliffs overlooking the mighty brown Mississippi.

May 12, Jack to his parents

... I am now a Major in William Doran's army. Our army has nearly $30 in their treasury. I went to confession a few days ago and yesterday I went with Grandma to lunch at the Byrons' and after school I had my hair cut. LaVern Kelly and I have made up a party at Crapo Park the Saturday after next and we are going to have 15 boys and girls and the boys are going to chip in about 20 cents apiece and we'll get two dollars for the ice cream and the girls will bring cake ...

Some people came to Burlington to stay. Jack's grandfather, Michael Fleming, probably took the most popular route to Burlington – 1,400 miles upriver by steamboat from New Orleans, on a trip that might have taken weeks, past the mouths of the Red River, the Arkansas, the Ohio, the Missouri, the Illinois and the treacherous rapids at the mouth of the Des Moines, past Natchez, Vicksburg, Memphis, St. Louis, Hannibal, and Keokuk. Though he grew up in County Cork, Ireland, Michael was one of the pioneers of Burlington, where he would eventually become a judge in the magistrate's court. One of Jack's ancestors (on his mother's side) had fought in the American Revolution, another joined the Illinois Brigade in the Civil war, and yet another was an oil man in Pennsylvania. The Flemings had a sense of themselves as people of substance, who had many threads woven into the fabric of American life.

Jack's father, too, was a Burlington success story. After almost thirty years at the National State Bank, John Fleming resigned in 1900, a year before Jack's birth, to become trustee of a wealthy Burlingtonian, Mrs. E.D. Rand, and executor of the estate of Charles Rand. In this role, he was in a position to make loans and investments, which led eventually to his appointment as president of the Burlington Savings Bank, a bank he'd helped found in 1904.

He was also a leader in the Catholic community in Burlington, serving as Grand Knight and president of the local Knights of Columbus and a member of the national board of the Catholic League. Three of Jack's aunts were nuns, one a mother superior and an innovator in Catholic education in the Midwest. For Jack, Catholicism was not a religious option; it was a family business.

Jack was both a choirboy and an acolyte at St. Paul's Church, where his mother would look at his sweet face at a Christmas service and, on a scrap of paper that I found in the box, write this:

Will my sturdy starched acolyte again
Raise strong young voice in the Christmas songs
Will slowly dawn appear, in high arched windows
While fathers stand with pride beside their sons?

When his sister Esther married six months later, in December, 1910, in a wedding the Burlington *Hawkeye* called a "brilliant nuptial event," Jack served as altar boy, standing where he could watch his sister marry a West Point graduate, an Army lieutenant in full military dress, recessing out of the church under the crossed swords of ushers gloriously attired in gold and blue. My cherub-cheeked father was no doubt swept up in the occasion and the allure of the military life. It was to be a lifelong yearning of his, to wear a uniform, and it had a profound effect on my father's self-esteem when he finally went to war at the age of 42.

Jack had a lot to live up to. In 1910, when these first letters were written, his father was a staunch community leader, and his only brother, Phil, would in another year graduate first in his class, the Class of 1911 at West Point, a singular honor that would launch Phil on a luminous military and political career. Jack's family history was populated with prominent men and strong women. But in 1910 Jack was still free to be an active, happy boy.

May 15, Jack to his parents

I went to the K. of C. children's' party Saturday and Bill Doran, and Joe Murphy, and Joe Bruce and a few other Bills and Joes and Jacks came. I ride to school on my bicycle whenever it is a good day. I do not leave it at school but I leave it in the basement of the Tama building. Francis rides with me sometimes too and he keeps his bicycle at Mr. Slant's sporting goods store.

Another singular event in the spring of 1910 was the appearance of Halley's Comet, and Jack didn't miss it.

May 18, Jack to his parents

I saw the comet. Tonight is comet night, I am going to wake up and see it. Have you seen it? I'll bet you have with nothing to keep you from seeing it but sleep. Write me soon. When Papa comes home I suppose he will be blarnyin' about all the countries in Europe and speaking every kind of language except one certain kind. I am wishing you will have a happy time.

At this moment in Jack's childhood, the family was beginning to disperse. Phil was already gone from home, never to return except as an increasingly distinguished visitor; Esther, following her December wedding, would move to the Philippines, (among many Army postings); Agnes had left home to pursue her own life

– she would marry and become the mistress of a sprawling Wyoming dude ranch; Polly was graduating from high school, and only Mary, his closest sister, would still be in school with Jack in Burlington. Jack's father would soon be sixty years old and his mother would soon be fifty. The city of Burlington thrummed with activity and commerce, with trains whistling through the city center between the residential neighborhoods on North and South Hills.

That Jack's mother doted on him, her last child, is unassailable. Decades later, when he was about to go into World War II, still the maternal cheerleader, she wrote him, *Jack my darling son, what a happy day it was the day that you were born. I never had so many congratulations – people had been so sorry for me because I had four daughters. I didn't like that at all as each one was precious, but I was rejoiced that there was another John J. Fleming and you were the dear delight of the whole family.*

Though Jack could not repress his charm – his letters give evidence of that – I wonder if his siblings were ever able to see him as anything but a child, a charming, lovable child, but not someone to be taken seriously. My father suffered from the belief that he was not as competent, not as strong and certainly not as successful as he wanted to be. It depressed him. Perhaps he internalized a sense of inadequacy in comparison to his family, or at least a sense that he needed to rely on his winning nature, which, if nothing else, would always get him by.

In the summer of 1910, Jack and his grandmother and sisters would reunite with their traveling parents at West Point, where it had been arranged that the children would spend the summer in residence until their parents' return. They would visit Phil, just finishing his third cadet year there, and Jack would watch the cadet drills, perhaps practicing to take the tradition back to his friend William Doran's army, in which he had reported his promotion to major.

But before they left, Jack went to his sister Polly's graduation from high school.

June 9, Jack to his parents

Tomorrow we are going to the High School graduating exercises. Only three days before we will start to Chicago. I am very anxious to get to West Point and see Philip and after a while to see you also. I just got home from doing some shipping for Grandma and having my Bicycle crated. Polly got about five dozen silk stockings for graduation presents. I hope you have a grand time and will soon come home.

> *~ Your little honeybunch,*
> *Jacksonia Flamingo*
> *The great pianist*

Jack was never a great pianist, but he was clearly a little honeybunch. That must have made it that much harder for his parents to send him away, at age thirteen, to a Catholic boarding school for young boys. I wonder if he had already exhibited a need for a more disciplined academic environment. I wonder if today he might have been diagnosed with a learning disability. Jack's two oldest sisters had been sent to a girls' Catholic boarding school in Pennsylvania, a school their mother had attended, to finish high school, while Philip and the other girls were educated in Burlington. Jack was the only one of the Fleming children to be sent away to school at such an early age. Was he having trouble in school, or were his parents just tired?

1914 to 1919
Jack at Boarding School

Jack to his mother from St. Mary's College, Kansas
April 1, 1916

Dearest Mother,

I received Papa's letter with the check, which was plenty for my needs and my ball-glove, which I have ordered. I also got Polly's letter, and you can wish her a happy birthday and many of 'em for me, and tell her that I hope she will long remain in her present vigorous, robust health. She's very welcome to the silk stockings – I "knew all the time" that I was giving them to her...

I received a letter from Esther several days ago, and she said they would go through here sometime next week, but, on account of the children, can't stop off. She wants me to go down and meet the train, however, and see them all, which I certainly will do, if I can get permission...

I am a captain in baseball in Second League. The Leagues haven't started yet, although a number of practice games have been played. The regular teams are made up now, and on paper, my team looks pretty good. The first game will be played tomorrow.

The first varsity game is April sixth, with the Chicago Sox. Of course, it won't be their first team. From then on, there will be a game almost every rec afternoon. When does the season start in Burlington?

~ Love to all, your loving son, Jack

My father was sent to Jesuit boarding schools for his last five years of secondary school, starting in the fall of 1914, when he was 13 years old and beginning eighth grade.

Certainly, it would have been important to his parents that Jack have a Catholic education. So for two pre-prep years, eighth and ninth grades, Jack attended St. Mary's College in St. Mary's, Kansas. St. Mary's was founded in 1849 by St. Louis-based Sacred Heart nuns as a mission school for the Pottowatami Indian tribe in Kansas. As the Indians gradually disappeared from Kansas territory with the influx of white settlers, the Jesuits converted the school to a boys' boarding school.

Jack's letters are filled with energetic engagement in his world, and the recurring themes that marked his correspondence – friends, sports, movies and plays, and money, money, money.

There have been several ball games lately. Tuesday we played Kansas Normal, whom we beat 8 to 2, in a game which was pretty much of a slugfest – I mean there was lots of hitting...In Second League in the Small Yard, which I am in, the games now stand 5 to 4 in favor of the "other fellow." We have been having some very good games...We had a very good movie Easter night – Mary Pickford in "The Foundling." It was the best one we have had this year...P.S. I need a little money as I have to pay for my basketball fee, and some other things. What do you think? Ringolds sent the trousers by Express Collect, and I had a pretty hard time scraping up the money to get them! Did you forget to get a gym suit at Schmeltzers when you were in Kansas City? If you did, I wish you would send me some money to get one here. There are a lot of things I want to get anyway, and I have to pay for some pieces (music)...and bottles of Dioxogen and Listerine, and some corn plaster... Has that box of crackers and jam or peanut butter been sent yet? Give my love to all the family.

P.S. Don't forget about the money.

It interests me that though there were Catholic schools in Burlington, Jack's parents chose to send him to boarding school. Among the eastern upper classes, it was common for families to send their boys to boarding school like Phillips Academy in Andover, Massachusetts, Phillips Exeter, St. Paul's, Groton, or Choate. American boarding schools were founded on the model of English public schools, German *gymnasia*, and French *lycées*. Their purpose was to prepare boys for higher education in one of the growing number of colleges and universities in the country – and for a life of moral purpose. The training for a moral life provided the rationale for students to live where they learned, so that they might be under the vigilant guidance and influence of school masters undertaking their training. They were to create a "natural aristocracy" of learned Christian men who would be exemplary citizens leading the great American enterprise, as opposed to an "artificial aristocracy" growing in America, a class structure based on land ownership and commercial success. This last was a development the founders of these schools regarded as antithetical to the democratic American ideal.

Catholic boarding schools no doubt had similar missions, with the special purpose of putting good Catholic boys under the supervision of religious educators who would provide a classical education and reinforce Catholic traditions among privileged Catholic children. My grandparents chose to entrust Jack to the Jesuits, who were known for their intellectual rigor.

I don't know what my Fleming grandparents' social ambitions were for their children, or if their choice of schools for Jack had anything to do with social ambition. So far, the children had all married well. Esther and Polly married Army officers who were West Point graduates. Mary and Phil married children of prominent, well-to-do protestant Burlington families, and Agnes married a handsome, glamorous rancher. Though I suspect that in Burlington they might have suffered from anti-Catholic sentiment that was common among the displaced easterners who came to live there in the 19th century, they didn't seem to suffer from social stigma and they were clearly proud of their Catholic heritage. In any case, when Jack moved on from St. Mary's, he found himself among a wealthy, socially elite group of Catholic boys, and that made an impression on him.

By the fall of 1916, Jack and a few of his St. Mary's classmates had transferred to Georgetown Preparatory School, the secondary school program at Georgetown University in Washington, D.C. I think that among prominent Catholic families, St. Mary's may have been regarded as a good "pre-prep" program, in the manner of English junior boarding schools, to prepare the boys for the more rigorous academic program at Georgetown, the country's oldest Catholic boys' high school. Interestingly, before Georgetown was a university, it was a "classical" secondary school in the European style, in this case focusing on the study of Latin and Greek to produce well-educated Christian men. It was from the secondary school's beginnings that Georgetown University grew.

As Jack was entering tenth grade at Georgetown, Woodrow Wilson was near the end of his first term as president of the United States, the "Great War" in Europe had begun two years before with, thus far, no hint of American involvement, and the Panama Canal had been completed, to much fanfare, the previous year.

In 1916, the "prep boys" at Georgetown were housed with the college boys on the university campus. Jack's room was in Healy

Hall, the historic university building with a tower that is still a familiar feature of the Georgetown skyline. From his room, Jack would not have been able to see the boats still carrying freight up the C&O Canal, but he might see – and use – the trolleys still rumbling along tracks embedded in Georgetown's cobbled streets, returning at night to the car barn on M Street at the foot of the Georgetown campus.

For the trip to Washington, D.C, Jack took the train from Burlington, changing trains in Chicago where his Uncle Ed Fleming, a freight manager for the Pennsylvania Railroad, could usually arrange a berth for Jack on the Penn Limited for the rest of the ride east. Jack was fifteen years old. He wrote after he arrived, October 4, 1916

Dearest Mother,

I arrived here safe and sound last evening, two hours late, however. I have met quite a few fellows already, besides four boys that went to St. Mary's last year, so it isn't as bad as it might be. In fact, I like it very much here. My room, No. 46, is on the top floor of the Healy building, facing into the court between all the buildings. We had a short class this morning, after the opening exercises in Gaston Hall. The Prep School and college are all together here, just like one school, the only difference being that the College boys have a little more privileges than we do. I am going out for the prep football team tomorrow. I hope I make it. By the way, Georgetown U. plays Navy next Saturday...

Jack began to see, and aspire to, the life style of rich and sophisticated boys on the Georgetown campus.

Say, this is a very dressy place, he wrote home in October 1916. *Quite a difference from St. Mary's. It looks as if those flannel shirts and extra trousers aren't going to do much more than take up space in the wardrobe. Just think, one-half of those fellows part their hair in the middle, about one-fifth of them wear tortoise shell rimmed glasses, and about one-fourth invariably wear polo shirts. The "proper" styles of shoes are very dark tan oxfords. And it appears that money doesn't mean such an awful lot around here. If you would tell someone you had a couple of dollars, they would probably say, "Oh, gee, hard luck, is that all?"*

Jack was acutely aware of the visible signs of social status, in dress and even in the décor of his dormitory room. This first contact with the glamour of the east coast was not going to improve Jack's relationship with money:

I am getting to like Georgetown very much and certainly would prefer it to any other school I know of. My room is all right but it is rather bare. A couple of small rugs, or one big one (if we have any around the house not working), a bunch of pennants, some pictures and photographs, some kind of covers for my dresser and trunk, a couple of pillows, a nice heavy blanket to go over the top of my bed and possibly a couple of curtains would make my room look much more attractive and homelike. Why, quite a few of the boys have Morris chairs and Victrolas in their rooms.

And there were other costs of living on the Georgetown campus that Jack needed to warn his parents they would find on the "home bill." *First, a pair of football shoes, $6.00, which I had to get, $15 for what is known as the "Pressing Club," for which I can get my suits cleaned and pressed as often as I want during the year; and $2.00 for the use of the tennis courts during the year...*

It must have been an academically challenging experience for the prep boys – the curriculum included instruction in Greek, Latin, English, mathematics, religion, history, physical geography, and modern languages. Jack was excused from a required course in elocution, as by this time he had begun to stutter. By the time I knew him, the stuttering was only occasionally noticeable, accompanied by a reflexive jittering of his fingers when he was nervous or upset. Near the end of his life, when my father began to have *petit mal* epileptic seizures, the stuttering and the jittering manifested themselves as a part of those events.

By November, Jack knew he was in for some very hard work if he was going to succeed as a student at Georgetown:

I had a good bit of my spirits taken out of me this afternoon, at the reading of the month's marks. They were Average for Latin, Greek, History, English and Catechism – 86; Algebra – 82; and Spanish 70. I will say I expected more, and that they are as unsatisfactory to me as I know they will be to you. In Algebra, however, it is a surprise to me that I got even 82. What I did learn, I had to hammer out for myself, and didn't get by any teacher's explanations. My Spanish mark was a complete surprise to me. Why, I thought I was doing fine in that, and expected a very good mark. I cannot imagine where the trouble is in that. Still, I guess that's the trouble, thinking I know so much. The highest mark in Spanish class was 75. I have to admit that I could work quite a little harder on my other subjects, and I promise to during the following month, as I know nothing pleases you more than my making good marks, and I certainly want to please you. I am sorry, mama, and I am going to try to do better. By the way, 60 is the passing mark here, and those who fall below 70 in any subject have to study in Study Hall instead of their rooms ...

But if he didn't exactly shine as a student, Jack was an enthusiastic participant in sports, willing to sacrifice teeth and tissue to the effort:

...Last Monday we played Western High School, and beat them 19-0. I played part of the game. I am not exactly a regular, but I usually get in for a good part of every game. I am in good condition beyond one or two bruises. I did, however, hit my nose and upper lip pretty hard in tackling yesterday, and knocked a chip off one of my teeth. The Preps are supposed to have one of the best, if not the best, team in the city. We average about 160 pounds. My weight now is about 145 (stripped)...

With his sunny nature, Jack was very popular with his fellow students:

By this time, I know a majority of the Preps and several College fellows. We may go down town any afternoon, but we must be in by six o'clock, that is, in time for supper. We are never allowed down town after six without special permission, while the College boys may go down Wednesday and Saturday nights. I have been down town several times already, but not since football practice began as we have to go out every afternoon for that, and work hard.

At Georgetown as, later, at Cornell, Jack won the approval of the "right" crowd, and that seemed to please him. By the beginning of November 1916, still in his first semester at Georgetown Prep, he had more to report:

...I have some news for you, mother. I was asked by that crowd of fellows which I mentioned in my last letter to join their fraternity. I was very glad to accept them, and have been taken in already. In my opinion, they are the best crowd in Prep School. There are, by the way, two frats in Prep School, this one and another one, the second of which Joe Thompson is one of the leaders. They are both fine bunches, but the other one spends a little too much money. I am not supposed to tell this, but I was asked by them, too. The initiation fee was $3.00, which I paid. I would like to get a pin, but of course that can wait. The pins cost $7.50. My friend Eddie Kaiser, of Detroit, has been asked, too, and will be taken in soon, I am glad to say. He and I have been going around together quite a bit. He is a dark haired boy of about Frank Schramm's size and build – a good-natured kid, and funny, too. He is a month or so younger than myself. He wants me to "double up" with him, that is, get bedrooms next to or opposite each other, and make one a bedroom and the other a study room. I would like to do it myself but I don't know whether we can or not. What do you think about it?...

to which he added, always interested in the new car, the family's first, at home,

58

I am glad that the machine is running so well. Having any tire trouble?...

The year 1917 started off at an ordinary pace:

January 6, 1917

Dearest Mother,

I arrived here safely yesterday morning at 10:15, the train being an hour and three-quarters late. Practically all the other Georgetownites living in the West were on that train also, besides the Misses O'Shaugnessy. In Chicago, I went to breakfast at the La Salle, and went up to Uncle Ed's office afterward. I am glad to say that he managed to get me a lower berth, as you said he would. He said that he would send you word that I got to Chicago all sound. By the way, I got some socks at Fields while I was there...

In March, Jack and a friend took a trolley down to the Mall and walked toward the Capitol so that they could witness the second inauguration of President Woodrow Wilson.

...We had a fine, although a cold and windy day for the Inauguration. Syl Mullen and I went around together – saw the President take the oath of office at the Capitol, administered by Chief Justice White, who is a graduate of Georgetown, and of course saw the whole parade. The West Point Cadets and the Middies from Annapolis were in the parade, and I must say that the Cadets marched the best of the thousands of troops that were in it.

There was a military snap in the air, and within a month, on April 5, 1917, the United States declared war on the Germans. In May, the Army, in desperate need of recruits, called for registration for all able bodied men between the ages of 21 and 31. They soon amended their call to include men from 18 to 45 years old, and by the end of the war, 24 million young Americans had registered for army service. Of those, almost three million soldiers were inducted into the armed services. Four Army divisions spent the winter of 1917-18 in France. Neither Jack's brother Phil or Esther's husband Harding were on the western front during the war, but both, now more senior officers, were busy training recruits at U.S. Army bases to be sent to the front. By the end of the war, Jack's sister Agnes's husband, Wendell Van Auken, would also be in uniform as an Army Air Corps pilot.

The declaration of war and the Army's need for recruits caused a fever of military activity on the Georgetown campus. In April, the college began to think about training on campus and started to organize a campus officer training corp. By August 1917, the government, hoping to prevent the depletion of college rolls, announced the organization of Student Army Training Corps (SATC) on college campuses, encouraging students to stay in school with the idea that educated college students were a military asset by virtue of their continued study. But that didn't mean that that war fever hadn't hit Georgetown, and it hit hard. In October 1917, Jack wrote his mother,

Military training has been taken up seriously here, and there are three hours of drill a week. Major Bookmiller of the Infantry, a West Pointer, is in command, and uniforms have been ordered for all. The uniforms consist of woolen blouse and breeches, spiral woolen puttees, one O.D. shirt, and a Stetson campaign hat, with blue and gray cord. Our measurements were taken a week or so ago. Altogether, the uniforms will cost about thirty dollars. Service shoes are not included in the equipment, but I don't think I will need any, do you? I'll bet you won't know me when you see me in my uniform! I'd like to get one of those short sheepskin coats to wear with the uniform during the winter. Many of the boys already have them. Do you think there is any possibility of my getting one?

What joy, the sartorial Jack got his own military uniform!

Major Edwin V. Bookmiller, professor of military science and tactics, oversaw ten hours of military training per week on campus – six hours of drilling and rifle practice, and four hours of academic training, including aviation and navigation courses. Students under the age of eighteen could enroll in the training, but could not enlist in the Army. They could be trained, but without arms or other equipment, save the much coveted uniform, puttees, Stetson hat and Sam Browne belt.

The campus newspaper, the *Georgetown College Journal,* was filled with news of the war and Georgetown's participation in it. The newspaper published letters from the front and kept a running survey of Georgetown men in arms. The first Georgetown soldier to be killed was reported in April 1918. Ads were filled with images of soldiers in uniform using the razors or smoking the cigarettes advertised, and the college press produced a *Domesday Booke of 1918,* in which they published letters from Georgetown University men serving in the American Expeditionary Force.

Jack was consumed with war news, and worried about the impact of war shortages on his family at home:

A few days ago, the Georgetown Unit was inspected by Lieut. Col. Pitcher, acting for the government, to report on the favorability of our becoming an R.O.T.C. He was very well pleased, and promised that his report would be all in our favor. The latest thing that the Unit has procured is a Colt Machine Gun.

Hoping you have lots of coal and sugar, Your loving son, Jack
Jack's money issues were getting worse.

October 29, 1917
Dearest Mother,

I received your letters with the checks for four dollars enclosed very gladly. Tell Dad that the five dollars which I got from Father Becker was just for spending money, but that I did not intend that he should put in on the home bill. I meant to pay him back out of my allowance. I am very sorry about it because Dad cannot afford to give me more than he is giving me, and I promise not to let it happen again. Anyway, I can get along very well on two dollars a week. It seems to me that no matter how much the other boys may get, they don't have it any longer than I have mine. The more one gets, the more one spends, and then doesn't have much to show for it ...

As more of his roommates turned eighteen and left the campus to enlist in the Army, Jack was moved from dormitory room to dormitory room, and he felt left out, frustrated not to be able to enlist himself. It was inevitable, then, that Jack would be utterly disappointed when he heard the bells and whistles announcing Armistice from church towers and firehouses all over Georgetown and Washington on November 11, 1918. Jack would not celebrate his eighteenth birthday for another two months. For him, going to war was to be a dream deferred though, as it happened, not denied.

November 11, 1918

Dearest Mother,

Well, it looks as if it was all over but the shouting, doesn't it? You know how I feel about it, but I am glad for your sake that it is over, because I know it will save you a lot of worry. I suppose it is very selfish of me to wish that peace was not declared, but I can't help it. Being able to enlist was the only thing I was looking forward to, and now – I don't know what to do, unless I go ahead and enlist anyway. As it is, I feel as if I was branded as a fourteen carat slacker for life. Just my luck, though, and I don't suppose Phil is especially happy about it either.

A lot more of the boys went away to camp about a week ago, and they moved me to another room, with two fellows my own age. They were both waiting to enlist, too.

All the whistles are blowing now, definite peace, I guess.

It took Jack half a life, until he went to war himself in 1942, to shake the idea that he was a "fourteen carat slacker." As popular as he was, Jack was still a decidedly vulnerable boy who thought because he didn't wear a uniform for his country (as his brother and brothers-in-law did), because he wasn't an outstanding student, and a stuttering one at that, he wasn't as worthy as other people. Perhaps this was at the root of his inability to save money – perhaps he used money irresponsibly in order to look and feel like his more glamorous friends. And his money problems compounded his self-esteem issues because they always led to his father's disappointment in him. But Jack *was* unfailingly likeable – lovable – and his need for love, along with his vulnerability, made him a perfect match for my mother.

And now to Peggy's story...

1903 to 1919

Margaret

From Peggy's father, Harry Talbot, to her mother,
Fanny, July 1919

Dear Fan,

I received your letter. I suppose it will always and forever be the same old story, some complaint about poor Margaret. Put her in a cage and stand guard. I know then no one will dare come round ...

I would like to introduce Peggy as a charming, playful child like the little boy, Jack, whom she was destined one day to marry. But in her case history is unfair. My grandmother Fanny, Peggy's archivist, does not leave me the material evidence to do that for her. Since there are very few letters in Peggy's childhood voice, we have to take her parents' word that Peggy was a difficult child.

My mother, Peggy, christened Margaret Alexander Talbot, was Margaret to her mother, though her father affectionately referred to her as "Pete" and her adored Aunt Ninny, who lived with the family, called her "Pussy Willow." By the time she was a teenager her friends were calling her Peggy.

Peggy was born in 1903 in Buffalo, New York. For as long as I knew my mother, she lied about her age by one year, saying that she had been born in 1904. It wasn't until late in her life that I noticed her real birth date recorded on her driver's license and learned the truth. I don't know if the lie originated with Peggy's marriage – she had some idea that she ought to be three, not two, years younger than her husband. Trying another theory, I wondered if perhaps she had been conceived before her parents were married, which fact would have allowed other mysteries of the Talbot family dynamics to tumble into place, and that she had altered her birthdate to conceal this aspect of her provenance. Records show, however, that her parents were married in March 1902, fourteen months before Peggy was born. More likely, Peggy began to lie about her age after I was born. I think she may have been embarrassed to have had a baby at forty. Thirty-nine probably sounded better to her.

Peggy was a pretty, blond little girl with soft brown eyes. In photos, she is dressed in white organdy with big collars, stockings and little leather Mary Janes, and she poses with a soulful, faraway gaze. Other photos show her with her hair tied back with big floppy bows. I imagine that she was a very feminine child, who loved girl toys and fantasy play. In the spring of 1909, Fanny gave Peggy a sixth birthday party fit for a princess. Fanny noted the details of the party on a piece of scratch paper: there were twenty-three children, seventeen mothers, and three teachers, along with her Aunt Ninny and "Mamma!!" The menu included a birthday cake with six pink candles, fancy cakes, ice cream and candy curls, and Peggy received a small mountain of birthday presents, including a purse, a bracelet, a fan, beads, modeling clay, a peg board, an egg cup, hankies, a possum, a glass gypsy kettle, dolls, flowers, and a book called "The Pansy Wedding."

I know from this letter, the only one her mother saved from this period, that Peggy was a little fashion maven:

August 6, 1914
Dear Mother:

I hope you enjoyed your trip through the Hudson and met Daddy all right. How is everybody at home? I went in swimming this morning and the water was lovely...

Mrs. Noble decided to get the ribbon from Strawbridges. She is going to send for it herself... I am training my hair in a pompadour. Mrs. Noble says it is very becoming to me. I have no side combs and will have to break my dollar to get them if you don't send them to me. Please have them wide.

I guess I will close now with love, Margaret

When she was three years old, Peggy and her family left Buffalo and moved to Glenside, Pennsylvania, a suburb of Philadelphia, where her father, Harry, a lawyer, had a job as staff lawyer for an insurance company. Glenside, at the turn of the 20th century, was a relatively new community. By 1855 there was a Glenside railroad station on the Northern Pennsylvania Railroad line and, thirty years later, the railroad and investors began a major real estate development project that would result in the construction of 1,000 houses in what one contemporary brochure called "Glenside Farms, A Model Home Town." The discovery of typhoid in Philadelphia city water had hastened a general exodus to the Philadelphia suburbs in 1898.

The Talbot family moved to a neighborhood that was probably no more than twenty years old, though Glenside had been popular as a summer retreat at the end of the 19th century, when Philadelphians would put on their Sunday best and take the train out to stroll among the electric fountain displays or hear Victor Herbert and John Philip Sousa in open air band concerts at Willow Grove Park. Glenside was just on the edge of the countryside, where farms were still sending hay wagons full of produce for the market at Reading Terminal in the city.

What Glenside was not was an enclave for Philadelphia's upper class, who lived in a parallel universe in nearby Chestnut Hill, Penllyn, and Philadelphia's Main Line, across the Schuylkill River that bisected the city and its western suburbs. Philadelphia society was already legendary as a piece of American culture (in the box there is a letter to Fanny from a friend, describing someone as a *"bred-in-the-bone Philadelphian, which is to say, Englishman of long before the Plymouth colony"*). The Talbots, new to the city, could have lived without much interest in this social group at all. But coming from Glenside would be significant later, when Peggy would find herself in such close proximity to Philadelphia's upper class that it would fuel in her a powerful ambition to belong to this world. But for all of that, Glenside was not a good address.

I imagine (and dimly remember) the house in Glenside, set back from the street with a front porch festooned with potted plants, including a night-blooming cereus, a cactus that produces an ephemeral display of blossoms just once a year in the dark of night. I remember this plant, because my grandmother woke me to see it on an overnight visit. Inside the house, a dark entrance hallway led to an old fashioned kitchen at the back with a wooden ice box, a gas stove, and a flat ceramic sink set in a wooden counter. Off the hallway were two parlors, closed off with pocket doors that slid into the wall, a bathroom wallpapered in gray with flamingos dipping their beaks into reedy ponds, and a staircase to upstairs rooms I never saw. I remember lumpy Victorian furniture with embroidered doilies on the tables and antimacassars on the backs of chairs, and I'm sure the house must have had some evidence of my grandfather's annual hunting trips – mounted trophies and animal skins.

But, this was not a happy household. In her twenties, when Peggy was a new mother herself, she wrote this poem describing her childhood:

Kind hearted Harry
And famed fussy Fan
Found of themselves
A very strong clan
Their whole objective
By acclamation
Was simply to thwart
The next generation
At nine o'clock sharp
Every night of the week
They'd lock up the doors
Put the children to sleep...
At eighteen and twenty
The story was sad
The children grew worse
They even grew bad
Pennyless Peg said
My feelings are sore
Tumultuous Tom
Tumult is in store
Peg chose matrimony
A dubious call
Tom went off to college
To cushion his fall.
Fanny and Harry
They stomped and they shouted
They threatened submission
I think they both pouted

The poem concludes with a bitter comparison to her parents' affection for their grandchild, my brother Tommy, an affection Peggy never felt:

Then toddling Tommy
Came into the world
A cunning young tyrant
Whose hair is all curled
Fan says – Birthday Baby
Just have your own way
And heartless old Harry
Please don't go away
The moral my children
Is simply and true
They won't do to the next
What they did to you

Peggy made it clear to me that she didn't like her mother, and as I read the letters, I have to conclude that Fanny didn't like her daughter, a spirited child with a fierce, defiant nature, who at some point in her childhood began to be a problem for her mother. I can actually hear the edge of an imperious tone Peggy used with her mother in that one letter I found, surprising from an eleven-year-old.

When did this breakdown happen? And why? Her parents and their own history provide a key to the trouble, so I begin there.

"Fanny," though a popular name in the late 19th century, seems like an incongruously jolly, happy name for my grandmother, making me think of Can-Can girls from Toulouse-Lautrec paintings. The facts are more prosaic. Fanny was born around 1865, just at the end of the Civil War, and grew up in Buffalo, New York, the daughter of an immigrant English tailor, John Procter, and his wife Margaret Quirk Procter. The family had emigrated in about 1860 from Devon, England with Fanny's five older siblings – she, Fanny, was the first and only child to be born

70

in the United States. They lived in a house near the dockyards on Lake Erie's waterfront, not far from the Erie Canal, which since 1825 had been open to barges transporting goods from abroad through Buffalo and New York City. Buffalo, the terminus for the Canal, was the point at which goods were shifted from canal barges to larger ships that would take them through the Great Lakes.

Fanny's mother died early, and this seems to be significant: Peggy had been told she had a "nervous breakdown" on a train. The train is the only detail of the story that I know, and I don't know if her early death is connected to this breakdown, but I wonder if this grandmother, this Margaret for whom Peggy was named, suffered from mental illness. I keep this in mind as a significant piece of information as I look at my mother's emotional history. Did Margaret Quirk begin – or continue! – a family pattern of emotional fragility for Fanny, and for Peggy, in the succeeding generations?

By the time she was grown, Fanny was motherless, living in a household with her father, her oldest sister Anne, fifteen years her senior, who was a school teacher, her brother George, a "cutter," perhaps of cloth in his father's tailor shop, and a brother John, who was a carpenter. At the age of eighteen, Fanny began to teach school herself.

Fanny married late, when she was thirty-six years old. Her husband Harry Talbot was ten years younger than she, twenty-six. That was only the beginning of their differences. She gave birth to Peggy, her first child, when she was thirty-eight, and to her second child, Tom, when she was forty years old.

Harry, a Canadian, had become an American citizen in 1899, and at the time of his marriage had just finished his studies in law and joined a Buffalo law firm as a partner, trying cases in municipal court. An unlikelier couple could not possibly be imagined, as they introduce themselves to us in letters.

I suppose that Fanny, though a petite pretty woman with blue eyes in a heart shaped face and a swirl of honey colored hair on her crown, had considered herself to be a spinster, unlikely to marry. She would teach school, keep her father company, read Shakespeare, which she loved to do, and spend her summers attending lectures at the Chautauqua Institution, near Buffalo. I get a sense of Fanny in 1899, at thirty-two, in a letter she wrote to an acquaintance from Chautauqua (Fanny had a habit of keeping handwritten copies of some of her letters): *I have so often thought of you and the little folks to whom I became so much attached that "summer long ago" in Chautauqua. I have found a little book containing a song I promised to send for them, but was never able to write down the music as I know it only by ear.*

I spent two weeks in Chautauqua this summer. Hoped I might find you there. I cannot say I am really fond of the place as I always feel lonely among so many people.

Chautauqua, still operating in its original location not far from Buffalo, was an educational experiment pioneering the idea of adult learning as a vacation activity. The institution, a tightly packed gingerbread summer community, was founded as a summer school for Sunday school teachers, but it appealed to people like Fanny, earnest and serious, hungry for intellectual stimulation in a proper Victorian setting. I know what Fanny means about feeling lonely among crowds of people, but that she should mention it seems sad to me. I think she was a shy, solitary person.

For Fanny, to marry in her thirties must have been the answer to a romantic dream. Among the fragments she saved from this period is a small envelope containing a calling card engraved with the name "Miss Procter," two theatre ticket stubs from January 4, 1897, and a small photo of a man in spats and high collar holding an umbrella – was this Harry or some other beau? She also saved a newspaper article with advice on clothing for train travel (perhaps for a hoped-for honeymoon) and later the bills for her wedding, which provide interesting details: a catering bill for the wedding dinner, at $1.50 a plate, to include salmon *farcies*, sweet bread croquettes, chicken salad, peas, jellied tongue, macaroons, cream royals, Delmonico ice cream, wine jelly and, of course, a cake. Candles were thrown in but china, silver, linens and decorations added $5 to the bill.

She also saved her wedding dress, a pretty, cream-colored *peau de soie* dress with a high neck, mutton chop sleeves and a bodice puffed out like a bird's breast. I know this because I wore it at my wedding. Peggy, whose own wedding dress was a little black silk number, short and waistless in the style of the flapper era, had saved her mother's dress as she saved so many things, to create a history for herself. There was also among Fanny's wedding memorabilia a bill for a brougham carriage (a horse-drawn carriage for two) to take the couple from the church to their new home, and a millinery bill for the materials – buttons, fabric, gimp, braid, crinoline and "serving silk" – to make a blue traveling suit. These bills and lists, which have survived more than 100 years, lying in a box, allow me to imagine Fanny sitting on a horsehair divan in the parlor hammering out the details of her wedding, an event she may have thought about for years. Was the menu very *haute cuisine?* Did her father and brother put together the travelling suit in their tailor establishment, or did they only make men's clothes? Was a brougham carriage a grand statement? I wonder what Harry thought of all this to-do.

Peggy's father, Harry Talbot, grew up in the Erin Township of Ontario, Canada, near Eramosa, a community the Talbots had settled two generations earlier. The Talbots, who were Irish Methodists, had come to Canada from County Kerry in Ireland in 1832, bringing with them their expertise in cattle and horse breeding. The Talbot men, including Harry, were physically imposing, tall, large framed men with an activist, athletic, strong willed masculinity. Eventually, Harry's father and four uncles moved to western Canada to pioneer the western prairie. One uncle was a prairie veterinarian and another was a senator representing the province of Alberta in the Canadian Senate in Ottawa. They were a noisy, outspoken, energetic family.

Harry's parents, Tom and Jennie Talbot, raised seven children, five girls and two boys, of whom Harry was the oldest. In their sixties, Tom and Jennie followed the rest of the family from Ontario to Alberta with some of their children, to homestead in Lacombe, Alberta, establishing a large farm. Harry stayed east to study law just across the New York-Ontario border in Buffalo, New York.

Through her letters I have come to know Harry's mother, my great grandmother, Jennie, an immigrant Scottish girl from Thurso. I've gotten very fond of her, and I wish she could have been more of a presence, brave as she was, in Peggy's childhood. I like her for picking herself and her family up to move from the established culture of Ontario into the unknown western territories, and for embracing her new life with enthusiasm that infuses this letter, written when Peggy was about one month old:

Lacombe, Alberta, June 17, 1903

My dear Harry & Frances & Baby,

I hope you are all well and that baby is growing nicely. I suppose she will know you by this time. Babies soon get to know their parents. Have you named her yet?

The girls and Alex (Harry's siblings) *go to school every day. I am to tell you how many turkeys I have, well I have 48, but I expect the coyotes will have some if not all of them. We do not see coyotes very often. I have over 50 chickens and 19 ducks. I would like to have 200 chickens. There is quite a lot of trouble looking after them. The girls have just come in from school.*

We have two fine little colts – Alex named them Jess and Bess – and three young calves, all females. I just forget their names at present, and Alex is not here just now to tell me. With love to you both, and kiss the baby for me. I remain your affectionate mother,

~ Jennie T.

And to augment the picture of life on the prairie, here's another fragment, written to nine-year old Peggy in February 1912:

... Last night we were over at your Aunt Jeannie's – thirteen of us in a sleigh. It was a lovely night when we left home but before we returned it got quite cold and dark. We got back at three o'clock in the morning. And tell your father old Maude was one of the horses we had to draw us there. Alex drove most of the way. We had a good time and a good lunch, card playing and dancing being the chief amusement of the night...

~ Much love, your grandmother   (Jennie Talbot)

While Fanny seems to have been timid and cerebral, Harry Talbot, in an early letter, presents himself as an adventurer, though not without a taste for culture. He wrote this letter to Fanny, his wife of two years, in 1904, while on an extended train trip across the country to visit his parents in Canada. Fanny was at home with baby Margaret in Buffalo:

Kenyon Hotel, Salt Lake City, Utah, September 12, 1904

Dear Fan,

Well, here I am taking in the sights of the Mormon City. I arrived here about 4:30 p.m., and leave tonight at 12 o'clock. Have seen the most interesting sights of the place and had one of the men very kindly show us around. We had the rare good fortune to hear the great organ. The organist played especially for us. There were only three of us there, the Mormon, another young man, and myself. It was wonderful. I have never heard anything like it. The organist matched human voices singing. From the time I left Denver until I got into Salt Lake City, we were passing through mountains continuously. The grandeur I cannot describe. The Adirondacks cannot compare with them. The Royal Gorge was

75

beyond description. Our train passed between rocks rising thousands of feet above us, and creviced every few feet. Today we have been passing through a desert. We see huts every few miles. How people can live there is beyond me…

Does baby miss me? With love to all. Kiss baby for me.

~ Yours, Harry

Harry also had an appetite for elaborate hunting trips into the wilds of the American and Canadian west, taking him away from his family for a month or more at a time. Photograph albums show Harry lounging around a campfire in hat, hunting vest and boots, shotgun in hand, or posing triumphantly with his kill. There are always other men in the photos and the setting, though unidentified, is decidedly rough and rural. Following is a poem Harry's law partners wrote for him in 1904 during one of his hunting trips:

Your wife and child are sad indeed
A husband and father they sorely need.
The negligence business is on the bum
No poor old "sucker" has lost a thumb.
Everything in fact is dull and slow,
Why in the devil did you go?
Come back again and give us life,
Come back again and see your wife.
Come back again and see "Bessie Place,"
Come back again, let us see your face!
Our heads with grief we sadly bow,
The Municipal court knows no attorney now.

Harry's willingness to leave his family for long periods was to become a malignant sign, but at least in this early letter, his affection for his wife and daughter seem genuine.

In 1907, when Peggy was four years old and her brother Tom was two, Fanny took the children to Chatham, Massachusetts, on

Cape Cod, for what may have been an annual event, an extended summer vacation, leaving Harry at home to work. This warm letter from Harry, reporting on his July 4th weekend activities, leaves me feeling that in 1907, all was well with the family:

July 17th, 1907

Dear Fan:

I received your letter on Tuesday, and was very glad to hear from you, and to learn the little babes were all ok. I wish I could see them. I of course miss you very much and wish you were back here. I went to Atlantic City on Sunday to avoid being lonesome. I went in for a swim, and got caught in the undertow. I could not get in and the lifeguard came to my assistance. I was not quite exhausted but was getting so pretty rapidly. I could have remained afloat of course, but I lost my head. They took in two others while I was there. They had to take them in their boat, but I simply hung on to the boat and was towed in. I did not get back Friday night for the concert. I remained up town to see the illumination for a while, and when I got back, it was over. I will close now with love to all and a kiss for yourself and babes.

~ Yours, Harry

Two years later, by 1909, the household in Glenside had grown to include Fanny's father, John Procter, now an old man retired from his work as a tailor, and her widowed older sister, Anne. Though she was long gone when I was born, I know about Anne, Peggy's Aunt Ninny, because she was tucked so firmly in her heart that even in old age, Peggy had nothing but the most affectionate feelings for her. Anne elicited the same affection from her sister Fanny. My name, Selby Anne, is Peggy's nod to her Aunt Ninny. Fanny's family became Anne's family and Harry did not object to this invasion of in-laws. I presume that the presence of this kind of extended family in the household was a late Victorian custom.

Soon, when things started to fall apart, I suspect that Harry found their presence convenient.

Harry's letter to Fanny and Peggy, vacationing in Chatham during the summer of 1909 (when Peggy was just six) makes me wonder: was Peggy's relationship with her mother already difficult?

August 11, 1909
Dear Fan,

I received your letter last week, and have received one from you today. We are very glad you are enjoying yourself and while we will be glad to see you when you come home, yet you might as well remain until you have finished your visit. We are getting along all right. Tom is looking and feeling well. I have just asked him if I could tell his mother that he is a bad boy and he says no write her that I am a good little boy, and to come home soon, and bring Pete. He misses both of you, but manages to have a good time...

How is Pete getting along? You do not say much about her. I expect to have to go to New York Monday next week. Will try and not make it the day you are to arrive. Travel at night, and avoid being sick. Your father and Anne are well. When you are ready to come home let us know, but stay until your visit is out. Love and kisses to you and Pete. Regards to all friends.

~ Yours, Harry

By 1912, and perhaps earlier than that, Harry was working in New York City, in the New York office of an insurance company on Wall Street, perhaps the same company he started with in the Philadelphia office. He leased an apartment in the city, where he lived during the week.

But though he went home on weekends, his separation from the family was, it turns out, even more profound. Separated during the week, during the summer, when Fanny took the children to Cape

Cod, and during Harry's hunting trips, Fanny and Harry had begun to drift apart. Within the next few years, Harry began to keep company with a woman whose name – Mrs. Cecilia Sophian – remarkably lives on in the family. There is even a photograph of Harry, Mrs. Sophian, Peggy and Tom in New York, on their way to a baseball game, probably in about 1915. Peggy, lanky and somber with a large bow holding back her hair, was about twelve years old in the photo. Tom, perhaps ten, stares soberly from under a visored cap. Both are standing in an uncomfortable grouping with a bosomy Mrs. Sophian standing with her arms draped protectively over the children's shoulders. It was Peggy who identified Mrs. Sophian for me in that photo, and where they were going.

I wonder how that must have felt to Peggy. At twelve, she had to have some concept of sex, not to mention some Freudian feelings about her increasingly absent father, the parent who seemed to have an easy affection for her, at least then. What damage might this apparent liaison have done to my mother? And did Fanny, sitting in Glenside, know then about Mrs. Sophian? Was Harry asking his children to participate in a secret?

Peggy and Tom, then, grew up in a household with extended family under their roof, but with an increasingly absent father. Though like other children they made good friends among their playmates in the neighborhood and at the Glenside public schools, and summer vacations on Cape Cod, it is clear that between 1909 and 1912, things had gone very wrong in the family.

That was bad news for both Fanny and Peggy, who was increasingly resentful of her timid, proper mother. As it turned out, Peggy was not a successful student, nor, as later letters show, was she obedient or respectful of the limits her mother tried to impose on her.

As early as 1915, when Peggy was only twelve, Fanny was in search of someone else – a school – that would take responsibility

79

for her little girl. She launched the search with a letter to the Episcopal bishop of the Diocese of Philadelphia.

To Bishop Phillip Rheinlander
Reverend Sir:

I have a little daughter twelve years of age, whom I would like to send to an Episcopal boarding school. Will you kindly inform me what schools there are in this vicinity?

~ Very sincerely yours,
(Mrs. H.A.) Frances P. Talbot
Glenside Pa

Judging from Harry's irritated letters to the family, by the time Peggy was fifteen, Fanny, Harry, and Peggy were in open warfare. Peggy seems to have cared little about school and a great deal about her social life. Fanny appealed for Harry's absentee supervision in letters to him in New York, to his enormous annoyance.

January 31, 1919
Dear Fan,

...I am returning Margaret's school report. It certainly is very discouraging to think of a child so indifferent to her own interest. If she is not an idiot she will live to regret to her dying day her conduct. Some people have to learn through rough experience and I suppose she is one of these poor fools.

You may show her this letter. And she is not to go out to a solitary party in the evening until her report is satisfactory to me. She is further to study one full hour at home each day including Sundays. If she disobeys, I will cut off all her allowance and I wish you to do the same. I can tell her more. If she does not do better this is her last school year. I'll put her to work at anything anyone will hire her for. She will earn her own living or go to school, whichever she wishes. She can do the choosing.

~ *Harry*

Though Harry made a lot of noise and bluster that kept the family at bay, he seems to have been intimately involved in the care and discipline of his children, if from afar.

...Tell Margaret to write me as to how much I owe her and how she is getting along. It is not necessary that Margaret go twice during week to the movies when she has plenty of other amusements. She only must give up the movies one night. I cannot see any particular harm in her going. Ignorance has inspired more fuss than knowledge and you cannot protect a child by shutting her in. Tell Tom to write me.

~ *Harry*

Margaret must keep up her music practice.

Things came to a head in the summer of 1919, when Fanny and the children were in Chatham, a summer in which Peggy did everything she could think of to drive her mother crazy. Harry's "put her in a cage" letter, written in July 1919, continues:

I am doing the best I can for you. If you do not appreciate it, come home and stay there. I have to stay in the city and work. The least you can do is to quit getting me wrought, if so I cannot work. I do not wish Margaret to go with any roughs, and if any of them molest her let me know, and the Cape will have a little excitement. Tell Chapin to tell this boy I will certainly put him out of his misery if he annoys Margaret. As for sending Margaret to a camp, I simply cannot afford it. She has the only camp she will get this summer. If there is any nonsense, send her to me here in New York. I will take care of her and she may rest assured of that. I am glad Tom is enjoying himself and I sincerely trust your next letter will not be so discouraging. I am doing my best but guess the task is hopeless. Spent last Sunday here in the city as I intend spending all of them. It is lonesome but I can stand it...

~ Harry

Since dictating the above I have received your letter, and am glad you are more contented. If Margaret does not wish to do anything, let her be unless she gets too bad. Then ship her to New York where I will cause her to remember this year forever. I have a little 12 hour a day job for her, besides which she will keep my apartment.

Fanny seems to have been utterly unable to understand Peggy, let alone manage her. An introvert and an intellectual, she must have been both baffled and even a little disdainful of her fierce little material girl, who loved crinolines and hated rules. The earnest, dutiful Fanny seems to have offered Peggy little empathy, little color, laughter, and enthusiasm for life.

Desperate, and unsuccessful at getting Harry to agree to a summer camp for Peggy, Fanny wrote from Chatham to make one last pitch for boarding school, an idea she'd been trying to sell for four years. This is Harry's answer:

August 20, 1919

Dear Fan,

Your letter received. Before you go looking for schools you better ascertain how you can finance your suggestion. In my present earning capacity, my income is such that it would be impossible to send Margaret to any paid school even though her life depended on it. There is one thing I am going to tell you all now. I am not going to permit you or the children to cause me to spend my old age in the poor house. If my children are not so constituted as to appreciate the advantages offered to them the future coming to them is theirs and not mine. There is nothing about them that warrants... better than other children get. I know my resources and I know my duty. The trouble is that you do not seem to have the power to make the children mind you. I have to make the living and manage the children too. What do you have to do? You speak of sacrifices, but I see you making no suggestions. I cannot send Margaret to school and run the house in Glenside. I can afford to spend for 3 people a year and this is every cent I can afford. I am spending this now with the house and expense attached to it. I do not spend any more money on myself for pleasures than you do, but I have to live, and I intend to lay by a little for my old age no matter what the circumstances.

And then comes an apparent crack in Harry's resistance...

I do not wish at this time to spend money giving to the schools you have in mind, although you may make such inquiry as you can. I intend to take the matter up in some practical way and see what can be done. I am sending you therefore $125 and trust this will be enough to pay the rent and bring you home. When do you propose coming home? I must go to Glenside next Sunday and Labor Day to get my things in shape for my trip. I intend to leave Sept 5 or perhaps now that you all have been away for two months you think I should give this up and turn the money over for Margaret's school.

~ Harry

This would turn out to be Harry's last bluff on the subject. By September, Peggy was enrolled in boarding school.

Putting the pieces of the Talbot family portrait together, I have a picture of a prim, unhappy, and overwhelmed Fanny. My brother Tommy, who knew her, found Fanny dour, self-pitying, and spiteful. I knew her only at the end of her life, when she had retired to her bed for several years, but I'm not sure that's quite fair. Like her daughter, she admired pretty things and a genteel lifestyle, but she also yearned for an intellectual life, and found herself, in middle age, with two tigers by the tail – Peggy and Harry. Her son Tom was the great love and comfort of her life. It must have been terrifying for her to try to manage these large personalities, especially if she was already familiar with family conflict as a result of *her* mother's histrionic nature. Peggy told me I reminded her of Fanny, and though I'm not altogether flattered by that association, it makes me feel some sympathy for her.

I have a harder time understanding Harry. On the one hand, I like his restless energy, his humor, his curiosity and interest in so many things. I like the fact that he had some real sympathy for his little girl. His cruel temper and disdainful tone, though, make it hard for me, in the end, to find him a sympathetic character in Peggy's story.

Poor Peggy – she had to make sense of a world in which love was uncertain and survival was a matter of fierce will. Who knows what innate emotional equipment she had to deal with it all? No wonder Jack looked so good to her when he came along.

1919 to 1922
Peggy at Boarding School

Harry to Fanny, July 1919

...If Margaret is to go away to school what she is to have is a school which will give her at least the equivalent of a high school education and a vocation. Margaret will never stand in my judgment a so-called college education, but it is imperative that she know how to earn a living. Therefore, the school that you must have in mind must combine these two features in addition to a proper atmosphere...

Fanny chose the proper-sounding Moravian Seminary for Girls, and in the fall of 1919, Peggy was enrolled there as a boarding student. The school (and its successor coeducational school) is still located in Bethlehem, Pennsylvania, about an hour's train ride from Philadelphia. It was founded by the Countess Benigna Zinzendorf, whose family were patrons of the Moravian Church in Moravia (Czechoslovakia), as a boarding school for daughters of traveling Moravian Church workers. Tom, meanwhile, was still going to school and living at home, and would do so until he finished high school, a successful student who went on to Dartmouth College.

Bethlehem was one of two communities founded in the New World in the 18th century by the Moravians, a Christian sect that grew out of the early 15th century church reformation in Czechoslovakia. With a missionary spirit and the support of German aristocrats, the Moravians settled on a farm in Pennsylvania, where they created the community of Bethlehem, and on a large tract of land in North Carolina, site of three communities including Salem, now Winston-Salem.

The idea that she was going to a "young ladies seminary" must have made Peggy's skin crawl. But, if Fanny studied her choices, she might have been very hopeful about what a Moravian school might be able to offer Peggy. Early in the church's history, the sect came under the spiritual influence of John Comenius, a pioneer in education who even in the 17th century believed in the progressive idea of formal education of women. The seminary and its sister school, Salem Academy in North Carolina, were among the first private schools dedicated to the education of girls established in the United States.

Peggy, however, was not impressed, nor was she interested in the education Moravian Seminary was offering or in any transformation of her wild spirit. That she was not happy at school is confirmed in four letters written from Moravian. From this first letter, it's easy to understand why Fanny was anxious to get Peggy out of the house. This is the attitude she was putting at a distance:

October 1, 1919, from Peggy in Bethlehem
Dear Mother,

My velvet dress and things I didn't wish I am returning. I despise the place etc. and you for it. Where is my mail? I don't care about anything. I can't go out until I get some clothes and will not have you pick them out and send them to me. I will go to New York and get them or have nothing. Don't send what I don't want. It will only come back.

Why doesn't anybody I care about write? I don't think about anything, but why my chosen family doesn't write. And only hate you for all. Please have my silver slippers fixed. The heels, and cleaned. Don't send the others.

I have marked my clothes with indelible ink and am sending to laundry.

I will have to borrow money, send my allowance.

~ Margaret

What an angry, unhappy child. Taking into account that she was furious about being sent away to school, it is still remarkable to me that Peggy's letter shows such a profound absence of affection for her mother or fear about the consequences of being so rude to her. Peggy was in control of that relationship – and Fanny truly was tyrannized by her daughter. Had Peggy adopted her father's behavior as a model for her own? My mother could be a tyrant. It seems that she learned this behavior at home.

In another letter written that first autumn at Moravian, this time to her brother Tom, Peggy put her own construction on life at boarding school:

Every time we go out for a walk, we have to go by two in a line with teachers as guards. We look like either an orphan asylum or a bunch of convicts. Oh, you'd be surprised to see me trotting along so meek and mild.

It's especially entertaining to think of Peggy menacing, plotting anarchy as she trots along in formation, but it is surely an exaggerated picture of life at the Seminary. The girls, who in 1919 were housed in Colonial Building, the former single brethren's house of the original Moravian community, lived in room "companies" of 16 to 20 girls under the supervision of a housemother. At Salem, the seminary's sister school, the girls had private space in alcoves with an iron bed, a wardrobe, a dresser, and a chair, with a curtain that could be drawn. They would awaken to a rising bell at 6:45 am, and would complete a Bible reading, breakfast and chapel before the day's classes. After dinner, they would study, with lights out at 10:30 pm. The girls at the seminary participated in plays ("A Flower of Yeddo," "The Second Act of Tennyson's 'The Cup'"), concerts (piano, vocal, violin solos and a saxophone duet) and Greek dances draped in togas and, like Isadora Duncan, frozen in tableau scenes in imitation of the gods and goddesses frolicking, as depicted on a Greek vase. They went to dances with boys at Lehigh University and Bethlehem Preparatory School. There are even records of a trip to the spring rowing regatta on the Schuylkill River in Philadelphia. In 1919, the campus, touched by the outside world, was saddened by news of the death of a science teacher, who had entered the World War as a private in the United States Field Artillery in France.

Peggy's letter to Tom continues:

Gee whiz!! What do you think I did, got hysterics in church last Sunday a week ago when the preacher started to talk about St. Mike. Can you blame me? You know we have to go to church twice and vespers once on Sunday.

Received that peachy box of fudge you sent me and my my but didn't it taste good. My roommates all thought it was awfully good too. Thank you ever so much for sending it.

I expected Daddy last Sunday and was disappointed when he did not arrive.

~ Love to all, Peggy

Religion was definitely an integral part of the education of students at Moravian Seminary. The Moravian Church takes a gentle approach to human failings, believing, like the Quakers, that we are all reflections of God. Through the centuries, the church has adopted some quite beautiful traditions, including a "love feast" at Christmas, at which the community shares sweet rolls and coffee in a liturgical setting, and some dramatically beautiful services with candles in a darkened sanctuary that Peggy sometimes found extremely frightening. She was not unknowledgeable about Christian traditions. She was confirmed in the Episcopal Church.

Recollecting her school years, Peggy often spoke of an "end of the world" service that was very traumatic for her. There is, however, no "end of the world" service in the Moravian church calendar. The "St. Mike" service to which she refers is the end of September service of St. Michael and All Angels, which honors Michael the Archangel, Biblical victor over Satan. Moravians use this service as an opportunity to pray especially for those in charge of the education of children. Knowing Peggy's sometime terror of Moravian services, I wondered if the "hysterics" she mentions in the letter to Tom meant that the service made her cry in fear, but it hardly seems likely. The comment might also mean that she was laughing hysterically, that this may have been a joke shared by Peggy and her brother, possibly about a "Mike" in their acquaintance who was no saint. But more interesting to me is the idea that Peggy would have been frightened by the services at all. The Moravian church services are known for extraordinarily beautiful and moving music. Was she, with her mother's encouragement, afraid of some judgment, the judgment of God for her sinful ways? As powerless as she was, Fanny might have pulled out that threat as a way of scaring Peggy into better behavior.

Peggy's mention of her father is another sad reminder of his unreliability for her. This letter indicates that he was using his distance, and the mail, to continue expressing his disappointment in her, and that it hurt her:

Peggy to her father from Moravian Seminary, no date
Dear Daddy,

I don't know what to write. I've been thinking all day but you sounded so cross in your letter. Really, Daddy, I have been trying and I'll try even harder. Of course I want an education. I want it more all the time. One can't really be refined without one and you know how I hate ordinary people. It's hard for me now because I didn't work last year and I'm right sorry now I didn't. You may not believe this but it's the truth.

Professor Shields my teacher in music said I was doing well, that ought to be some consolation, because you wanted me to learn to play.

Thank you for the money Daddy. Write soon.

~ Pete

Where did this fine and fancy girl who didn't like "ordinary people" come from? There is no evidence in the letters that suggests her parents had these notions about their place in society. Peggy seemed to be inventing a better self who was a refined *lady,* who was above the riff raff, a stylish and elegant persona.

Meanwhile, Harry had a reason to be unhappy. Peggy's academic performance did not improve at Moravian Seminary. In another unfair turn of history, her report cards reside in the archives of the school ninety years after they were recorded, available to me, in the 21st century, to report. Her first year at Moravian, Peggy had a full load of classes: in Rhetoric, Literature, Algebra, French, Chemistry, Composition, Latin, Grammar, Latin coaching, Geometry, Sewing, Vocal Music, and Cooking. The second year's report does not include grades for any mathematics or science courses, or Latin, but she had added History, Gymnastics and Piano. In the first semester of her third year, she was only graded for History, Chemistry, and Latin, and then only for the months of October and November. For each of her three years at boarding school, her year-end average grades hovered in the sixties (with the exception of a 56 in Chemistry and a 47 in Geometry), having gotten worse instead of better as each year progressed from October to May. Meanwhile, in piano and voice Peggy excelled, earning year-end marks in the 80s.

In sewing, Peggy was a star, with a year-end grade of 95. This letter to Ninny, demonstrates how much she cared about her sewing projects, and though she adopts an affectionate tone, she can't quite hide her petulance, even with her staunchest ally.

Moravian Station, Bethlehem, March 5, 1920
Nin dearest,

Received your sweet missive this "après midi" and was very glad to hear from you.

I don't like those goods. I only want and can make my particular "bloomers" out of "white satin" the same amount and same as the "crepe de chine" so I will be unable to sew any of my sewing in my "curriculum" until I get it. So please send it.

It has been awfully stupid here since I have gotten back and nothing much to do. Our musical comes up Tuesday a week and I trust you will have my dress (white organdy) sent in time also that blue middy.

I have a great many things to do so will have to make this short this time.

Write soon dear and please don't mention Sidney. The less said the less I hate, I knew if ever I did dislike a man, I would be forced on him. I am going out and have a good time at Easter or I <u>won't</u> care whether I pass or not, it has been so <u>long</u> since I've had one I have to think to remember. It's all right to go with a group of girls here and there but I'm sick of it and darn sick of it.

~ Write soon, Love, Pussy

It's interesting that Peggy, chameleon-like, adopted a different tone – and signed a different name – for each recipient. To her mother she, Margaret, is angry, defiant, and hateful. To her father, as Pete, she is a supplicant. For her brother Tom, she, Peggy, adopts a teen *patois* and a conspiratorial tone. To her Aunt Ninny she, as Pussy Willow, is sugar sweet. Who was the real Peggy?

In the fall semester of her third year, Peggy did not have a grade above 60, which may explain what happened next. She left Moravian after that fall semester, in December 1921. Perhaps she was asked to leave because of her grades, or perhaps she was asked to leave because of her behavior. She was always pleased to retell the story of her greatest act of rebellion at boarding school: she was caught smoking on the roof of the dormitory at Moravian Seminary. Her punishment was to be shunned for a week by the school community, including her classmates, which for Peggy was a fate worse than death. Someone (her parents, or more likely the school) decided that Moravian could do no more to educate Peggy.

Instead of going home, though, Peggy was admitted to Moravian's sister school, Salem Academy and College, in Winston-Salem North Carolina. Salem Academy is located in the other historic Moravian community settled by the sect in the 18th century. Though at that time few girls in the south were given a formal education, the establishment of Salem Academy, like Moravian Seminary, reflected the Moravians commitment to education and belief in the education of girls. In the mid-19th century, even as the Civil War was in progress, Salem added college courses to its program for girls.

At Salem, Peggy had a surprisingly successful last semester of formal education, encouraged by the school in the "cultivation of gentleness, forbearance, and patience." Though she failed her Bible class, she actually earned some B's (in Domestic Science, English, Sight Singing, and Geometry!), and even a passable D in Chemistry. Though Peggy arrived on campus too late to be included in the yearbook for 1922, and I don't know how else she spent her time, I do know that she made two of her lifelong best friends during the semester that she was a student there.

In May, 1922, Peggy, then nineteen years old, received a degree certifying that she had completed a high school education. By that fall, she was back at home where, in spite of her mother and probably at the behest of her father she had access to a car, a Model T Ford, a social life, a fur coat, and a practical course of study. She was enrolled in sewing machine classes at John Wanamaker's department store. Through his bluster and oddly attuned to current fashion, Harry acted on Peggy's behalf as usual:

To Fanny from Harry in New York, October 7, 1922
Dear Fan:

I enclose check for $66, $3 for Tom and $5 for Peggy. I will be home Saturday week. I cannot get into my new apartment until the 16th. Tell Tom to take care of his dog or he gets no more pets from me.

Regarding Peggy's coat, find out if Strawbridge & Clothiers have as yet mailed it, and when. And have Peggy write me about the length again. Friends tell me, and the latest models show the fur coats of young girls to be short, no longer than Peggy's. These are the latest Paris models.

~ Harry

In a mere six months Peggy would be embroiled in her grandest, most flamboyant, dramatic and defiant gesture ever. We go back now to the summer of 1923.

1923

Summer

Mr. and Mrs. J. J. Fleming, Jr.

Peggy to Jack, Glenside, PA, June 22, 1923

Darling,

I'm just in a daze – I can't realize that yesterday – so short a time ago – we were so <u>vitally</u> with each other. And now you're on your way to Burlington...

I'm all "non compas mentis" (misspelled, but you know I'm not a Latin student, sufficient excuse from myself for myself). I can't snap out of it, even a little...I put my little ring on a ribbon like you wanted me to. And every step I take it hits me – my <u>soul</u> – and then I have that crying instinct...

You know, I don't feel like we'd eloped like common people do. It was just natural – our minds were married and being spiritually married, it seemed the only thing to do...I'm developing a deep interest in household things – hope you like my ideas.

Just all – all yours, Peggy

On a Thursday afternoon, June 21, 1923, four days after the end of their happy reunion at Senior Week at Cornell, Jack and Peggy were married at the Cathedral of St. Peter and St. Paul in Philadelphia, kindling a firestorm that by the end of summer threatened to consume both families. Their marriage certificate notes that the ceremony was performed by Rev. J. J. Hickey in the presence of two witnesses, Rod Porter, who had introduced them, and Barbara Kenny, who may have been a friend of Rod's, but who, in any case, doesn't figure in Jack and Peggy's story except in this important moment.

That they by chance chose the summer solstice, Midsummer Day, a pagan day of mischief in western culture through the millennia, for such a bold passion-driven step seems particularly apt for my parents and their story. Then, too, the setting, the Roman-Corinthian building on Logan Circle in downtown Philadelphia rather than a justice of the peace in Elkton, Maryland (the elopement capital for Philadelphia lovers through the generations) must have helped reinforce Peggy's rather grand idea that they were not "common people."

Jack's besotted state notwithstanding, he must have insisted that they be married in a Catholic church, and Peggy must have made no objection. This later proved to be a very wise move. Not only might it perhaps take a little of the sting out of the Fleming family's reaction later, after they learned Jack and Peggy's secret, but more importantly, the church actually came to the rescue when family members were dispatched to undo the damage. That didn't happen until later in the summer.

I like to think of Jack, handsomely turned out in a suit he'd worn to bring Peggy home on the train from their Cornell week, standing at the altar with Peggy in her raffish little black silk, a sleeveless dress with a dropped waist, a lace collar and a black ribbon rosette with trailing streamers fixed to the scooped back. I know that dress – Peggy saved it for posterity. A perfect stylish early flapper dress, it was much later consigned to a costume box and my daughters, then little girls, rustled around the house in it, bare toes peeking from under trailing black silk.

I see Peggy and Jack standing timidly but earnestly with Reverend Hickey and their friends. I wonder what the priest thought as he took this young couple's vows. I wonder if he checked over the paperwork a few times to be sure it was legitimate. But, why wouldn't it be? They were of age, at twenty and twenty-two. Perhaps they stood at the main altar, dwarfed by the vaulting coffered and gilded dome above them, their faces lit in blue and crimson and amber from the sunlight piercing stained glass windows. Or did they say their vows at one of the chapels at either side of the main altar, looking up at mosaic renderings of the Annunciation, with shafts of light from clerestory windows catching dust motes drifting through the massive space? Was the church dark or lit up by the giant hanging lamps, sending light glancing off the polished pews and marquetry floors? I am guessing, given that they were such a small wedding party, and part of an event sprung on Reverend Hickey on a sleepy afternoon on the first day of summer, they were consigned to one of the more intimate, and less intimidating, marble altars that line the sides of the sanctuary.

Jack to Peggy from the Ithaca Hotel, Ithaca, N.Y., Friday afternoon June 22, 1923

My own darling wife –

I am completely lost – desolate – without you, Peggy – and wanted so to address the envelope "Mrs. J. J. Fleming Jr." Last night, darling – I could hardly tear myself away from you – I wanted just to hold you close and let all the trains in the world go to the devil – and in the train I just sat in a daze – lost in thought – I don't believe I moved a muscle till Bethlehem, where the conductor almost had to shake me – to tell me to move if I wanted a berth. I lay in the berth – for hours I think – with your picture in one hand – and our Certificate in the other – to prove to me that it was a wonderful reality, and not just a beautiful dream. O darling – I am so glad that we did make up our minds to get married – I believe I am the happiest – and the lonesomest – man in the world...

Peggy once described to me the scene that led to their decision to elope. They were standing forlorn in a train station, she said, perhaps waiting for the Lackawanna train from Ithaca back to Bethlehem, then the Reading to Philadelphia at the end of Senior Week. Peggy said she complained about her mother and her life at home, and Jack said, "Why don't we just get married?" "All right," Peggy told me she said, imitating a rather desultory, matter-of-fact voice. The story, in Peggy's retelling, has little of the romantic intensity these letters betray. They made this impetuous decision when they had known each other for less than three months.

When the jig was up and their secret was out three months later, Jack insisted to his brother Phil, and later to his new mother-in-law Fanny, that though he and Peggy were legally married, they had not consummated their union. From their correspondence later that summer – efforts to find time to be "completely married" and for "that honeymoon we planned" I believe that Jack's assertion was technically the truth. Peggy was also worried, I think, about unintended consequences of sex. In July, she wrote not too obliquely:

Our 'attitude' toward the immediate future needs careful consideration. So much depends on your getting your diploma. I would hate to be the means to any indirect case that might compel you to have to drop out. This being a very delicate, and not at all tasteful subject to me, the less said the better.

But, she went on, *Darling, I do love you so! And you know I want to really be <u>all</u> your wife, Jack. I just don't want to have anything interfere with your ambitions.*

None of this would matter had that technicality not taken on significance when the families got involved in Peggy and Jack's drama at summer's end. But I am struck by the relative squeamishness of her language about sex. In fact, my mother and father were always squeamish about sex – I have painful memories of my own encounters with them on the subject, including my mother's attempts, during daily interrogations in the car on the way home from school, to find out what I "knew" about sex, before giving me a birds and bees book to get the story straight.

Jack and Peggy were, after all, children coming of age in the 1920s, the Jazz age, an age of new sexual freedoms, informed by veterans of World War I, male and female, who came home with more enlightened "French" ideas about love and sex. Then, too, Jack and Peggy's early relationship seems loaded with sexual intensity. In July Jack wrote from Ithaca:

Sometimes feelings come over me, sweet wife, that are almost too much to bear. Last night Chad came and got me – drove out to Glenwood and out there, in the darkness by myself, looking at strips of star-laden sky between two tall rows of black tress, I just had to clench my teeth and my fists till the nails cut into my palms, I wanted you – longed for you – so terrifically...It's really really time, isn't it, that you are my wife and I am your husband?

And Peggy wrote from the New Jersey shore, where she spent much of the summer with her family:

Darling, could you come this weekend? Oh, I understand this physical torture feeling. I feel as though I'd scream sometimes if I couldn't be with you the next second. I want you so.

In the hours they spent together right after their wedding, did Jack and Peggy go have a celebratory drink in Rittenhouse Square with their friends? Did they park along the Schuylkill River and neck? They apparently didn't rent a hotel room. By evening, Jack was on that tortured train ride back to Ithaca to pack for the summer and go home to Burlington.

Before Jack left the campus he made one last ditch effort to salvage his Cornell career, visiting the dean of engineering, who was *"very friendly, but not at all encouraging. As a last hope, I dashed around to a few doctors, and got up a petition to the effect that the headaches which I have now and then were a partial cause for my poor work."* He was not hopeful, he reported, as he also learned that the committee that would meet to decide his future at Cornell had not yet convened. So Jack left Ithaca for Burlington not knowing whether he would return. He had a secret wife and a pocketful of unpaid bills to present to his father. He was waiting for the train at the Ithaca Hotel when he wrote Peggy:

It all seemed so unimportant, sweetheart wife. You occupied my every thought. Have you your little ring on a ribbon around your neck now? Always remember that it is there, darling...that little ring holds our souls so closely together, even when we are so heartbreakingly far apart.

Peggy's wedding ring was a little silver filigree band, unusual and pretty. She wore it until, many years later, after she had begun to slip into senility, it was mysteriously lost. She said that it had flown out the bathroom window. Jack and I took her to a jewelry store, wheeling her in a wheelchair past glass jewelry cases with displays at her eye level. She seemed unable to choose between a plain gold band and a garnet studded band and my father, wanting to please her, bought both. When Peggy died, I found the gold ring in a box. The garnet ring was on her finger.

Jack and Peggy intended to keep the marriage a secret, though it was not clear what their plans or timeline were for telling the world that they were married. I suspect that they didn't think that far ahead. Why? What were they afraid of? The simple answer is that they were both financially dependent on their parents, they were unusually young and naïve, and though they were determined to have each other, they were terrified about the possible consequences of their behavior. One possible consequence, a fear

Jack shared with his family, was that the news might literally kill Jack's mother. Mary Fleming was *that* good at keeping her children in line.

The truth is, neither one could keep the secret for long. Almost immediately, Peggy reported that she had told her friend Lottie Quittner. Lottie, a Catholic, promised to take Peggy to church and help her think about becoming a Catholic (a conversion that never happened). Jack told a half-truth – that he was secretly engaged – to his friends Warren and Henry, both of whom also had girlfriends to whom they were secretly engaged. More secrets! Henry was telling a half truth, too – Jack found out later in the summer that Henry and his wife had also secretly married on June 21st.

But the biggest revelation, within a week of coming home to Burlington, was Jack's confession to his sister Mary and her husband Henry Chittenden.

Jack to Peggy, Burlington, June 29, Thursday
My own darling –

...I told Mary and Henry, and they are pulling for us, but I'll tell you the whole story. I went over Monday night, and found them alone for the first time – in bed, in fact. But I roused Henry, and he came down. I said "Henry, can you keep a secret?" And without further words handed him our certificate. He read it – asked me if I was joking – read it again – and fell back against the wall, speechless. It knocked him flat. Then he said, "My God, wait till I mix a drink – and tell me all about it." I did – and he gave me a lecture on the difficulties of supporting a wife, and the seriousness of the step, and all that – but that he was all for us.

At first he didn't want to tell Mary on account of the shock it would be – it happened that they had been talking about me, and Mary had suspected that I was thinking of marriage, on account of some questions of living expenses and all that I had been asking her crowd. But I finally prevailed, and we called her down, with conversation as follows. Myself – "Be prepared for a shock!" Mary – "engaged?" Myself "Worse than that." Mary – "Not married?!!" Myself – "Yes." Mary – "Peggy?" Myself – "Yes." Then Mary sank into the nearest chair, and another round of drinks, and then the story over again, with all of us half laughing. And Mary and Henry still incredulous. Then we talked about you – and marriage in general – and secrecy. They told me not to tell another soul, lest the family find it out, and they took the certificate, and said that I ought to leave your letters with them, too – because Mother has been known to read letters – so I am doing that. Of course we can trust them perfectly. They will always stand behind us – and Mary wants to write to you. It's gotten under Mary's skin too – she says she dreams about us, and is afraid someone will read her mind. But I don't see how I will ever tell Mother – she is so nervous and intense that it will completely knock her out – and Dad, too. But let me worry about that later.

The idea that Jack's mother, Mary Fleming, was a fragile woman given to the vapors seems not quite right to me. Among the grandchildren who knew her (I didn't) she was reputed to be a sharp witted, durable enthusiast, a grandmother that would gather up her old fashioned long white skirts to traipse *up* a sledding track in pursuit of her athletic grandchild, my cousin Jocelyn, while on a visit to West Point – the same grandmother who carried on a vigorous correspondence with everyone in her family, actively engaging her grandchildren in topical exchanges, and who enthusiastically displayed the most stars on the front of her house in her neighborhood in Burlington during World War II – seventeen, one for each child or grandchild serving in the war. Nevertheless, Mary Fleming had conditioned her family to believe that an emotional shock would cause her to collapse. She was apparently not above judiciously using guilt as a family management tool, and she was obviously very skilled at it.

Jack's June 29 letter continues:

Last night, I went to my room early – to write to you – and Mother came in, and had a long, long talk with me – that was a terrible nervous strain. First of all about work at college, and bills, and I am so much at fault there. And she took the blame on herself (making it terribly hard for me). Then about you, sweetheart. She has an unjust prejudice against you in connection with my staying over – and that almost roused my temper. And then, out of a clear sky (Mother is a mind reader) she asked me if I loved you – and I said "I think I do" – I couldn't bring myself to downright lie about it. Then she talked of going slow in picking a wife and making sure and all that, but in a kindly way – rather in a tearful, not vindictive way, Peggy.

Darling, I hope and pray that someday you will love each other – and I think you will. Then a little about all her children and their love for her, and its shortcomings – and then a little crying, and emotional scene. Oh, I can't describe it, but the whole thing left me a wreck. I can tell you about it so much better when I see you.

Peggy's mother and her Aunt Ninny also got suspicious during the summer. Peggy wrote in July...*Mother and my aunt are getting quite inquisitive. Asked me if we were engaged! And keep giving me little things for a home (to inspire confidence). Isn't that a scream?*

Needless to say, Peggy's relationship with her mother-in-law did not begin smoothly. Peggy was adept at using guilt as a management tool, too, a tool she applied during the summer, reminding Jack that they were *married* now, and she had a right to expect to see him.

However, with the exception of two brief rendezvous, one weekend at the beach in July, and one painfully abridged visit in August, Peggy and Jack each spent much of the summer pretending they weren't married, which meant going to parties and dating, while my mother kept her wedding ring tied to a ribbon

103

around her neck and hidden under her clothes and my father ignored the girls he brought along to picnics and tennis games.

Peggy in Glenside to Jack in Burlington, June 25, 1923
Darling:

Your letter came – how I love it, the first letter from my husband. How thrilled I am when I write or read that word and realize its full significance. Each other's in God's eyes – wonderful!

Darling, Frank came. I couldn't help it, you were here when all that was decided and I know you understand. I wasn't alone with him at all. We did the usual things, swimming and "Thirteens" in the evening. Everybody noticed how changed I am. All I thought about was the time when you told me you loved me. And how I loved you...

Jack to Peggy, Burlington, June 30, Friday

... I have just been on one of the favorite local pastimes, a picnic, with Warren and Hilda – and Laura Blaul. We went out on a point overlooking the river, and I had the world's dumbest time under such ideal conditions. I hardly spoke to Laura, just gazed into the distance. And Warren and Hilda purposely made me feel worse, damn them, by being as affectionate as possible. We took Laura home early – she might as well have been there all the time – and I've been driving Warren and Hilda around. I wouldn't let them sit in the front seat with me. They took great delight in saying "Don't you wish Peggy were here?" – just torturing me. They think they know how much I miss you, darling, but they don't know the half of it. The only way I keep my spirits up is by saying it won't be long till summer school, and Ithaca is near Philadelphia. And Chad still has his Ford.

Two good things happened: first, it was decided that Jack would go back to Cornell to summer school to try to reestablish his academic career; second, because he passed eleven hours in the previous semester, the college decided Jack could continue at Cornell for another year to earn a bachelor's degree in civil engineering. His father put him on a very tight financial leash, however.

From Jack on the Pennsylvania Railroad, Thursday
Sweetheart –

Two weeks ago, you and I were having those first sweet short hours of our married life – those few little hours that went by so quickly... But Peggy darling, I'm on my way east now, and every second brings me closer to you, although I don't know when I'll be able to get to see you. But you know I'll make it just as soon as I possibly can. Father has made it unusually hard for me by promising me the absolute minimum amount of money necessary to get through this summer. He wants me to devote every minute of my time to working and give up all pleasure entirely – and he says that holds for next year, too. Of course I can see his point of view after almost busting (but I didn't, thank God) – and after giving him that staggering total of bills which I had. Thank heaven I'm getting all those off my chest, too. But we can talk about plans for next year and all that when I see you – that wonderful time, darling – because I'm going to – nothing can keep me away.

Jack was astonishingly cavalier about his recurring debt, especially given the burden of guilt he carried whenever he got in trouble for it. His father was a banker, in the business of managing money conservatively. It's a wonder that none of his father's financial conservatism rubbed off on Jack. He seems hopelessly innocent on the subject.

Jack to Peggy, Ithaca, July 9, Sunday
Peggy my own –

Ithaca again, and everything reminds me of when you and I were together here – the house, the library, and I'm so lonesome for you...The afternoon was spent dashing around registering, and I got a job. Darling, I swallowed my pride (I haven't much anyway) and am now saving my board by working in the kitchen of one of the co-ed dormitories – a regular hash slinger. Sweetheart, it's the only way I can save money to come to you – and I've got to do that...

To which Peggy, ever the grand lady in training, responded...*Darling you are so precious to work like that. I don't like you to do it, but I want you so...*

For all her grandness, to her credit, Peggy was from the beginning of their relationship the more practical partner. All summer she wrote Jack to remind him to be careful about money and to pay attention to his work, and to keep in mind how important it was to his future – and to his parents, and therefore to her reputation – that he graduate from college. And in later years, though life with her was often chaotic, though she desperately wanted the fine things money could buy, though she never developed much of an interest in "household things," Peggy bore the burden of being the responsible one, the keeper of the checkbook – a role that didn't come naturally to her, but one she took up because she had to.

Peggy was with her family at the Talbot beach house in Spray Beach, New Jersey, when Jack wrote this:

Jack to Peggy, Ithaca, July 13, Friday
Darling-

At last! – definite plans. It's all settled and wild horses wouldn't hold me now. Chad and I embark in the same old Ford next Thursday afternoon – heading straight for Philadelphia, and then sometime Friday – a week from today – we ought to reach Beach Haven, and you!...I know how a prisoner must feel that's been imprisoned for ten years away from everything that means happiness to him. It seems that long since I've seen you – since that day that we will always remember.

The big problem now is to get the work caught up and ahead – I'm carrying all my puny shoulders can stand and no one knows better than you that I can't afford to bust any more courses. But you needn't worry, darling. I'm working harder than I ever worked before here. I haven't time to get bored and what's worse, I haven't found the time yet to go swimming. Just now we're busy with plans for the dance that (we hope) will finance our trip. And what's more darling, I haven't had any dates, and I don't want any. All that I want – all that I love – is you.

It took Jack less than a week in Ithaca to secure a plan to see Peggy. The following letter from Peggy in response to this news also brings into high relief the family circumstances that drove her need for a passionate partnership with Jack, and perhaps were the source of the lifelong intensity, both positive and negative, of their relationship.

Peggy to Jack, Beach Haven, July 15
Darling:

That's great about you coming this Friday. Now please <u>don't change</u> your plans.

Had a rotten weekend. My father's "?" (maybe she is just a friend) is staying at the Baldwin. Oh gee it's all so <u>sordid</u> – my family makes me so unhappy. I don't understand it at all. I can discuss it better than write it, though. Darling, I'm so glad you have <u>principles</u>. You know the people that are tolerant of each other and love each other all through life are the happy ones after all, aren't they? Age isn't as barren to them. Darling I know I'll love you just as much when you're sixty, even if you aren't precious looking. It's different then but just as strong, if you were really meant for each other, isn't it?

I hope your dance is a success. Please dear, don't get in debt. Jack, I don't want any dates either, I just want you. This is a disgusting old place. Ugh. But we can go sailing and swimming and dancing and walk on the beach. Gee, please hurry Friday!

~ Just, Peggy

It's no wonder my mother was a wildly jealous wife, always on the lookout for predatory women among their friends who might have designs on my perennially handsome and charming – and I think faithful – father. Peggy came back to the subject of fidelity later in the summer of 1923.

Peggy to Jack from Beach Haven
Darling:

...I don't like Gertrude Atherton (a prolific American novelist of the first half of the 20th Century). *She says "fidelity is a virtue of the bourgeoisie." That's such a damn lie, because the bourgeoisie are seldom faithful. If they are, it's because they haven't the money to be otherwise. Fidelity – real fidelity of mind as well as body – is something that every sensitive soul craves. And oh how carefully you ought to treat it. That's why marriages for anything but love are so wrong. Jack, you are my inspiration. Even if all the character critics anyplace promoted infidelity as a personality developer, I'd want to, <u>couldn't help</u> but be, true to you as long as you wanted me. And you feel that way, too, don't you Jack? You want to be true, rather from will than duty, don't you? That's the perfectness of you – our ideals are so the same. I love you Jack.*

~ Just, Peggy

In his correspondence with his mother, Jack painted an innocent picture of life as usual at summer school. She could have no suspicion of the distractions he was enduring, or the fact that he was about to leave campus for a weekend with Peggy at the New Jersey shore.

108

Jack to his mother in Burlington, Ithaca, July 19, Thursday
Dearest Mother,

I was certainly glad to hear from you yesterday – and to receive the bathing suit. I suppose the racket will be along soon now. Orr and I have been rolling the court a little – have it all in shape for playing now – besides getting our exercise doing it. Chad Head drives up now and then of an afternoon – and a couple of times we've gone to a swimming hole out in the country, where only trunks are necessary (a 1923 man wore a one-piece suit covering his whole torso) *– a pair of which I located in the attic. Now, however, I can go much more easily to the popular gorges nearby.*

My work is going along quite smoothly, and tomorrow I have two prelims, which will indicate (as well as examinations can) just how much I have absorbed during these two weeks. I hope to do well, but of course, I can never be sure till afterwards...Phil and Dot (brother Phil and his wife Dorothy) *are certainly hobnobbing with the high hats, aren't they? That must be a wonderful life down there – if you have lots of money and no inclination to work.*

~Love to all, your loving son, Jack

In his evolving feelings about class and money, Jack seems to have been both envious and mildly disapproving of his brother's glamorous life. Phil, a rising star in the Army, travelled in grand company, even as a young instructor at Virginia Military Institute.

After an apparently successful weekend, Peggy and Jack carried on, each in their own environment, as if they weren't carrying a very large secret. Uppermost in both their minds was the next rendezvous, the week (they hoped) at the end of summer school on August 17.

Peggy to Jack, Beach Haven, July 28
Darling:

It's "Ocean Country" day – races and everything. We all went down to the Yacht Club this afternoon. Of course everybody was there. Gosh – in the middle of the afternoon up came a terrific thunder storm. I wasn't even scared. What was the use – you're studying. But darling just watching all these people play...I want to swim and dance – be an All American prom trotter, but with you. Feel a little frivolous – we could, couldn't we Jack? That's one mood and it's fun in its place.

Darling please try and stay for a whole week when you come – you're my husband and It's not as though you were staying away from school. Is it selfish to think you might stay with me? For me to want you to dear?

~ Just, Peggy

They were constructing their dream of a life together. But interestingly, Peggy imagined a gay romp with the prom trotters, college boys and girls who dance the night away, while Jack, in a letter written on the same day, imagined a romantic domestic scene.

Jack to Peggy, Ithaca, July 28
Sweetheart,

Your sweet letter waiting for me every day is the one thing worthwhile that draws me straight to this deserted house after the daily grind of classes, the only thing that keeps my spirits up...This morning Orr and I both had exams – and last night we both studied far into the night. And never in my life have I had so much difficulty in studying the prosaic qualities of concrete. My thoughts just wouldn't stay where I put them, but would leave the printed page before and go straight to you. Time and again I would find myself dreaming – of you and me in a comfortable little apartment, my head in your lap, just giving myself up to the joy of being near you, or walking through the dark pines of some northern woods, to the edge of a placid little starlit lake – or, to look farther into the *future, of a winter night in our house, with the snow beating against the windows – a big, big fire in front of us, and the children (I have <u>such</u> an imagination, sweetheart) safely upstairs in bed – or of a week in New York together, and getting our fill of theatres and such things...and then sinking back to realities, typified by concrete, which I finally did get studied, and passed the exam, I think.*

In his next letter, Jack offered his own free verse definition of the prom trotter.

Jack to Peggy, Ithaca, July 30
Sweetheart,

I didn't write to you yesterday – please forgive me, I'm so ashamed of myself and sorry, and afraid that you will feel hurt, but darling, I regret to say that I was in no shape yesterday, mentally or physically, to write to the girl I love – my wife. You see, from Saturday afternoon to Sunday morning was one long bender for a crowd of us – you know, one of those silly, collegiate affairs where a crowd of boys get together and try to drink as much as possible and ride around from one house to another, and sing and be noisy generally, and think they're enjoying themselves. Orr and I ran into some congenial friends Saturday, and the thing got started as such things do, and as a result I got just one hour's sleep Sunday morning - with church and working at Risley and all – and by evening, after an extremely foggy and grouchy day, I dropped into bed like I had been drugged, cursing myself for not writing to you, and for being such a college boy. Darling, I didn't love you or think of you one whit less, but it wouldn't have been the real me writing you...

How can we help but be happy forever? We'll be all-American prom trotters together (grim reality – if we can afford it) – but not the kind of prom trotters as the term is generally used. In fact, darling, I began thinking about the typical p.t. and was inspired

111

(?) to a little free verse, which I am enclosing. Tell me how terrible it is.

I abhor the prom trotter
When I think about her
Her soul a shallow saucer
Holding her lukewarm cleverness.
A hard drinking, insecure gold digger
With extremely light feet
And a lighter head
Always necking somebody else
And throwing a heavy line
That's usually just out of the shade
And, often, to insure popularity –
Way in it.
She talks of the wonderful parties at Yale
When she's at Dartmouth
And is constantly referring
To the "cute boy" she "plays with"
At Princeton
She has a pose of "just adoring"
Something or other unusual
Which would be all right
If it weren't a pose.
And next winter she is considering
"Dancing at the Lenox Grill"
If the management urges her enough
She calls you "sweet child" and more
Which pleases you
Till you hear someone else
Getting the same thing.
I abhor the prom trotter
When I think about her
Why is she so attractive

When I'm with her?

The subject of class fascinated both of them. With a mix of envy and disdain that they seemed to share, though Jack seems to have had more mixed feelings than Peggy, they both equated money with social status, and money was important to both of them. But being "natural" was an aspiration of a higher order. A poem he sent Peggy later in the summer offers more of Jack's observations of class in America (with vivid images of life in the 1920s), revealing that with all his mixed feelings, he was a privileged boy, knowledgeable about the lives of the wealthy (I think of his visit to Long Island with his friend Lib), and disdainful of the poor:

How would you like to be a High Hat
And have a country house
And drink cocktails
And have dinner at eight
And "Weekends"
And family portraits in oil
And wrought iron andirons
And Rolls Royces
And "arrive on the Berengaria"
And be a Yale man
Or a "prominent Junior League worker"
And play polo
And marry often
And read "The Spur"
And "Town Topics"
And have something
To be snobbish about?
I wouldn't (Sour Grapes)

Isn't it funny
That so many people

Can live in the midst
Of player pianos
And front porches
And "Art Calendars"
And church socials
And inquisitive neighbors
And gossip
And linoleum bathrooms
And prim respectability
And colored statuary
And striped shirts
And Ladies Home Journals
And Mission furniture
And pampered Buicks
And hairnets
With rubber bands in 'em
And still be happy?
But then, happiness
Is a state of mind
Not environment.

I don't know much
About the city poor
But I do feel sorry
For the small town poor
You know the kind I mean –
Lazy coarse men
In blue shirts
And suspenders
Cursing at their shapeless wives
In Mother Hubbards
Alternately bending over hot stoves
Or screaming

At the dirty children
Playing with the garbage.
You've seen it –
Red table cloths
And cracked plaster
And filthy beds
And window panes
Patched with paper
And perspiration
And flies
And the eldest daughter
With the big feet
And blotchy face
After a hard day
At the laundry
Going to meet her "girl friend"
In the same pink shirtwaist
And the same "silk" stockings
Which display elegantly
Her muscular calf.
Did I say I felt sorry for 'em?
Well, that won't help 'em any –
And what's more
They don't want to be helped.
It's a blessing
They don't know any better
Then they <u>would</u> be unhappy.

Peggy salted her letters with grand ideas about their life together when their financial ship came in, but she was quick to add that money didn't matter. *"Jack, when we have our little room (with a kitchenette, even) how happy I'll be having bread and cereal with you – more than sweetbreads and orange ice with the Prince of Wales!"*

And speaking of money, Peggy momentarily abandoned her prom trotter fantasy to tackle some realities. It's not clear where her $25 weekly estimate came from, but she mentioned it in several letters, so they must have come up with the estimate together.

Peggy to Jack, Beach Haven, Aug. 2
Darling,

...I do understand about the bender...only don't drink too much, Jack. It worries me a little cause it isn't good for you. And I don't want you to get the habit even a little. And then you don't always know just what you do when you're tight – and sweetheart, you're my husband, and I love you so much.

Darling, I don't feel frivolous very often – about your free verse. I love it. It's very good. I wish you would do more of it. Jack you have awfully good thoughts and express yourself so well.

Darling I've been making out budgets with our $25 a week. It's going to be close working, but it will be fun, really. Not to get in debt and to see how much we really can get out of it. You know it takes genius to live on that and you're always happy when you're using your brains and initiative. "Necessity is the mother of invention." That's a much better attitude than if we were dissatisfied. We can "pan" our daddys for party clothes (I hope you'll like mine) and if anybody should give us a check, it goes for the rent. But then we can't count on presents. Want me to send you some budgets? And you try and improve them.

Anyway, you be making some up too. I feel very serious dear and I want you to also. Mary and Henry ought to be able to give us pointers. Only I'm afraid their ideas would be a little extravagant (sounds funny for us to say, doesn't it?) – but we will show everybody that two heads are better than one.

116

Peggy's practical turn was music to Jack's ears. I wonder who called Jack a child of the gods, but it helps me to understand the magical appeal of this handsome, sunny boy.

Jack to Peggy, Ithaca, August 4
Sweetheart

Your letter made me feel so happy, and cheerful, and proud of you...I feel so lucky that you are my wife – you – perhaps those people that love to kid me were right when they called me "child of the gods" I must be– when they smiled on me from Olympus and gave me you, forever...

And Peggy, I wish you would send me some of the budgets you doped out. I'm terribly interested. It's all so real and vital to us, isn't it? And I'll try my hand at it, too. In fact, I'll try and get some real practical information (I don't know just where) – because I'm afraid I wouldn't make very good guesses as to what different things cost. It seems so indefinite when one doesn't know absolutely. But it will be fun, won't it? And I know we can do it, and be completely, sublimely happy. Darling, next summer we'll start. What a wonderful time that will be. I wonder where it will be – our first home together? Chicago? New York? Burlington? Shanghai? The next year will tell, and anywhere with you will be heaven. Now, I'm using all my anticipation in looking forward to seeing you, two weeks from tomorrow!

Jack seemed more comfortable imagining what life would bring him than in actively crafting a life. Peggy was ready for an active "brain polishing" self-improvement campaign, together with her husband.

Peggy to Jack, Spray Beach, August 5
Darling:

Usually I don't agree with ministers, but I like Frank Crane – and I thought this article was rather appropriate, dear.

117

You know when men only get about $25 a week, they usually get a corresponding vacation – two weeks. Darling, wouldn't that be fun? There are so many things you want to do. But I think the nicest way to divide it would be a week in the summer, when we could find one of those "sun drenched" lakes noted for its inspiring scenery and be inspired together. And then in November to take a week and go to New York – sharpen our wits. Darling we don't want to be old back numbers altogether, or current books, plays, etc – do we? And a week in New York is the best little brain polisher there is. Of course we can improve on that as the income improves.

In recommending the Frank Crane article, Peggy fell into the trap she hated most, exposing her less discerning intellect. In recommending it, she sabotaged her own desire to be *au courant* with the latest in literature and culture, not an "old back number," like an out-of-date issue of a magazine. And Jack couldn't keep himself from responding in a patronizing tone:

Jack to Peggy, Ithaca, August 7
Darling –

One day closer to the seventeenth and you – how these days do drag by. And I do want to meet "the gang" as you so quaintly call them. They are your friends. And I want to know them and like them, darling...and sweetheart, what about that fragment of a honeymoon that we had planned? Can't we have each other all to ourselves even for just a little while? I love you so, and every second we have together is priceless - especially so when, married though we are, we see each other so unfairly seldom.

The Frank Crane article you sent me certainly had some awfully good philosophy in it – food for thought for both of us. But as a rule I don't like his self-satisfied saccharine drivel. Perhaps it's unjust prejudice on my part, and I'm missing a lot, but to me his is an educated bourgeois, irritatingly optimistic mind. And

118

somehow I always associate him with "just folks" and Gene Stratton Porter. I'd a thousand times rather read something bitter and tragic (which Dr. Frank doesn't believe in) by a Russian author, who doesn't write for the checks it brings in. But all that doesn't matter. I love you, darling...

Peggy didn't miss his tone...

Peggy to Jack, Spray Beach, August 11
Darling,

I thought I noted a sort of subtle current of criticism through your letter. I guess once a day was too much of a request for us to write each other, and I trust you think so too, from the number of letters I've received lately. I think you lost the motive of the article I sent you in your burst of dislike for Frank Crane. I'm sorry my tastes are so apparently bourgeois. I'll try to bring them to a level with yours, Jack.

Their plans started to fall apart during the last week of summer school, just before Jack was to go to Philadelphia for what they hoped would be a weeklong reunion.

Jack to Peggy, August 13
... I wrote home telling them of your invitation, giving them a chance to sanction my going, and what should they do but refuse me flatly on the grounds that I ought to want to get home, that I can't afford it, and that I had promised to give up everything and to devote my entire time to working for them – all ridiculous and unfair. I will be in Philadelphia just as we had planned – I'll let you know the exact time later – and as to how long I can stay, I can't say now. But I am afraid it can't be long. To be with you, sweetheart, that is all I ask. But the family's attitude makes me mad and hurts, too. And I wrote and told mother just how unfair I thought it was. And then, on top of that, the enclosed letter from

119

Mary – and damn it, our secret has preyed on her so that she has written to (brother) *Phil.*

Jack enclosed the following letter, from his sister Mary, for Peggy to read herself.

From Jack's sister Mary in Burlingon to Jack in Ithaca, August 9
Jack dear,

I know you have been wondering why I haven't written to you before this, but don't think I haven't had you in mind, because I have every minute. I've thought about your marriage from every point of view and please don't think me disloyal when I tell you that I can't bear the responsibility of being the only one of the family to know of it any longer. I have written to Phil to see you and talk to you – it's time that he took an active interest in your life, and it's only right, Jack, that you should discuss this with your older brother. You know why I worry so, of course – on account of Mother. I really believe that she would suffer a complete mental and physical breakdown if she found out you were married. She is absolutely incapable of taking a shock philosophically and I am so afraid she will inadvertently find out that I'm in a constant nervous strain myself. Please talk to Phil. It's such an awfully decisive step you've taken – I don't think you half realize yet what it is going to mean to you and all of us. I can't really conscientiously keep your secret any longer. I feel that it isn't fair to you or to Mother and Dad. Please try to forgive me if you can't feel the same way I do. I'm afraid Mother has written you not to see Peggy before coming home. I tried to talk to her but without success. I want to get this off on the afternoon train. I felt I must do this and do it at once. I'll try to write more coherently tomorrow. Don't let this upset you. Try to look at it perfectly reasonably and believe that I think it the right thing to do.

~ Much love, your devoted sister, Mary

Peggy, unaware of the impending change of plans, wrote happily, still trying to figure out how to please his family with a demure image, rather than one that is "gaminesque," which I take to be naughty and flirtatious. She was also still making a silk purse out of the idea that they would be poor but respectable, like southern gentility, in their life together. They were forever working out their ideas of class and money.

Peggy to Jack, August 14
Darling:

...Let's take a lot of snaps while you are at the shore. Harry promised I can have a big picture taken. Hope I look real naïve and refined instead of "gaminesque." Darling you don't know how that really worries me. You know about your mother thinking I was a little witch and you know I want to live up to the family traditions of respectability. I don't mean that sarcastically. I want my children to be innately "real." But they couldn't help but be with you their father. Let's bring them up like southern aristocrats "poor but proud" – maybe fortune will favor us and you'll make ten thousand a year in the future. Won't we feel like "John D." after our twenty-five a week. Then I can write articles on "how I helped my husband save."

Then she got Jack's letter, and the following scary news:

Jack to Peggy, Ithaca, August 14
Sweetheart,

... Today I got a telegram from Phil, talking of the "surprising" news from Mary, and that he <u>must</u> talk to me, and that mother's happiness and probably life depended upon it – which I think (and I hope to God) is considerably exaggerated. The thing has become an obsession to me. I don't know what to think, and I need you more than ever, darling, to talk to. My God, I don't see why we can't be happy without making other people unhappy, do you?

121

Now the siblings were working together to undo the marriage. Everyone seemed to have the impression of Peggy, sight unseen, as a lower class girl. Class, always class! I imagine the two sisters in Burlington, Mary and Polly, meeting over drinks on Mary's front porch to plot how to save Jack and the family from the embarrassment of an ill-considered marriage to an impulsive girl unvetted by the family, and one who apparently had a hypnotic power over their naïve little brother. I imagine them including Mary's husband Henry, a member of Burlington's upper crust, on an indolent late summer afternoon, looking out at the Mississippi River in the distance, and coming to a decision: the only solution was to bring in the big gun, their brother Phil, an Army officer used to assuming command. It was Phil's turn and, after all, he had taken precious little responsibility for his young sibling over the years.

Jack to Peggy, Ithaca, August 16
Darling Peggy

...Troubles to tell you, sweetheart. They all seem to come at once. In the first place, Phil insisted by telegraph that I meet him in New York Friday night, as that will be the only opportunity we will have of seeing each other – so I gave him my word that I would – and darling, only you can know what a sacrifice it is to me, giving up one precious night with you. But I will be there with you just as soon as possible Saturday morning, and I'll wire just when.

And then, a letter from Polly today, saying that Mother is in the hospital, with a serious attack of appendicitis, and that my last (rebellious and reproachful) letter had upset her terribly – and going on at length to the effect that we both (Polly and I) will have to sacrifice everything for our parents' sakes, for a little while, and that she knows how hard it will be to give up seeing you now. But I'll be damned if I'll give it up, seeing you, my own darling wife

122

even if it can be only for a few days. I'm afraid the idea of a wonderful week together will have to go. We'll just have to concentrate it all into a few days – as if that were possible – as if we could even concentrate all our love into a lifetime...

And then – insignificant, but tending to make life just a little more miserable, with finals coming on, and my mind miles away from them, anyway, I've got a hell of an attack of tonsillitis. But that's disgustingly material, and such things don't count with us, do they?...

To say that Jack and Peggy's reunion on the weekend of August 17, 1923 didn't work out as they had planned would be an understatement. It was a weekend they would never forget, a climactic scene in the history of Peggy and Jack.

1923

Late Summer

Jack and Peggy, the Flemings and the Talbots

Jack's brother, Philip Fleming, to his sisters,
from Lexington, Virginia

Monday, August 20, 1923

Dearest Esther and Mary, -

I returned yesterday from what you may regard as an unprofitable trip, and perhaps I can agree with you, for it cost me a good round sum and nothing that you desired was accomplished. I met Jack in New York on Friday, and while there had two talks with Monsignor Waring, one alone and one with Jack along. Father Waring is now Vicar General for the archbishop and as such handles all legal-ecclesiastical matters so he knows what he is talking about and he says that everything about Jack's marriage was so regular and complete that no church annulment is possible – and the fact that they have had no conjugal relations has no bearing – as it might under the civil law. But since a civil annulment alone would mean nothing to mother I did not pursue

125

that further, beyond finding out that neither Jack nor Peggy want it. They are determined to go through with this so we can only accept it and find out what is best to do under the circumstances. And I am convinced that Jack should tell mother and father without delay. It will be a terrific shock, but mother has a lot of stamina and it will be better for her to know what has happened than to worry about what may happen. Actual facts, however unpleasant, are easier to face than dreaded possibilities. And further I think it would be dishonest for Jack to go back to school without notifying his father of the conditions under which he is being sent. And Peggy says that her family may cast her out when they know she is married, so it is dishonest of her to accept their bounty and support for another year too. Jack has accepted a responsibility and I think he should start to work right now to bear it. Get him a job in Burlington and let him bring Peggy there...

Instead of getting on a train to the New Jersey shore for one more weekend with Peggy at the end of the summer school session at Cornell, Jack, on command, went to New York City to meet his brother Phil. Phil had come up on a train from Lexington, Virginia, to "do something" about Jack's rash decision to elope with a girl no one knew anything about. Phil was in his late thirties, sixteen years older than Jack, when his sister Mary called upon him to intervene in the drama Jack and Peggy had produced with their elopement.

Phil was now well launched as an officer in the Army, living what his little brother regarded as a rather glamorous life among the "high hats."

Phil was a small sturdy man but with the stature of command, and bushy black eyebrows – a Fleming family genetic trait – framing cool, intelligent eyes. Since Jack was only ten years old when Phil graduated from West Point, I suspect they hardly knew each other. Phil apparently shared the family perception of Jack as a hopelessly irresponsible boy, though it would seem, judging from Phil's letter, that Jack's charm was lost on him. That Phil managed to secure an audience with the Vicar General of the Catholic Archdiocese of New York to intervene in Jack's marriage on behalf of the Fleming family is impressive, testament to Phil's sense of himself and to his father's status as a lay Catholic leader in the Midwest. But even though I, too, think they were crazy and irresponsible, It makes me feel especially pleased on behalf of my besotted, fiercely attached parents, that Monsignor Waring would not be coerced, even by a rather stern military officer, into undoing the marriage.

Failing in his first mission, Phil went to Philadelphia with Jack to rendezvous with Peggy, who came up from the shore in a fashionably pleated skirt and blouse, with a touch of blush and lipstick. Hoping to scare them both to death, Phil took the two miscreants out to lunch. I imagine a meeting in the elegant lobby of, say, the Bellevue Stratford Hotel, my parents sitting stiffly, but close, on a lobby couch, Peggy looking frightened but determined, her legs crossed demurely, and Jack, in stand-up collar and tie, his thick wavy Irish hair slicked back, surreptitiously touching fingers on the seat between them, while Phil, perhaps seeking to intimidate them by wearing his Army uniform, lectured them about their rash actions. *"It wasn't a very pretty party,"* Phil noted in his letter.

Phil also provided the family with his first impression of my mother:

I have met her and had a long talk. She is a nice girl – no world beater, and not gifted with an unusual amount of common sense – she's a match for Jack there – but she has possibilities and she is in love with Jack. She would become a Catholic with very little urging – and that should soften the blow to mother and dad. She is rather pretty, about my height, thin, has hazel eyes, nondescript hair, teeth not very good, rouges a little, skin and complexion not bad but nothing to brag about, dresses simply and in pretty good taste. She did have one of those skirts that looked as if it were about to drop off her hips, but that seems to be the style these days. Her manner is shy and rather sweet. Her voice is soft and her grammar is good. She hasn't much to say – but then I gave her very little chance. They are obviously very much in love – certainly as much as two such children could be – and everything may work out all right. You won't be ashamed of her, and may like her very much – we'll have to, for there is no going back in this now, it must be accepted in good grace and go ahead. They married secretly to avoid their parents' opposition, never thinking that it would be harder to face later than then. They are simple idiots, without any idea of what a struggle life is...

He was right about them, of course, but I feel perversely proud of my parents' tenacity in the face of such severe judgment. Phil provides some details about their conversation:

Jack talked big about getting a $125.00 a month job in Newark next year, and living on that until I told him what ordinary things cost. She can't cook or sew but hopes to learn. I learned nothing of her family beyond what Jack can tell you. Peggy is afraid to tell her own family and wants Jack to undertake the job, but I think both families should be told at the same time – and soon. I advised Jack to consult with you two and Polly as to the most propitious moment for telling mother. She must be told now, for if the news should come to her through any other source than Jack – and it will in time – it might kill her. So don't let Jack put off telling. He has been weak so far, but he has to show some strength of character now. I have thought much about this and am sure that I am right – and Father Waring agrees with me. I took Jack to see him and his advice was the same as mine. Jack should tell all and then bring Peggy out to Burlington this summer to show that he isn't ashamed of her and to put a stop to whatever idle gossip may get about – and mother will worry much less than she is worrying right now, after she sees and knows Peggy. Jack should, I believe, get a job and a place to live in Burlington and then actually live *within his means and show the world that he hasn't made a mistake, and that he <u>can</u> make good. Peggy is a nice, sweet girl, and it may be a good thing for Jack that he has her instead of someone else – susceptible creature that he is. And if properly handled this may be the making of him.*

After their unpleasant party ended that Saturday, August 18, 1923, Jack went down to Beach Haven with Peggy for the rest of the weekend, keeping their secret from the Talbots. Jack promised Phil that he would depart for Burlington promptly. His sisters Esther and Polly, who in addition to sister Mary now also knew about the elopement, were to meet Jack's train in Chicago and drive home to Burlington with him and Polly's fiancé, Major Wilfred Blunt, a West Point classmate of Phil's. .

Peggy was undaunted by unfolding drama and just as ardent as ever...

Peggy in Beach Haven to Jack in Burlington, August 22
Darling,

...How is your mother? Please let me know right away. Jack I wish I could tell you that I had been given the power to express myself – half tell the way I feel. I'm so overpowered, so inspired. All that could ever want is just to make you happy. "Humility" – I guess that's it. It's too complex for me to analyze. I just know I love you, more than I ever learned of loving anything. And that I feel so thankful and grateful – cause we are each other's – all each other's.

Darling please find out as soon as you can about "our" plans. Jack, do just what you think is best about everything, and let me know immediately. You know how worried I am, and anxious to know. I hope in a way we can be with each other right away, although I do want you to finish school.

...I can't think of the best thing to do. I know what I want to do. We don't want our thoughtlessness to make us any more selfish, Jack.

But Jack loving each other isn't selfish and oh I love you so, darling.

What followed is incomprehensible. With the exception of one telegram, Peggy did not hear another word from Jack for almost three weeks. No news, no calls, no reassurance, no plans, even though he must have known that Peggy would be beside herself, with her future happiness hanging in the balance. I can only think that Jack, in the presence of his family, weighed down by the frightening task in front of him, to tell his parents what he had done, went into a kind of paralysis, a panic attack, a sort of catatonia. It turns out that along with everything else, he also got sick. By early September he was in the hospital for surgery on his tonsils – a turn of events Peggy was unaware of until it happened.

Peggy wrote daily letters, each more frantic than the one before: *You know you've been away nearly two weeks and all I've had is the telegram and a letter from Ithaca. Jack can't you understand how anxious I am? I wish you'd telephone me some night. I'd call you, only I don't think it would be good – you know with your family and especially if you haven't told them.* She began to offer suggestions for things Jack could say when he broke the news to his parents: *Please impress on them that we do understand how poor we'll be and that we don't mind. Just being with each other compensates – doesn't it Jack?*

Still the silence and uncertainty went on, and Peggy began to despair. She wrote: *Jack, I can't stand this indecision. I mean it. I can't sleep or anything, so please decide something definite immediately. If I give you the choice of any course you and your family choose, then you can at least let me know – and I won't have to worry all the time, and please write to me at least once a week. After you're married you do that from a sense of duty if not desire.*

Peggy and Jack's parents must have suspected something. Mary Fleming was felled by a "nervous condition" and Fanny Talbot's emotional radar was detecting a deception in the air. Peggy wrote, *The other day Mother gave me a long lecture on runaway and secret marriages. She asked me to promise I wouldn't. I evaded the question. Then she said, "Well Peggy if you do, don't keep it a secret, you know the construction people put on it regardless." Why do people always say that? It's so unfair. Darling we married each other so purely just because we loved each other. That paints me so much the smaller. I didn't even think of it. All I knew was that I loved you, everything about you.*

She finally concluded that Jack's family had poisoned his mind and caused him to stop loving her. *Perhaps it's an even more intense unhappiness to know we're married and you're sorry and don't think about me much...*

Here's Jack's explanation for his silence:

Burlington, Iowa, September 4, 1923
Peggy sweetheart –

Please, please forgive me for not writing – God, if you only knew how the thought has tortured me – and I'm so worried and nervous wondering what you will think of me. Please be forgiving to me, darling, and love me – as I love you – terrifically and intensely – I have thought of you constantly – always, Peggy, you have been uppermost in my mind – and the days went by that I didn't write – I was actually afraid to write because I had no excuse or explanation. O – it all sounds so weak – and I love you and want you so – it's just driving me crazy – you won't be too angry at me, will you, Peggy? – I couldn't bear it, and yet I know you have a right to be. Damn it – I'm in such a nervous state that I haven't opened your last letter yet – afraid to –

Here's the way things stand now. I can't tell mother till her nervous condition is better – the doctor won't let me – you see, she was on the verge of a complete breakdown - but is getting better now – and I know everything is going to be all right when the time comes – and everybody – all the family – is going to help all they can. And all my sisters and Henry are sweet about it – and want to know you and love you and take you as one of them – and are going to do everything they can for us. And Phil wrote to them telling how sweet you were – and how he liked you (you see, I knew he would) – and even wrote a note to give mother when I told her to make it easier for her – and us. Esther was the most understanding – she could see best what a hell of a strain it is being away from you – and facing mother every day – and wishing I could tell her – she was so sympathetic – I'm sorry she's gone. Polly has just become engaged to Major Blunt – so her mind is more occupied with that – and, by the way, that engagement is very pleasing to mother – and will put her in a good frame of mind, and help a lot.

By the way, darling, (it seems trivial but I guess it isn't) I go to the hospital in the morning to have my tonsils taken out – think of me. I haven't said half enough – but I have to mail this now – I can't wait – and I'll write lots more tomorrow, sweetheart – little wife.

~ Jack

The letter had a soothing effect on Peggy, but not before she had a chance to think about it.

Special Delivery, Peggy to Jack, Glenside, September 8
Darling,

If you only could realize what a relief it was to get your letter. I don't believe I ever felt so frantic. I didn't know what to do. Darling I'm not angry and I do understand but please sweetheart, try not to get another "don't feel like writing" mood and excuse me for writing that bossy letter. Jack you don't know how hard it was for me to not think you were a little selfish. I had to wait a whole day convincing myself. Then I knew you really were sorry and I felt like that had been an unfaithful thought on my part. And I'm so worried about your operation. You know that I think of you all the time, only more intensely every day...

I'm so sorry your mother's been so sick and glad she's better. Darling it's a hard situation, especially when we're so far away, but I know you'll tell her as soon as you can, and then please come get me...

While Jack was in the hospital, his sisters took matters into their own hands and told their parents about Jack's marriage to Peggy. The secret started to unravel fast.

WESTERN UNION TELEGRAM
Burlington Iowa, 9-10-23
Miss Peggy Talbot
Glenside, Pa.

Everything will be all right mother has been told and has written you so expect letter I was unable to write while in hospital but have written fully about plans they want me to finish school your family must be told am sending letters for them to you love dearest

~ Jack

Burlington, Iowa, September 10
Peggy sweetheart,

I adore you and long for you so, and I have so much to tell you; as you know from my telegram – and I believe mother wrote you, too – Mother and Dad have been told about us, and you can imagine what a shock it was to them. It came about this way – while I was in the hospital (I'm getting better now, but I did have a hell of a time, darling) – Mary and Polly decided it was an

133

opportune time to tell Mother – and they did. She was pretty much knocked out at first, and Dad, too – and they decided to make the best of it (which, after all, is the best way). Now, it is only fair, darling, for me – after being so deceitful – to do what will make them happiest, and they say they want us to be happy, and I know they do. Dad had his heart set on my graduating, and still wants me to go through with it – and keep our marriage secret from the world till next June, when you can come home with me, and they can help us get a start. But of course, this depends on your family, and they have got to be told now, haven't they? I'm writing a letter to your father, and darling, I know how hard it is going to be for you, going through this "telling" business. I wish you could tell them yourself, but I know you don't want to – and the only way left is for me to write, isn't it? ...

The important thing now is to get things settled. I've been made to see that I really have to graduate. I owe it to you – but how do you think your family, after they know, will feel about my going on with school? Your family must be told – there's no use putting it off, is there? I hate to think of the nervous strain on you, because I know what it is for me, but be brave, sweetheart. I know things will come out all right. O, I love you,

~ Jack

P.S. I am sending, under separate envelope, letters for you to give or send to your father and mother. Read them darling, and then get it over with.

What follows is Jack's letter to his new mother in law, and her response to him.

Jack to Fanny Talbot, Burlington, Iowa, September 10, 1923
Dear Mrs. Talbot –

When you have always been so very nice to me, it hurts me to tell you that I have been deceiving you all summer – because Peggy and I were married on the twenty-first of June. I know this news will come as a great shock to you – but I hope you will not blame me too much – and Peggy not at all – because it was at my impetuous and impulsive suggestion that we took this serious step. I hardly need tell you how much I love Peggy – and I have the honor of knowing that she loves me, too, and I know we will always be happy together. I realize how unfair it was of us to you – and to my family, too – to be so hasty in reaching that happiness as to be married secretly – and that I, without job or income, had no right to ask Peggy – but what is done is done, and I hope you will look on it in the best light you can, and forgive us, Mrs. Talbot. Your approval means very much to me, and little as I deserve it, I hope that, in time, it will come. As to plans for the present – I have written Mr. Talbot with regard to my going back to school – which, the opinion here is, would be best for both Peggy's sake and mine. What do you think? And I want you to know, Mrs. Talbot, that Peggy and I are legally married – but no more. Again, forgive a penitent son-in-law.

Sincerely,
Jack Fleming

The letter got just the right response from Fanny, whose reply is available to me because Fanny kept a pencil copy of it for herself. She was not immune to Jack's charms, though she clearly was uncomfortable with the fact that he was a Catholic. The Flemings, though troubled that Peggy was *not* a Catholic, had already crossed that bridge when Jack's siblings Phil and Mary both married Protestants. Fanny wrote Jack:

Fanny Talbot to Jack, Glenside, Pa., September 15, 1923
Dear Jack,

Your penitence disarms me.

I have always approved of you, Jack, and felt that if your infatuation for Peggy persisted, I must give way in minor things.

135

Of course, love is religion, and if you both are kind and considerate of each other, and render the best service you can to your fellow men – you will be following the teachings of Christ – regardless of creed and I hope that I am broad minded enough to follow that doctrine too.

You have the advantage of having made a good impression, while poor Peggy's fate seems to hang on a poorly taken photograph and her cooperation with you in contracting this hasty marriage. (This is evidently a reference to her discovery that Peggy was not well regarded by the Flemings – and I appreciate Fanny's loyalty, however reluctantly felt, to my mother.)

Now Jack, I don't want to be harsh and severe – I want to be just and <u>more</u> – to temper my justice with mercy. You two have not committed a crime – you have only been indiscreet, not even that, if you were in a position to be independent. You and Peggy want to be each other's, and there is no serious reason why you should not be, but we must get down to the practical side of it.

<u>I</u> want you to get your college degree – the hardest task I have before me now, is to tell Mr. Talbot. He may be reasonable, and he may not be – I dare not take a chance just yet – I must wait until I can lead up to it, so I cannot give him your letter now, but will do so as soon as I think it advisable – I will take the blame for the delay and exonerate you for this further secrecy.

Your parents have mapped out a very hard ten months for Peggy. With her passionate nature and her intense love for you it will be a mighty hard position for me to control alone. You will be away from Burlington – Peggy is living here in a suburban town among her friends and neighbors, who seem interested in every move she makes.

If you would promise not to consummate this marriage, until the announcement is made, and I have every reason to believe you are honorable, I would advise that you come to see her *occasionally to relieve this tense situation. I do not wish her to go to Ithaca at <u>all.</u>*

In the meantime, I would take a keen delight in getting Peggy some pretty things to start with. I would suggest that you have a little home by yourselves. "Be it ever so humble." Peggy is not a competent housekeeper at present, but if she has the proper spirit and your welfare at heart and I think she has, she will learn, and learn quicker by "doing."

Peggy's disposition is very different from mine – but her view point may be more human and honest, than mine – I have suppressed my hopes and desires until I am a nervous wreck, and I don't want her to follow in my footsteps. I want her to live in a happy atmosphere – and be natural, because for all her passionate, dictatorial manner, she is easily cowed and frightened. But she is loyal and not for one instant has she been sorry for this situation – her only grievance is the prospect of being separated from you. In fact, her loyalty to you is almost funny – and she has made some wild speeches in her defiance of my displeasure.

Perhaps Jack I may have said too much or too little – at any rate I hope you will both be patient and loyal and you will be happy.

Affectionately yours,

Frances P. Talbot

I sincerely hope you will start college and Peggy will keep you posted on any new developments. We hope your mother is better. This matter will be happily adjusted in time.

I grieve for Fanny, an unhappy woman trapped in a lion's den. There is so much that I, as Peggy's daughter, find interesting about this letter from my grandmother. First, I think that in her own way, Fanny loved Peggy and sought to protect her. All those years of despairing over Peggy's behavior, all the wild defiance Peggy had displayed, had not extinguished all of Fanny's affection for this bafflingly difficult child. That Fanny hoped Peggy would not, as she did, suppress her "hopes and desires" seems sincere, if self-pitying. Harry was surely the main source of her unhappiness, with his frightening tempers and flagrant infidelity. And then, to my astonishment, Fanny in one phrase captures the Peggy I knew, my mother, who "for all her passionate, dictatorial manner," was indeed "easily cowed and frightened." My mother was both terrifying and terrified, fearful in her needs and driven by fear, maddening as a mother, sometimes loving but often so hard to love. I am grateful to Fanny for putting Peggy's nature into a picture I can recognize.

Before Jack's letters arrived for Peggy's family, Peggy had already received one from her new mother-in-law, Mary Fleming. The letter is lost, but from Peggy's unhappy report in letters to Jack, we know that Mrs. Fleming said that the "victory" had been all Peggy's, "though we have never seen each other in our mutual conflict." She went on to say that if Peggy really understood Jack, she would never have "done it," because she would have known how unhappy it would make him – an accusation that cut to Peggy's heart. Mrs. Fleming stipulated that she didn't want Peggy and Jack to see each other at all during Jack's last year of college. I think Peggy had only a vague idea that she was in any "mutual conflict" with her new mother-in-law, nor that her mother-in-law was so very gifted at using emotional blackmail.

Fanny Talbot was, by Peggy's report, furious when she first learned of the marriage, but she was also furious at Mary Fleming's reproachful letter to Peggy. Still, in a letter to Mrs. Fleming, Fanny couldn't resist casting Peggy in a negative light.

Mother is furious. She wrote your mother and told her I was very self-willed and deceitful, and your family will hate me even more. I knew I'd get the blame from both sides. I don't care Jack, but if you stopped loving me even a little I don't know what I'd do. I never knew loving somebody could cause so much trouble. I'm not sorry we're married, though – do you think you are?

The last act in this drama was to tell Peggy's father, the fiery Harry, and to secure his approval for Jack's plan to go back to Cornell for his final year of college. To everyone's surprise and relief, Harry took the news very well, and happily gave his approval, thereby agreeing to keep Peggy – married – under his roof for another year.

WESTERN UNION TELEGRAM
Burlington Iowa, 9-15-23
Miss Peggy Talbot, Glenside, Pa.

Please tell your father yourself tonight and give him mother's and my letters absolutely necessary to have his decision now so I may know what to do about school no use putting it off further please wire outcome right away let's hope for the best love dearest
~ Jack
Harry responded immediately:

WESTERN UNION TELEGRAM
Glenside, Penn Sep 15 1923
John J. Fleming Jr., The Oaks, Burlington Iowa

While regretting your hasty unnecessary and unconventional action nevertheless forgive you stop go back to college will keep your confidence am willing to take my chances on you
H. A. Talbot

With that last hurdle overcome, the atmosphere improved in both the Talbot and Fleming households. The Flemings, in a change of heart about keeping the marriage a secret, decided to announce the wedding in the Burlington newspaper, and the Talbots sent out an engraved wedding announcement to all their acquaintances. Peggy and Jack resigned themselves to a life apart until Christmas vacation. Peggy was still chafing at getting "all the blame from both families" for the elopement, and still afraid of meeting her new in-laws, given her belief that they were disdainful of her. "I'm not just trash," she complained in one letter. Meanwhile, with the full participation of the senior Flemings, they began to plan a future in Burlington.

Jack to Peggy, Burlington, September 17
Darling,

Excuse the paper please, but it's all I can round up. I got a very nice letter from your mother today, sweetheart, and I'm certainly glad she approves of me, and takes such a fair view of religious matters, because the more our families approve of us, the better it will be for us, and for them, don't you think? ...But darling girl, I'm afraid we'll have to make up our minds not to see each other until Christmas – unless you can come up to Ithaca, and that I doubt if your mother will allow, unless you come together. Because my father feels he is doing all he can to give me barely enough to go to school, especially with Polly's wedding coming on, and if I can earn any money, I owe it to him to help defray my own expenses...with circumstances as they are, I don't see how I can honestly do anything but comply with my father's wishes, do you? It's going to be hell – it's going to be hell for both of us ...We were talking today about plans for next summer – sweetheart, I'm going into the (now almost defunct) construction company – probably as a partner – and start right in the contracting business. And I know, with you by me, that I'll make a success, because this country out here is growing fast, with all kinds of building going – and O, I'll just love working my head off with you beside me. And Peggy, we're going to have a little house to ourselves, and I think the family will give us, or at least help us to get one, that's how they talked. Of course we'll be poor as church mice when we start, but I don't care if you don't...

Mother Fleming, ever resourceful, figured out a way to keep her boy close by, even if it meant having Peggy there, too. Jack (and Peggy) fell for her newest plot hook, line, and sinker:

Jack to Peggy, Burlington, September 20
Sweetheart

...Your family certainly were wonderful about it all – and my family are now, too. Do you know what I've been doing all evening – planning a house – with mother and father!! And mother is so interested, and only you can imagine what a thrill I got when they brought up the subject. You see, part of our place here can be divided up into lots, and they want us to have a little house there. Of course it's awfully near home, but we can't be choosy about that, can we? We've been poring over "House and Garden" magazines, and finally found a peach of a house (golly, I hope they're serious about it, but surely they must be) to copy – sort of an English cottage, all one story, with a low, sloping roof, and kind of L-shaped. How does it sound, darling? Isn't it wonderful to be discussing a house all our own, just you and I, sweetheart? ...I think I have to leave for school on the 25th...

Peggy to Jack, Glenside, September 20

Jack, I'm so excited about our own home. Won't it be darling. I'm sure Daddy will give me the money to furnish it, and I'm going to get a Ford, and then we could drive out to Burlington next June. Is that a good idea? And I'll get a dog, you know a good one. So I won't be lonesome while you're "contracting." Jack isn't it wonderful about the company and an assured position, and you can build up. You'll have to work hard, and you know darling, I don't care how poor we are. Just so we're poor together. We'll read a lot. You know we mustn't let ourselves get tacky, and darling I'll help you all I can (not much). I'm glad you know we'll have nice people to play with. But let's have evenings when we're all alone too. It will be wonderful, won't it, Jack dear? I could almost cry with happiness when I think of it, darling....

Me, too. Jack and Peggy built a whole magical story together. But none of it, sadly, would be realized.

Jack to Peggy, Burlington, September 22

Sweetheart

I told Warren today, and he was certainly pleased and excited, and surprised. He thinks it's just wonderful, and insisted on permission to write Hilda right away. They're going to be married in February and they will be all settled when we get here...I'm going to tell Hennie next – he wanted to bet me the other day that he was married before I was, but I didn't want to take his money. His girl, Maureen Jeffries, is a peach...I get a new thrill every time I picture us living out here together. And as for evenings alone together, if I had my way, that's the way most of 'em would be. And I'll promise to learn to read out loud, and we can read to each other.

Thus began my parents' sixty-two years of married life, with my mother at home in Philadelphia, where she enrolled in sewing and cooking classes, and my father finishing his engineering degree at Cornell. Jack and Peggy did not move home to Burlington and build their dream house on the ample Fleming property, nor did Jack join a construction company as a partner in Burlington. And they didn't become a part of a new, young Burlington "set" with Jack's best friends Warren and Henry and their new wives. It sounded like a lovely, orderly plan, and I wonder what our lives would have been like if they had. Would their story have had a tidier ending in that scenario? Would they have realized the American Dream? Does anyone?

1923

Fall Semester

Jack in Ithaca to Peggy in Glenside, October 4, 1923

Darling,

...I have been working awfully hard – and I'm going to keep it up. Everyone says, even some of the professors that I know pretty well, "Look what getting married has done to Jack!" Some of 'em, however, especially my class advisor, are skeptical about my being able to take 42 hours between now and June, which I need to graduate. But I'll show them.

Jack and Peggy began their year of purgatory, with a brief release for Christmas vacation, with the single objective of getting Jack through college, so that by June 1924 they would begin their life together armed with his bachelor's degree in civil engineering from Cornell. Their letters, more than 100 of them in October, November, and December of 1923 alone, were first of all vehicles for keeping in touch. Their occasional long distance telephone calls, usually initiated by Peggy when she hadn't received enough mail from Jack, were as frustrating as they were thrilling. Peggy's voice seemed "too scratchy" and hard to hear, long distance service was expensive (Peggy notes that one call from Glenside to Ithaca cost $10), and precious minutes were spent talking to fraternity brothers who were sent in search of Jack somewhere in the Delta Upsilon house.

But the letters were more than news reports. They became an epistolary laboratory in which Peggy and Jack began to define their relationship and their future, to get to know each other better. Perhaps because, unlike other young couples, they were forced to shelve their married life for a year instead of living it, they had a year to imagine in romantic detail what that life would be. And though fate and circumstance and history always impose themselves on our dreams – no one gets to live exactly the life he imagined – it seems particularly poignant and a little bit sad to read of the life this fiercely passionate young couple planned and to learn once again how ephemeral were their dreams.

Their first job for the winter – one both of them focused on – was "that damn degree." Though they had, as Peggy complained, "a sheepskin wall keeping us apart," and Jack grumbled about "another day shot and another square inch of that damn diploma earned," they were in agreement about the importance of Jack's studies, and what his degree meant for their future. Peggy understood that her standing with the Fleming family depended in some measure on Jack's performance at school. *It's so important,* she wrote, *and I'm responsible for you. Don't let your family think I'm not a good influence.* Ever sensible to the impression they were making, she added. *And then it's sort of reparation to our families, and doing this for each other will prove to them what we don't have to prove to each other – 'that we do truly deeply adore each other.'*

Jack, whose discipline necessarily extended to the economical use of *both* his time and money, surprised himself. *Sweetheart, I'm getting so economical and frugal – a nickel looms up like the rising sun now. And you can't imagine how different I am in my attitude towards studying.*

It seems that Peggy *was* a good influence. After his first month at school, Jack reported that he had earned stunning marks for the fall term's first quarter: 90 in Heat Power Engineering, 91 in Highways, and 80 in Concrete Construction. *Darling I'm so proud of your marks,* Peggy enthused. *They're wonderful. I knew you'd get good ones but I never suspected they'd be as good as they are – and darling if you ever did get bad ones it would be my fault. Cause it would show that my influence wasn't sufficiently good to make you want to get good ones.*

Even without each other, both Jack and Peggy found plenty to do. Enforced by his father's constraints on him, Jack was stuck in Ithaca, but even so, was surprisingly resolute against a constant stream of temptations. He studied, went to church, wrote Peggy (never often enough), and went to class, wrestling with the intricacies of concrete and electrical wiring while college life swirled on around him.

Still a member of the DU fraternity, Jack grudgingly participated in freshman rush, and he managed to get to Cornell football games in the home stadium by securing a volunteer job as usher. Very occasionally a friend would talk him into going to a dance on campus or an evening out in Elmira, where he "sat alone outside and brooded," while his friends went to a cheap dance hall.

With his characteristic eye on class, Jack reported in detail on one memorable evening away from the books:

Last night, darling, Chaddock the faithful drove Sam Haldeman, Bill Hayes and me to Syracuse for the express purpose of seeing a supposedly good vaudeville show, and it was rotten. And there were some honeymooners in a box near us – I'm sure they were – and I couldn't keep my envious eyes off them – they looked so radiantly happy and oblivious of everything else – that they just made me blue and you-sick as the devil, Peggy. They were what I suppose we would call common, darling, but they were young and nice looking, with brand new country store clothes, and he had a brand new haircut and she had a brand new bob. The way they looked at each other lifted them out of their commonness. The faces of the people around me were far more interesting than the second rate acts that did the same old stuff on the stage – and got by with it. The audience all laughed just when they were expected at just the same crudities they have been laughing at for years. One act was one of these melodramatic playlets where the heroine talks with a cut in her voice and you can guess three jumps ahead, and you just know she's going to get her crook husband Jim out of a probably well-earned jail sentence by whining "Judge, you gotta wife and kiddies, too, aincha?" There was a woman near me with a mobile countenance who unconsciously registered and reflected every emotion – it was fascinating to watch her. I was sure she was going to burst into tears at the climax.

But most Saturday nights, Jack reported, he would spend "bellowing 'Pipe down!'" to noisy fraternity brothers down the hall, so that he could churn out a water supply report.

Peggy's chief laments were that she was at home, financially dependent on parents that "make me feel like a criminal," and that Jack didn't write her often enough. She reported with a petulance for which she soon apologized, *Everybody says 'Married? Where's your husband?' 'College.' 'Why doesn't he come see you, if he's in Ithaca?' I think people think you don't love me, Jack.*

In dark moments, she spoke of her own *horrid disposition. I don't love anything today except you. I'm a disagreeable brat, Jack. And I don't like me even a little...* And the letters provide a window on Peggy's mother Fanny's continuing animosity towards her daughter. Several times in her letters Peggy reported on some verbal assault, an unexpected tongue lashing that seemed to erupt from some deep vein of resentment in Fanny.

146

In sewing class Peggy learned to make a "teddy," a lingerie item contemporarily made famous in a popular song – "Oh gee, I miss my teddy!" She was assigned to make a man's shirt (Jack sent his neck and arm measurements, hinting that he would be pleased if she made it for him), a bedspread, and a dress. She thought of a twin pair of silk pajamas for the two of them, and though he was politely enthusiastic about that idea, they were never again mentioned, so my guess is that they were never made.

Peggy was particularly excited when she began to receive wedding presents – silver candlesticks, candy dishes, a silky quilt, a painting, and a "table sweeper" that she described with a little drawing in her letter. Even "Mrs. S," Peggy's father Harry's New York "friend" Cecilia Sophian, called Peggy to congratulate her on her marriage. Fanny was outraged and Peggy worried that Mrs. Sophian might be inspired to send her a present, a turn of events that would put Peggy in the awkward position of accepting it, thereby hurting her mother, or sending it back, rousing Harry's considerable temper. Surely not for the first time, Peggy was caught in the middle of her parents' unhappy arrangement.

Best of all, Peggy began to receive warm welcoming letters from her new sisters-in-law. Phil's wife Dorothy and Jack's sisters Agnes, Mary, and Polly each wrote her a friendly note, expressing the hope that they would meet her soon, possibly at Polly's Christmas wedding in Burlington. She sent Dorothy's letter on to Jack, which gave him an opportunity to offer an olive branch to Phil with the following request: *That was a nice letter from Dot – and when you answer it, darling, here's one thing you can do, for both of us. I never thanked Phil for the time and trouble and expense he took to come up to New York after summer school and meet me – or for lunch that day – or for his good and sound (after all) advice. Couldn't you bring that in, through Dot, in some way, Peggy?* This warmth from Jack's family was a welcome surprise to Peggy, but was probably premature. Family history has it that the

Fleming sisters, famous in Burlington circles for their snobbishness, felt that Jack had married beneath him, and they "felt sorry for him."

Esther, Jack's oldest sister, who with her husband Harding was stationed at VMI with their four children, made the most generous welcoming gesture by inviting Peggy to visit. There may have been an ulterior motive, an advance review of Peggy for the family, but it seemed authentic. The invitation was both terrifying and thrilling, and after some urging from Jack, Peggy accepted. *Sweetheart,* Peggy wrote, *please promise me you'll write me every single day, 'cause I'll be a nervous wreck, not knowing them, and with the disgrace of eloping with you – recovering my name to begin with...I want to visit her 'cause she's your favorite sister, and she was precious to ask me and be so sweet.*

The trip to VMI was a huge success. Esther, in her late thirties in 1923, swept Peggy into the life of the family for more than a week. Peggy wrote giddy reports of the children, Jim, Jack, Molly, and Tommy, of amiable exchanges in which Esther shared family gossip and funny stories about Jack's childhood, of evening strolls and bridge games and dinner parties and flirtatious VMI cadets. She sent a postcard of the VMI Parade with an X marking the room she shared with Molly. The stream of euphoric letters began with this:

Peggy to Jack, November 16, from Lexington VA
Darling:
...Whew! I don't know where to start. Of course I took an early train and not at all the one I said I would and arrived about seven in the morning before anybody was even up. Esther and Harding both kissed me. I nearly fainted. I think I need a book of etiquette – southern chivalry overwhelms my austere nature.

The trip provided Peggy some insight into the family's view of Jack and Peggy as a couple. *I think the whole family thinks we're perfect children – and we are – at least I never felt so unsophisticated and impressionistic. Harding is reading my book 'Lost Lady,' by Willa Cather. His criticism of the leading character is that she has masculine habits – you'll understand that when you read it. Anyway he went on to say that all men are naturally polygamous – that moral examples are guides – and I gather the point of the whole argument was that men are true because it's the thing to do – and not by desire. Esther's retort was 'I thought so, but I hardly expected you to admit it.' I was impressed. Jack, you don't feel that way, do you? But darling they love each other. That's why things like that and their different viewpoint is what makes us young to them.*

But Peggy was anxious that they cling to their less sophisticated, more "natural" values, fighting against the cynicism of their age, the fabled Jazz Age just defining itself, thanks to Scott Fitzgerald, even as Jack and Peggy wrote. *But darling, let's always be young. I'm glad you're a monogamist, 'cause I am – a Jackist.*

Jack was in complete agreement with her. *I read Oscar Wilde's "The Picture of Dorian Gray," he wrote. It's a cynical, horrible, yet sort of fascinating book. He is so darn clever, and it's just full of cynical epigrams – clever, but meaningless... He, too, condemns faithfulness as a middle class vice. If that's so, I'm horribly bourgeois, because I'm always going to be true to you...*

While visiting her new in-laws in Virginia, Peggy gained some perspective on herself, too, and articulated a touching fierceness about her feelings for Jack. *Sometimes I have inferiority complexes. But that's poor policy – after all you are what you think you are, and at twenty one can't be "savoir faire" itself – can one? Not this one anyway. Jack, you can make me so much more, so much better than anybody else in the world ever could. Jack, if I make a success of anything, I would rather make a success of making you happy than anything else.*

Among the subjects they examined in their letters were the books they were reading. Jack and Peggy used books to test their thoughts on the relationship they were building together. Peggy started reading Booth Tarkington novels, thinking that she would learn more about life in the Midwest in them. Jack agreed. *I don't know of a better propagandist for the Middle West than Tarkington. I was always crazy about his books,* he wrote.

Trading books back and forth, they also tried the novels of another Midwesterner, Willa Cather, and they read *Blind Bow Boy*, a novel by Carl Van Vechten published in 1923. They dipped into other works by Carl van Vechten, an essayist, novelist, drama critic for the New York Times, for a time an American expatriate in Paris in the intimate circle of Gertrude Stein and a photographer who, like Jack, had been born in Iowa. Both read the *Bookman*, a literary magazine of the era, which Jack compared favorably to another, denser literary journal, the *Dial*. For a student of the practical and tangible – concrete and pipes and wiring – Jack had a great yearning for literary diversions. In truth, all his life, he used reading to escape from the present and its demands.

Gee, it's great we both like to read, isn't it, sweetheart? Jack wrote. *Another link in the perfect chain that holds us together now.*

Jack and Peggy both believed in that "perfect chain" linking them. They had a mystical sense about their connection, believing that the intensity of their feelings for each other derived from the fact that they were one soul somehow separated at birth, that they were born loving each other, and that they were destined to meet, two halves of a whole reunited. When they recalled their first meeting and the immediate familiarity they both felt, they thought that "we didn't meet, but found each other again."

Jack wrote, *Darling, I can't help but marvel at how perfectly suited for each other we are – our intense mutual love that combines the mental, and psychic and physical in just the right proportions. – our mutual tastes and likes and dislikes – our trust and complete confidence and what I think is most important, our complete lack of restraint and repression, holding nothing back, suppressing nothing and thus being completely each other's.*

Chad asked me my philosophy of life, Jack continued, *and I told him that my happiness lay with you, and with nothing else – that rich or poor, as long as I had you to love and work for and have complete communion and partnership with, and with the wonderful inspiration of your love, I will always be perfectly happy, life can give me no more. And I told him, darling, of our intention to keep out of the ruts worn by so many couples before us – to keep active mentally and physically, and interested. I told him that we considered the present a job to be done, a sacrifice to be made, before we can reach that fullness of life... we'll create our own atmosphere above the commonplace – and domesticity changes at once to romance and adventure.*

Peggy reported talking about married life to an engaged friend. *When we were finished, she said she thought I had the sweetest idea of married life she'd ever heard. She said it reassured her, renewed her faith.*

Jack exulted, *I can just imagine people saying 'Look at Peggy and Jack – they're an ideal couple' – can't you, darling? And sweetheart, neither of us need submerge our personalities – instead we'll merge them into one. Why they are merged into one now, and each of us is a part of the other. Self-expression is all right as far as the single personality goes, but it can't reach the high planes of two personalities, complementary to each other and bringing out the best in each other and bound together by love and affection and comradeship. Why else did God make man and woman – why else did he make you and me, darling, but to belong to each other?*

It's comforting to me how healthy Peggy seems at this moment of her life. They both had a spiritual sense that God had led them to each other and, as Peggy said, "we must always be very grateful." Given that, the subject of religion, or more precisely the possibility that Peggy might become a Catholic, became a regular topic of their correspondence. Peggy reported, when she went to church with her friend Lottie that she was trying to understand the service, and found it "very impressive." She was moved when Jack reported to her that when he took communion, "about the most, in a religious way, that a Catholic can offer," he did it for her.

I feel wonderfully happy, Jack said, *and it seems that with you by my side, religion seems more to me than it ever did before. After all, darling, the right religions are founded in love, and when you know what love is, shouldn't it follow that religion will take on a new meaning? I couldn't even ever feel right if you didn't go to church with me, when we are going to be together in everything else. I wish my religion could be our religion – do you mind my saying it? I wish you would become a Catholic.*

This was Jack's boldest statement on the subject, to which Peggy responded, *Jack I said once if it would even make you specifically happier I would be a Catholic. If you wanted me to – and I am trying to understand – doesn't my going to church when you're away prove that?*

Peggy never did become a Catholic, and though my brother, Tommy, was raised in the Catholic Church, I was not. Perhaps it was a promise made in the first flush of their passion that Peggy, in the end, could not deliver on. To go through a conversion, Peggy, an Episcopalian by baptism and confirmation, would have had to consult a priest, and to take classes over a six-month period, before being admitted to the church with a first communion. Perhaps it took too much study, an activity in which Peggy had no confidence, and no doubt the idea of talking to a priest about her motivation in becoming a Catholic would have been frightening to her.

For me, their most poignant exchanges were about the life Peggy and Jack conjured as a young couple in Burlington, living in that house they expected the Fleming parents to build on the property. Jack drew floor plans and sent them to Peggy, who cut out pictures from *House and Garden* magazine and sent them to him. She wrote:

Jack you know I want our house to be different, have a personality. I would like some antiques, wouldn't you? Instead of all this very modern furniture that makes every home look exactly alike...and then to have a lot of good books will help too, don't you think so? But Jack we must have a davenport. I sort of like tapestry chairs too. Do you like them? And we'll have to have a gate leg table. Jack tell me what the little breakfast nook is like – all painted? Do you s'pose we can have built-in book cases? I love planning it all, because it is our house...

I want our house to be a home, the place we all love best to be. Don't you? I adore the plans you sent me. I think the little back bedroom that's away from everything, and has so many outlooks would be darling for our room. We'll wake up in the morning and look right out at the garden. Let's have an old fashioned garden. They're so conducive to romance... Why it lifts it out of the commonplace, doesn't it?

While Peggy fantasized about furniture, and the exact placement of each of their wedding presents, Jack said he got a kick out of thinking about structural details – hollow tile and stucco and roofs and basements. They imagined their life in Burlington – picnics at Crapo Park or along the Mississippi with Jack's childhood friends Henry and Warren and their wives; going to the big Midwestern university football games in Iowa City; Jack, like other Burlington businessmen, coming home for lunch, Peggy picking him up in the Ford at the end of the day (Peggy saw Jack as "one of Burlington's most respected men"); candlelight dinners, perhaps inviting the family. *It will be fun to have the family to dinner,* Jack wrote, *but oh so much more fun to have dinner all by ourselves in our own little house. And I don't care if it does upset the table arrangement (as they have it in the movies) – I won't sit far away at the opposite end of the table, but close to you.*

Jack said the decision was hers, but he hoped that they would not have twin beds, at least at first. Peggy hoped they would never have separate bedrooms, even when they were old. He wrote:

When I think of, and try to picture, the sweet intimacies and little details of life together, the waking in the morning with you close to me, cozy breakfast together, and when I come home from work...Sometimes, too, I think of children. I really think it's best to have them while we're young, don't you, sweetheart? You know, I read somewhere an argument against 'we can't afford to have children.' It was, we can't afford not to have children – that we wouldn't know the fullest joy of love until our love was consummated in parenthood.

Assuming that they were telling their families the truth (I think they were) and their marriage had literally not been consummated, and with a vacation reunion not far off, the subject of sex gained momentum in Peggy and Jack's correspondence. Jack offered to send Peggy a book on "it." He had become friends with a married graduate student at Cornell, "Pierce," who loaned him an out-of-print book on sex and gave him permission to share it with Peggy, as long as Jack promised to insure it for $50 with the post office.

I'm very interested in 'the' book, Peggy wrote. *But darling is that book of Pierce's very technical? I don't like things that take the romance out of 'it.' Darling, I really do think we have some fairly good ideas. They're very natural and darling, that makes marriage more spiritual, doesn't it?* She wondered, or pretended to wonder, if too much technical instruction might not breed contempt.

You know intimacy doesn't breed contempt, don't you, Jack responded, *and you are just teasing me, aren't you? Why darling, that phrase was built for things, or persons, that are attractive in appearance, but when you know them, through and through, intimately, you find they're not what you thought they were. And when two people love each other, isn't that entirely the opposite? The more intimate they become, the greater is their love for each other. Intimacy is a part of love, I think, sweetheart.*

Peggy read the parts of the book that Jack specifically recommended, and looked forward to further explanation from Jack when they were together again. *I knew I was ignorant,* she said, *but I never dreamed I was so ignorant.*

Jack and Peggy toyed with the idea of being together for the Thanksgiving vacation. *I feel sure mother would not take it as a breach of contract,* Jack wrote. *Her idea is not to keep us apart, but to let nothing interfere with my doing well this year and getting through, to which she rightly attaches the greatest importance for the present.*

In the end, it was Peggy, the realist of the two, who said no. She knew from experience how hard it would be for them to say goodbye after only a weekend together. Through the fall, they had written of the discipline they exerted on themselves to drive out thoughts of loneliness for each other. Seeing each other, especially so briefly, would rip apart the positive attitudes they were trying so hard to maintain. Jack wrote mournfully, *It's terribly, terribly hard to give up the Thanksgiving idea. I've been thinking about it so and planning and dreaming about it, and now to have it all go smash. But I suppose you are right, darling – we'd pay afterward for every wonderful second of it. And for so short a time, to have the awful effort of trying to get back to normal again. While we're making this year a year of sacrifice, I suppose we might as well do it right.*

From a modern perspective, it is hard to understand why Jack and Peggy, who were, after all, legally married, who were both in their twenties, were so in thrall to their parents. Why did they each need permission to make plans for a vacation together? Why,

155

indeed, did they keep their marriage a secret all summer, and why were they living apart at all? Were they in fact unusually young for their age, unusually unable to fend for themselves? Even from the perspective of the 1920s, a time when youth made a religion of flouting authority, Peggy and Jack seem frustratingly willing to accept the separation they were enduring at such pain. I think it was about the money. Their parents' support came with those rules, and as they were not financially independent, they had to follow them. In the end, it was their need for their parents' financial support that made Jack and Peggy so compliant, and in fact, they might well have considered themselves lucky to have that.

While a Thanksgiving reunion did not happen, the families had agreed to allow them to see each other at Christmas. Peggy was invited to Burlington and sister Polly's wedding. After Thanksgiving, the letters became electric with the building momentum towards Christmas and their long awaited reunion. Each letter is marked by a countdown – *only 17 more days until you are in my arms!* – and plans began to fall into place. Peggy would join Jack in Ithaca and they would travel together to Burlington for Christmas and all the festivities surrounding Polly's wedding.

Jack's mother sent this telegram on Thanksgiving Day:

Missed you today but looking forward to Christmas Peggy must come Moran sending check for one hundred dollars for wedding present to make sure would like to have her stay through January with Mary and us much love don't let up on work.

Mother

A joyous Jack sent it on to Peggy:

Jack in Ithaca to Peggy in Glenside, December 1

...Look at the enclosed telegram, and feel exuberant as I do! It means that now we'll have enough money and we're really truly going home together and not the least shade of doubt about it. ...I

don't know who Moran is, as the postal telegraph has it, but whoever he is, God bless him... the very thought of it completely shatters my sober, studious frame of mind. I want to find a radio and broadcast how much I love you – or borrow an airplane and write it on the sky. Three weeks from today – our six month anniversary – only this time I won't have to take the westbound train alone. We won't have to tear ourselves apart in any railroad station. We will be together, and oh so happy – you and I.

Meanwhile, Peggy wrote:

What do you s'pose, I had a letter from your mother – a darling one asking me to come for Christmas and in it, don't faint, a check from "Gran" (Jack's grandmother, the mistaken "Moran") *for a hundred dollars!!! Isn't that adorable of her – Harry was so impressed that he immediately said I could spend Christmas in Burlington! What'll we buy with the hundred? And Jack, your mother said I was to meet you and go out with you, so we can travel together! Aren't you thrilled and it isn't even three weeks till the twenty first. That's the day you get out, isn't it? I'm a wreck about meeting them all, but I won't feel so nervous with you darling...*

...I just thrill every time I think of traveling together, she said. *Won't it be gorgeous? Mother and Ninny bought me some lingerie for Christmas. I'm all aglow.*

And darling, don't you s'pose we can stay together on the train. How can we fix that? I'm afraid – rather I can't sleep very well, all alone, especially on a sleeper...

Jack already had that figured out. On December 6, he wrote:

...Darling I reserved a drawing room to Chicago for us on the twenty-second – it will be expensive, but don't you think we deserve it? A perfect little honeymoon...we'll probably have to use some of Gran's present, but I don't think it could be put to a better use, do you, darling? ...and you can leave Philadelphia Friday night and get here Saturday morning – then I'll have to go to two

classes in the morning and then we can have the day together till train time – four thirty...by the way, I had a letter from Phil and he'll be going down from Chicago on the same train we are – he said, apologetically, that he would try to be a more agreeable companion this time.

On the 14th, he provided more details for their rendezvous. Enclosed in that letter was a letter from his mother, full of excitement about Polly's wedding plans:

Dearest Jack

I was so glad to get your letter. The time seems very near now. You mustn't miss that Sunday train or Mrs. Starr will be desolated. Mrs. Starr thinks of nothing but this party of hers. If only Esther and Harding could come and Dorothy would – that is a very big disappointment. Polly wanted her in the wedding party. Everyone is so nice about the wedding. The Chittendens (sister Mary's in-laws) are certainly helping to see it through. They are going to Placid later but wouldn't go until after the wedding festivities are over. They are entertaining the Nicholsons. Are having all the older ones to dinner Saturday night. Everyone is delighted that Peggy is coming. Tell Peggy to bring a dress for Sunday night in a suit case for her trunk might not get here in time...

~ Much love – God bless you, Mother

Gran was so pleased with Peggy's darling note.

Peggy wondered what kind of dress she should bring in her suitcase for Mrs. Starr's party, to which Jack responded:

I suppose mother means an evening dress – or dinner dress (is that what you call 'em?) Mrs. Starr would give nothing less than a formal dinner – and that's what it is – far from being a party. Mrs. Starr is an old friend of the family, and is a high tension talker. An invitation for the Bachelor's Ball on Christmas night came for us today. I've been told it's going to be one of those functions that the whole population, young and old, attends...

158

So this was going to be a holiday full of glittering formalities. Jack was prepared:

Jack to his mother, December 20

Just the day after tomorrow, and Mr. and Mrs. John J. Jr. will be happily heading westward...I suppose Polly is all prepared now, and when does Blunty arrive? Oh, I'm glad to say I finally got a cutaway. Tell Polly to bring on her wedding, because I'm all set. I just need a pair of spats now. But perhaps Herbie has an extra pair. Well, three-seventeen Sunday and Peg will be home for the first time, and I'll be home again.

I like to imagine that my parents' trip went according to plan – that my father, after tossing in his bed at the DU house on Saturday morning, December 22, 1923, went to the Ithaca train station in the dawn hours to wake my mother in Berth Upper 12 on Car 1025 of the Lackawanna train from Bethlehem to Ithaca. I suspect that he found Peggy awake. I think of them, barely able to speak, suffused with the emotions they felt, making their way to the room they rented at the Hotel Ithaca, then wrenching themselves away from each other so that Jack could attend those last classes before the Christmas break.

1924

Spring Semester

From Peggy in Glenside to Jack in Ithaca, January 9, 1924
Darling,

The morning after a hectic night! Jack, I really did weep myself to sleep. I'm so damn lonesome for you. It isn't natural or anything. I just feel tense for you, all of me...Every time I'd wake up I'd involuntarily say "darling" and reach out for you, and oh, the terribleness of not finding you near me. It seems like a bad dream. After having had you...Gee, twenty four more days till we'll be together again. Please do work hard, Jack...

From Jack to Peggy, January 9, 1924
Darling wife –

...When I left you on the train, I hardy know how I got up the hill. I couldn't think. Those two wonderful weeks came and went so terribly quickly. The happiest time I have ever known, and now I'm back among faces I don't want to see, and surroundings that are

161

*hateful without you… And in the morning, there's no tousled head
on the pillow beside me, no eyes to read the love in…*

*P.S. Guess what a dumb thing I did, with my last dollar – I took
a chance on a raccoon coat – I hope I win, mostly because it would
please you, sweetest…I'd like one anyway…*

It seems safe to assume that Jack and Peggy had a successful
honeymoon in the Pullman stateroom on their December train trip
west to Chicago and Burlington. At home, they were swept up in
Jack's sister Polly's glamorous Christmas wedding, and
participated in enough social occasions to leave Peggy with at least
a dozen "bread and butter" letters to write when she got back to
Glenside. I wonder how Peggy fared with her in laws. Did they
find her more acceptable than they had anticipated? Peggy
mentions no resentment at her reception in the family. It would
seem that they embraced her as a "fact" if not necessarily as an
asset. Jack's euphoria must have been infectious. The additional
intimacy of sharing a room as husband and wife at home with
Jack's parents no doubt accounted for the prolonged acute pain
they each suffered as a result of their enforced separation from
each other. *The craving, the yearning for you that fills me all the
time is so strong that it just overpowers. I can't do anything. I
can't sit still. I want to wring my hands…concentration takes an
almost impossible effort,* Jack reported a day or so later, while
Peggy likened Jack's daily letters *to little oases on a vast desert.
I'm always so thirsty for them. When you're away there isn't
anything else that even counts.*

Just as adding sex to the equation must have intensified the
agony Peggy and Jack felt when they were apart, there was also the
worry that Peggy might have become pregnant. Birth control was
available in 1924 and, at least among more sophisticated
collegiates and flappers, it was yet another tool that allowed newly
independent modern women more personal freedom. But it seems
that Jack and Peggy were not using birth control, though they

certainly did later. Perhaps Jack's Catholicism – or their inexperience with these matters – took that option off the table in the early years. *And pretty soon you'll be able to tell me about something else very important to us, won't you sweetest?* Jack asked cryptically in early January. *Darling look you were right about NOT worrying,* she reassured him in a return letter. *In a way I wish you weren't, only I guess it is best for the present.*

Over the next months, their ardent letters were salted with the recurring themes of work, money, and their loneliness for each other – and glimpses of their daily lives apart. While Peggy waited for the months of separation to end, she continued her sewing classes at Wanamakers, an effort that by June had earned her a "sheepskin" of her own – a certificate for the successful completion of a dressmaking course from the Wanamaker Institute of Industries. Like the twenty-year-old girl that she was, she spent the night at friends' houses, played bridge (*for the Every Woman's club – how very provincial!*) and Mahjong, promenaded with other "Philadelphia flappers," as she described them, at Willow Grove Park, played the Victrola, "listened in on" the wireless radio (*We got Chicago!*) and went to the theatre with friends and the movies with her brother, Tom. She mentioned especially two now legendary films of the silent era, flickering images moving at unpredictable speeds to the accompaniment of a local pianist, "The Thief of Bagdad," a swashbuckling adventure movie starring Douglas Fairbanks and the foxy Chinese flapper, Anna May Wong, and "Flaming Youth," a risqué movie with the marquis tag line "How far can a girl go?," starring Colleen Moore, the starlet who came to represent America's idea of the flapper, slouching carelessly in a sultry pose, with bobbed hair and suggestive eyes looking at the camera.

Peggy was also continuing to get wedding presents, including presents from a surprise luncheon and kitchen shower given by one of her friends. After seeing the groaning board of presents for

Polly's wedding in Burlington, she was pleased to begin to acquire some of the nice things she wanted for the house they dreamed they would occupy come summer. Without question, the present that thrilled Peggy and Jack most was a hammered silver cocktail shaker, a necessity for all "grown up sports" in the opinion of Lois Long, style editor of the journal of sophistication, *The New Yorker,* that would begin publication a year later. Their excitement about the present is almost touching. The cocktail shaker seemed to represent a kind of confident lifestyle to which they aspired but was (and, as it turns out, would always be) out of reach.

Bill Belden's present arrived! Jack reported. *They had it sent here...Bill's mother gave him one just like it, which I have fondly admired for hours. It's a quart-size hammered silver cocktail shaker, with F engraved in the top – it's a knockout and I know you'll be crazy about it, darling.*

Sweetheart wife, he wrote a day or so later, *Bill christened his cocktail shaker before dinner this evening, and of course I had to join in and partake of a couple appetizers. Isn't it a peach, tho? The shaker, I mean. And won't it look wonderfully on our buffet – or Danish dresser – gee that just makes me think more about our little home – won't it be just perfect, tho...*

Peggy was wildly enthusiastic. *I think Bill's the sweetest man to buy us 'the' cocktail shaker,* she said. *Hey Jack, can't you feel little prickles of 'savoir-faire' running up your back every time you look at it? That's the most sophisticated present yet. I'll make you milkshakes every day, and then when we want to put on the dog properly for very special guests – like Bill and Mary and Henry – why, lo and behold we'll have the proper facility and just a little bootleg...*

When the shaker arrived in Glenside, Peggy reported, *Mother's a scream about it. She says (trying to hide the fact that she's worried about our soberness) 'Oh, that will be lovely for hot water!' I'm really awfully proud of it, aren't you?*

While Peggy mostly played, Jack worked harder than he had ever worked. He was tired of college life, in anguish over the course work ahead of him, and constantly remorseful that he couldn't seem to make do with the money his father gave him for his life at school. He wrote his mother, shortly after returning to school in January,

You knew what a happy time it was for me, and you can imagine what a wrench it was to come back here – a severe change in life that was just as hard as the nice two weeks before were pleasant. I was pretty despondent for the first few days, and to get back to conscientious work was an awful struggle, but I'm working harder than ever now – in the face of a discouraging amount of work to do in these next two weeks. It's all right when I'm working. It's at other times when I feel so low. I don't crave the companionship of any of the boys. I seem to have outgrown them – or they me – or something. Perhaps it's because I've been here so long, and so many have gone, that I feel out of it. But I don't care. I'm here to work for a degree and I'm going to get it. I hope you'll pray for me, mother.

With his parents and now his wife counting on him to succeed, Jack was under terrible pressure. Because he had lost a semester a couple of years earlier, and perhaps because he had failed a course or two, Jack had a heavy burden of class hours during his fifth year of college – 22 of them in the spring semester. After applying for permission to carry such a heavy load, Jack reported toiling over endless reports, doing lab experiments and prepping for tests and exams in electrical engineering, physics, highways, heat power, structural design, bridges, chemistry – and most painfully, public speaking. Jack's stutter is probably what led him to make this decision,

I've dropped Public Speaking, and I'll have to petition to get a degree by substituting for it. Please understand this, Peggy, darling – no one else can – but I just couldn't stand it. To sit

165

through the class was misery. The thought of making an ass of myself (I guess that's the basis of it all) shot my nerves all to hell – affected me almost physically. It obsessed me all the time – I knew it would never do me a particle of good. So I dropped it and I couldn't start again now if I wanted to.

In the face of so much work, Jack studied through many nights, only to exhaust himself. While he seemed to do well on tests, and even earned exemptions from some exams for his good work, he was, however, overwhelmed by the volume of reports he was required to produce. He reported working twenty out of every twenty-four hours, then not surprisingly having crippling headaches. He suffered from exhaustion and frantic nervous energy alternating with a kind of lethargy, and he was filled with remorse over his inability to concentrate on the tasks at hand. He seemed to slip into a depression as winter turned slowly to spring in Ithaca.

Somehow I feel this morning as if I weren't much good – weak – not destined to much success, he wrote Peggy. *No – I take that back – without you I'm afraid I would be that way, but with you to work for, I'll outdo my own limitations. I want you to be proud of me. I want you to have things. Oh, hell, Peggy, I'm ashamed of myself. Yesterday afternoon I meant to sleep for an hour and slept all afternoon – then after dinner Jim Trout, my Sigma Chi confrére induced me to go to a movie. Then I came home and worked frantically to try to make up for it until late into the night – and then, on top of it all – if I didn't sleep through two classes this morning. I wish I could sleep like an ordinary human being, and not go into a stupor, as I seem to do – so I can tell you, I feel pretty damn rotten this morning.*

Jack's blue moods, his punishing schedule, and his headaches worried Peggy, and she tried to look after him from a distance. Before an anticipated vacation, she wrote, *I don't know what to do, Jack, about all your studying. I hate to have you stay up all night and miss so much sleep. And get run down. It isn't worth it darling – please darling don't let yourself be nervous – you don't know how you make me feel when you say you're exhausted and nervous. Just desperate, cause I don't know what to do. I wish you didn't have all this work, and it's so important that you do pass it all. Your family would have a fit if you didn't and so would I. I'll just have to keep you in bed twelve hours a day and feed you up on malted milk and more tonic.*

Rarely, Jack was coaxed out to go to a movie, but he did indulge in his favorite diversion – reading. He told Peggy about a novel he fell into, reading it cover to cover in one night, which he described as *the nearest thing to the truth about college yet – in some spots it's so real it's uncanny...* Peggy's father bought her a copy of the book – *The Plastic Age*, published in 1923 by Percy Marks (and adapted for a 1925 movie) – and Peggy was similarly fascinated by it. *I can't describe the potent effect it has,* she wrote. *That man certainly does know the present day youth, doesn't he? Jack some places I can almost cry at the human feelings he puts into it.*

The book tells the story of a young man's four years at a prestigious men's college. It's a story about college life – classes, team rivalries, fraternities, singing groups, and affection for the *alma mater* – and the youth culture that was a phenomenon of the Roaring Twenties, when colleges witnessed a surge of enrollments and young men – mostly men – more interested in parties than the Peloponnesian Wars took colleges over, changing the experience of campus life. But more interestingly, the book is about class and social acceptance (did Jack feel any social stigma due to the fact that he was a Catholic? The book addresses this very subject), about first loves, and about disillusionment in an age of transition from a Victorian ethic to the freedoms of the modern age. At the center of the book is a "bull session" among the boys, in which they deconstruct the debauchery at a recent fraternity party –

where the girls and boys are drinking heavily, dancing provocatively to jazz music, and losing their virginity in borrowed dormitory rooms. Some of the boys are left breathlessly disillusioned by this scene and bitter at the lies – even extending to religious beliefs – that their parents told them in a more innocent time. Not everyone, it seems, was ready to embrace the new hedonism of the age. The book touches on a search for truth and meaning that history has left out of our view of the cynical, insouciant Twenties – and because it touched my parents so, I have to believe that it tells truths that they recognized and understood.

Though Jack and Peggy seemed cautious about both sex and alcohol, at least at the beginning of their relationship, many of their activities reflect the fads and fancies of their famous decade – beginning with their impulsive marriage, an act that rocked both families to their core. They were both conversant with Freud and his promise of self-improvement through suppression of impulses. They both knew Fitzgerald's novels (though Jack was less impressed with them than Peggy) and Omar Khayyam's then fashionable poetry. They went to movies and played bridge and Mah Jong and did crossword puzzles, all fads of the age. They listened to wireless sets and played popular songs like "That Old Gang of Mine" or "Yes, We have no Bananas" on the Victrola. They liked raccoon coats and fashionable clothes. After a fit of uncertainty, and a fit of consternation on Jack's part, Peggy even bobbed her hair – a shocking fashion statement symbolic of the libertine ways of that out-of-control generation of modern women, who smoked, drank liquor, swore, had sex, worked for their own living, voted, and generally exhibited too much daring and too much independence.

But were Jack and Peggy typical of their age? I think they might have been, had they not each been so unsure of their own strengths. It took courage, not to mention money, to be so brazen, so brave and carefree as the characters in Scott Fitzgerald novels.

Both Jack and Peggy were uncertain, at the core, that they were really able to be successful in the world. Peggy, who was well versed in defiance and rebellion against authority, might have been a classic flapper type had she been more interested in living as an independent woman – working, partying, even voting. But Peggy didn't trust her intelligence. She wrote Jack, *I felt so mentally and dramatically 'needy' in Burlington. Like the poor little girl from the country who didn't know anything!! Darling I hate to get so far behind the times that I can't have opinions – and don't even know what people are talking about. It makes me feel so inferior to you. You have such a wonderful mind.*

After years with well-heeled boys at boarding school and at college, Jack had the tools to embrace the *zeitgeist* of his age, but he was too worried that he would not be a success, a worry supported by his constant remorse at disappointing his parents, himself, and – most worrisome – possibly Peggy with his inability to get his work done, not to mention his inability to hold on to money. Given the fact that everyone in Jack's family seemed to share this low opinion of his abilities, it's not surprising that he doubted himself. He even wondered if he had made the right career decision. He wrote Peggy, *I often feel that I don't belong in engineering. It's so practical, material and unimaginative, yet again I want to do things in engineering, without losing any ideals of beauty.* I understand his early conflict about his career path – he was a person drawn to literature and the arts, yet he had a quick technical facility as an engineer and draftsman.

It was money he couldn't handle. Money, and their empty pockets, were a regular theme in their exchange of letters through the winter and spring. It was an obstacle to their ability to see each other on school vacations (there were two – in February and April, spent in Glenside, where Peggy and Jack were now allowed to sleep together, in Harry Talbot's little-used bedroom). It was also a source of mounting anxiety for Jack, who played a shell game with his father's monthly checks for school, using new money to pay old debts. He even cashed a $40 check from their joint account when, in a flash of hope after a wrenching separation from Peggy, he took the advice of a married friend and looked at married student apartments in Ithaca – a hope that was soon dashed by his parents. *When I was in the midst of the apartment dream,* Jack wrote, *I cashed a check on our account for forty dollars, to make the necessary payment. Then, when it fell through, I thought it would be wise to pay my debts – now – instead of letting them drift along and fall on our necks later, as might have happened. Ten each to Ed and Sun, and an old store bill. I bought us a wrought iron lamp, and I think I ought to pay Chad, and the cleaners what I owe, don't you? I hate to have them hanging over me, because that means they're hanging over both of us. And we want to start with a clean slate. Tell me what you think about that.*

Peggy didn't know quite what to think. *Darling it's all right about the forty dollars. I know you had to pay the debt and I don't mind so much cause I'd rather have you do that than owe money. But precious do you think it's exactly fair to have to spend "our" money which we have to do so much with – such as buying furniture etc on what your father ought to be paying for as long as its covering your schooling – like store bills and cleaners bills. I wouldn't say even a word, Jack, if we had a lot. But you know darling how much we have to do with it. And I'm just telling you all this so you won't spend the rest unless you have to. Don't be mad darling.*

In these exchanges I recognize a dominant theme of my own childhood and a familiar source of family tensions. In later years Peggy, the more emotionally fragile parent, nevertheless held the keys to the family purse, watching over it like a prison warden.

The story of the apartment is itself a story of the family's assault on Jack's confidence – and a story of the continuing power struggle between Mother Fleming and Peggy, even though Peggy wasn't putting up a fight. In February, after an extended break in Glenside with Peggy, he sent the following telegram on Valentine's Day,

Can get tiny apartment here for thirty eight monthly shall we take it darling and how about our families must sign lease Saturday if at all so wire answer immediately with forty from our account for deposit we could manage with your allowance how about it all my love Jack

The next day, he followed up with a letter, describing the apartment. *Now for what's burning my mind – darling, the idea of our getting an apartment here has obsessed me ever since I came back from you. I've been able to think of nothing else. I mentioned it to my married Sigma Chi friend Hal Davis, and he was all encouragement – said he knew just the place for us, and I just couldn't resist going and looking at it. It isn't much, precious, but we wouldn't care, would we? And anyplace with you would be heaven. It consists of two rooms, not directly connected – a sort of alcove kitchenette, and a bath down a flight of stairs, which would also be used by an older couple. It is so-called furnished, with the exception of silver, in old-fashioned style – huge gilt frames and much bric-a-brac, but it's clean. The other families in the house are instructors and their wives –no children. Thirty-eight dollars a month includes everything – light, heat, gas, electricity, water, and there's a fireplace. Oh darling Peggy wife, I know this letter reads matter-of-fact, but can't you see the love and longing and excitement just popping out all over? So I went right ahead – I couldn't resist – and made tentative arrangements – and wired you – and your precious answer came today – and I'm night-lettering home, and praying, tonight. I said we would want it March first – but I think we could have it before then. You see the young man that owns the place works in Chicago, and has to go back tomorrow – hence the need to sign the lease, as there is another man that wants the place... I know I can work ten times better. It*

171

would be pretty hard sledding and economizing, but I know we could do it, don't you? And anything is worth being together – the loneliness is unbearable for both of us.

Peggy, euphoric over the idea, secured her parents' permission, but Jack's family would not hear of it. On the 16th – Jack's birthday – he wrote: *Darling, the answer to my night letter home came this morning from Dad, to the effect that my sudden request had made mother sick, and he could not consent, and of course we just have to give it up in the face of that. Another hope shattered, another dream that couldn't come true. Darling, I don't see why they should take it so strongly, do you? Oh Lord, I suppose they think that's breaking the agreement, and I've bungled again and hurt some feelings. Why must I always be causing sorrow? We would have been so happy here together. It would have been so wonderful, but there's no use crying, is there, precious girl? Let's just try and forget we ever thought about it. Isn't that the best way? Anyway, it's just going back to the original plan, of a whole year of sacrifice and loneliness. But my mind, in a few days, had become so set on it – hadn't yours? And the quick mental readjustment is pretty damn hard – oh, well. We have each other, dearest Peggy.*

Peggy, as ever, was more philosophical. *Please don't feel discouraged Jack. It was natural that we'd feel we wanted to be with each other. You don't know what a temptation it is for me just to hop on an Ithaca bound train and just make you a home, and live with you regardless. But we mustn't. And then darling isn't it sort of natural for our families to mistrust our ability even if we do know we could do it. And I know we could. I'm sorry to upset them so. I don't see why it should though when they know all they have to do is say no if that's what they want.*

I agree with Peggy. Mother Fleming was good at manipulation, but in getting "sick," she outdid herself. From the perspective of hindsight, I also wonder if Jack wasn't right – that he could have gotten through his last semester more successfully if he had had Peggy by his side. But Mother Fleming, who had played a heavy hand in several exchanges over the winter – complaining that Peggy's letters to her were not chatty enough, sending Peggy wires to check on Jack's whereabouts – was not letting go of Jack without a fight.

The apartment was the first of a devastating series of disappointments Jack and Peggy suffered in the spring of 1924. Next to go was the dream of a house – the house they had furnished, decorated, and landscaped in their minds – that the Flemings would build them on their city block of property in Burlington. Deducing – from silence on the subject – that the dream house was not going to materialize (at least not by June), Jack and Peggy must have transferred their hopes to the small house the Flemings owned on the same property – a little white clapboard Victorian structure that had once housed family retainers and by 1924 may have been a rental property. After repeated pestering from Peggy, who smelled trouble, Jack wrote his father asking for a direct response about whether they could have that house. His father's letter is lost, but here is Jack's report,

Precious sweetheart I'm enclosing the answer I got from father about the house – and you can see for yourself that it's not at all satisfactory. I see they're still clinging to the idea that we're going to live at home for a while. Of course that's absolutely out of the question and when they realize that, that will put a different light on matters. Damn it. I wish I could talk to them – a person can't explain and argue properly in letters. But darling, please don't feel discouraged. It's a long time (too damn long) between now and June, and I'll get it fixed up before then somehow. We'll have a darling place to ourselves or bust and it will be the knock-outest place that was ever inhabited...

A sort of compromise was reached. Jack reports, *As to Burlington plans, mother says not to worry, as they'll be away over a month and we can have the house to ourselves while we're finding a place of our own – our own – gee, that's what we've been looking for ever since we first set eyes on each other, isn't it?*

The next disappointment was the evaporation of the job Jack had hoped to go home to in Burlington: *"Darling girl, I got a letter from Dad today, too. With some damn discouraging news in it – which I hate to tell you. My father's partner, Mr. Riling, is not going to resurrect the construction company again. Lord, after we'd planned on it so. And I'd looked forward to something that I was going to be in for myself, with unlimited prospects of expansion. I had my heart set on that company. You know it, sweetheart – and now, crash goes that for us. But to counteract that news, dad said he was trying to get me a position with the Illinois Power and Light Company – a huge corporation that is doing transmission line work now, especially.*

In the face of all this disheartening news, Jack did what any red blooded college boy with a hole in his pocket would do. He bought them a car – *an unhandsome, but rugged Ford runabout – 1922, starter, speedometer, demountable rims, and everything!* The car was purchased for $100 from a fraternity brother who had just lost a bundle of money betting on Cornell crew races. To make the purchase, Jack borrowed the $100 from another fraternity brother. From that purchase, Jack and Peggy set about spinning a new web of hope for their future, beginning with a long road trip home to Iowa after graduation. *Darling girl, we'll have to revise Omar Khayyam's recipe for happiness to 'a Ford, a radio, a dog, and thou beside me in the wilderness' (the arid steppes of the Middle West)*, Jack wrote, after a friend offered to make them a radio. Peggy charmingly responded, *You'll have something to play with then – several things – me first, I insist. And when you're bored with me, why then the car and the dog, and now a radio. When we get sick of the town talent, we can just wire in the Ritz.*

But the worst was to come. With the oncoming spring, the realization dawned on Jack that he really was *not* going to finish his work in time for graduation. His remorse over his studies, his debts, and his penchant for disappointing the people he loved seem to have pushed him alarmingly close to an emotional collapse. It's hard to imagine the sunny boy of the Jacksonia Flamingo days writing this,

...life as a whole seems to give few people small glimpses of happiness. Mankind seems gifted mainly with troubles and worse. And in my short life the only pure happiness I have ever known has been with you and from you...the days (such a few of them and they've passed so quickly) that we've been together have been the only ones I've known really worth living...And later, I'm nervous, worried, restless. I can't do anything. God, I hate myself for it. I can't work, that's the damnable part of it. I can't stay in one place, my nerves are continually on edge. I brood, about not getting my degree, not getting my debts paid, what is going to happen. I feel a nemesis pursuing me that I can't escape from – a continual sensation of crumbling walls that are slowly falling on me. Worst – worst of all – is that I'm not proving worthy of you. We're bound together forever and always, and what I do to myself I do to you, and I'm not proving worthy. What will you think of me darling, that's the question that drives me crazy. Please please love me whatever happens. Stay by me......I just hate myself for letting myself drift into a pretty deep chasm, partly for the shame of it, partly because I am dragging sweet you in with me. God I know how people feel when they want to shoot themselves, when they make a mess of things.

Peggy did her best to cheerlead from a distance – *You know we're going to be a success. I'm not worried baby – cause we have to start out with a little bit – and I don't mind. I just hope you aren't going to mind supporting me, Jack I promise I'll help as much as possible – and I mean to be as economical as a Scotchman - almost stingy – till we get on our feet.* But with each frantic letter from Jack, she began to worry in earnest. She was not happy with the prospect that he actually might *not* graduate – she just hadn't believed his pessimism, so when she got this telegram, she began to panic.

Telegram, Jack to Peggy, May 31

Have not had time to write darling haven't even slept for thirty six hours am working terribly hard but doubt graduation on time will write tonight crazy to see you all my love

Worried about the pressure he was under, she still couldn't let up on him. She responded with this telegram:

Sweetest, if you only can realize how worried I am. It's awful! Hectic telegrams about not having slept for such lengths of time, and even at that the doubt about your graduation. I don't want you to work so hard, and yet it's so damn important for you to do it. It means so much, doesn't it?...

Jack to Peggy, June 2

... I cannot graduate on time. I hate to face it, but it's the truth, I suppose we'd better try to be philosophical about it. You are right, Peggy sweetest, you and I will just stay here till I do. I think I can get half day work building the stadium here. That will support us – because I don't like to ask dad for any more help, although he would surely help me – and most emphatically, you must not accept any more from your father, darling girl.

Dad sent the $150 – of which $100 went to Sam and the $50 to the man I had borrowed from – the way it leaves me is obvious. That was supposed to cover all our expenses west – and, with a little mathematics, I find that our trip would cost us a minimum of fifty dollars. I certainly hope we won't have to lose our Ford – to *get ourselves through, but we can talk it over when (at last) we're with each other again – for good, too, precious girl. And that's going to be a week from today, because after my last exams, I'm heading straight for you. And then we'll come right back here to Ithaca – all right, darling? And I've got it all arranged so we can stay here in the house – all that week anyway.*

The following exchange, with a decided shift in Peggy's tone, offers a first glimpse of the relationship my parents had when I knew them – Jack anxious, fragile, and ashamed, seeking forgiveness, and Peggy, disappointed and judgmental, taking charge.

Peggy to Jack, June 6 – special delivery
Jack dear,

Of course I'm very disappointed and just a little aggravated about graduation. But I suppose I might as well take it optimistically, as it can't be helped. Jack I'll tell you what I want you to do – write your family immediately about it. I know they won't like it because I just had a very sweet letter from them in which they expressed much excitement and anticipation of your graduation. Also tell them that you'll be able to make up your work and get your diploma in about two weeks. Then they'll probably be more sympathetic, Jack.

You know Jack I know that you'll be able to work much better if I'm not with you. This is really much more of a punishment for me than it is for you – because I am crazy to come up for senior week. But you must finish as soon as possible – by the twenty-first at least, because I want you to be here about a week before we start. There would be no place for me to stay after senior week, and if you are alone you can work every minute. This is certainly a very great disappointment to me!

Also Jack, if you can't get the money to drive to Burlington I will – so don't sell the Ford – I planned to take the trip in it. And I want to. I know it isn't your fault about the money.

I told mother and she's disappointed. We decided not to tell Harry. Do your best precious. I don't want this letter to be snippy. I am simply trying to make the best of the situation. I love you Jack, Peggy

Jack didn't miss her change in tone.

...your somewhat cold and censorious letter today was justified, I know. But I'm so damn super sensitive to every word you say – it didn't add much toward my peace of mind. It's all such a hell of a mess. I've simply got to see you and talk it over, darling girl. I wrote home all about it – and just as you predicted, I got a very sympathetic letter from mother. Mother agrees with you, sweetest - in insisting that I stay here till I finish up. And I promise you I'll slave til I do. But, darling Peggy girl – I just must see you, and I'm coming as planned tomorrow. Perhaps you are right about your not coming up – I don't know – but you had your precious heart so set on being here for Senior Week – and (selfishly) I ache so to have you here with me – and I've disappointed you so much already I hate to do it anymore...and I'll hang on to the Ford, too, sweetest – we've planned too much on that trip to give it up now, haven't we? But gee, all these things can't be decided by letters – even by telephone – but you see that we've got to see each other?

The semester's letters ended with this exchange, so I don't know what happened, except for a later reference to the arrival of the diploma by mail in the winter of 1925. Jack must have eventually completed the delayed reports that he needed to write in order to graduate, because he did earn his degree in civil engineering.

It would seem that Jack and Peggy spent not just a month and not just the summer, but a full six months, until after the turn of the

New Year in 1925, living with the senior Flemings at the family house in Burlington. It must have been a miserable beginning to married life. Jack had a spell of illness (again!), possibly an ulcer, in the autumn of 1924, and Peggy did her best to care for him. But she did not feel very welcome in the Fleming household. In Peggy's version of the story, she was closeted in a third floor room, a garret, appearing only for frosty meals at the family dinner table. Circumstances didn't look promising for a good relationship between mother-in-law and daughter-in-law. Perhaps the tension that existed between the two women helped Jack and Peggy to give up the idea of living in Burlington. Jack's fragile health, too, may have been a reflection of frailty in his emotional health. Jack seemed to respond to life's vicissitudes with a succession of fevers, colds, and flues – and ulcers.

The following letter describes an October trip to Chicago to interview for a job with the McNulty Brothers, Chicago contractors, thanks to the intervention of Jack's Uncle Ed Fleming, General Agent for the freight department, in the Chicago office of the Chicago, Burlington and Quincy Railroad Company (which also ran the Colorado and Southern Railway and the Ft. Worth and Denver City Railway):

October 8, 1924, from Jack in Chicago to Peggy in Burlington, on Uncle Ed's office stationery
Peggy Darling –

As you see, I'm now in Uncle Ed's office talking things over – but I'd better tell you things in proper order…Well, the trip up was uneventful – except that I started feeling rotten and chilly and feverish. I went to Uncle Ed's office – found him out – then to Ken's office, where I stayed till five while he tried to get hold of Jack McNulty – to no avail. But Ken was enthusiastic about the job – and thinks I can get it. I am to call him at 12:15 today for definite arrangements as to seeing the McNultys. Well, after I left

Ken, I went out to Uncle Walt's and had supper. We did a X-word puzzle. Then we went to see a new apartment building next door, where they had two-room kitchenette apartments for $70, which Uncle Walt thought reasonable. By that time I was feeling rottenly – but I didn't say anything, and excused myself to go to bed at nine (after a good shot of Coscora)...Uncle Ed thinks it would be too hard for you to jump right into housekeeping. He thinks we ought to get a furnished room either with a kitchenette or to eat out for a month. However, I'll know better what to do after I see the McNultys.

It was the McNultys who launched my father's career. By January 1925, Jack and Peggy were in Chicago, beginning their life together in earnest, and awaiting the birth of their first child.

1925

John Joseph Fleming III

Chicago

Jack in Chicago to Peggy in Burlington, January 3, 1925

Peggy darling,

I didn't get a chance to write my letters on the way over because the train was so packed after Galesburg I couldn't move. And I've been busy as the devil since I got here – but I'll tell it in order.

I went to the McNultys – and found W.P. in – who had forgotten me. However, we fixed things up and I go to work Monday – as a carpenter's helper – to harden me up, he said. He also said they would be watching me, and told me to wear long underwear, as it is outside work.

Jack and Peggy began the year 1925 in Burlington. Now armed with his bachelor's degree, which had arrived in the mail, Jack went to Chicago just after the New Year to secure the job promised by the McNulty brothers in October, and to find lodging. Peggy, who must have been three months pregnant in January, stayed in Burlington for another two weeks with her in-laws, helping them close the Burlington house and pack for a winter vacation at the Riviera Hotel in Biloxi, Mississippi.

He found *a huge double front room and board for two, $25 a week – single $20 a week – another nice smaller double room $20 and $15 respectively for two and one. Don't you think that sounds good? And (big attraction) she (Mrs. Lyons) has had many Lafayette graduates staying there, sent by some steel company. So, darling – I think I'll try it there, for a week anyway – til I can tell how it will be.*

Jack chose the lodgings in the front room, with a view of Lincoln Park, at Mrs. Lyons' boarding house on Roslyn Street, for which he paid a single rate of $18 a week. Lincoln Park, located at the edge of Chicago's wealthier North Side, is one of the city's largest parks, bordering Lake Michigan at the north end of the city's Gold Coast, location of Chicago's fanciest addresses. Jack and Peggy could walk a block or so to the park and stroll in the gardens, visit the zoo or go to a concert in the newly renovated conservatory.

The room is really a peach, he reported to Peggy, *very large, four windows (three in a bay), mahogany furniture consisting of big comfortable bed, dressing table, chiffonier, desk, three chairs, two small closets, wash basin (running water), plenty of lights (including a bed lamp), and northern exposure, and a lovely view. How's that?*

They viewed the boarding house as a temporary solution to their housing needs, and Jack spent his evenings looking at apartment listings in the Chicago papers, marking them on a map of the city for a weekend search.

He was also snobbish about the other boarders – or perhaps he thought Peggy would be. With his characteristic class consciousness, tempered with gratitude, he reported, after coming home late from a night out and Sunday morning Mass, *Imagine it, my landlady gave me a large and hearty breakfast at 2:30! And the dinner this evening wasn't bad, much plain wholesome food. She seems anxious to please. I think I was lucky to get this place, although the three other boarders are terrible, yet awfully interesting as types. First, Plumber Duffy, a 300-pound philosopher who eats like a horse; second, Tailor Duffy, with pretensions to dandyisms, third, Stenographer Bandaline, a blah young lady from Terre Haute, where 'dancing is their only exercise!' Wait till you meet and eat with them!*

In truth, their accommodations were a far cry from the love nest in Burlington that they had spent the last year imagining. Gone, for the time being, were the cozy breakfast nook, the old fashioned garden, and the antiques on which the cocktail shaker would rest. On the other hand, moving to Chicago meant breaking away from family and jumping into a fresh, independent future. It must have been exciting to move to the urban heart of the Midwest, the Windy City, the "outdoor museum of commercial architecture," where the skyscraper had been born (and the term "skyscraper" invented). These were the buildings that had gone up at the beginning of the century, replacing sections of the city destroyed in the devastating Great Chicago Fire in 1871. By the 1920s, architects were vying to build the sleekest, most original buildings, garnished with Art Deco facades and interiors decorated with surrealist and cubist paintings. Chicago was a city buried in ready cash from the bootleg coming from just across the Canadian border. It was a city of con men and dice games on the street, a city that reveled in its decadence.

While Burlington offered family and old friends and 4th of July picnics by the Mississippi, the Chicago that became home to Jack and Peggy as newlyweds was, in 1925, the wild center of the Prohibition era Jazz Age. Louis Armstrong, Fats Waller, Earl "Fatha" Hines, Bix Beiderbecke, and Hoagy Carmichael were performing in Chicago, redefining improvisational black New Orleans Jazz music to create a flashier hot Chicago sound. Jelly Roll Morton's hit song that year was "Chicago Breakdown."

Jack and Peggy were beginning their life together in earnest just as Adolph Hitler published the first volume of *Mein Kampf*, and the Communist Party announced plans to move the Soviet Union from an agricultural to a manufacturing economy. In the United States, Tennessee became the first state to outlaw the teaching of evolution, Charlie Chaplin made "The Gold Rush," Edna Ferber won the Pulitzer Prize for her book *So Big*, and the country went mad for real estate in Florida. In fact, so many people migrated south to make a stake in the Florida housing boom that thousands were living in tents while they waited for housing construction to catch up.

The country, with Calvin Coolidge in the White House, was only in the middle of Prohibition, the thirteen-year national bar against the manufacture, transport, and sale (but *not* the purchase) of alcohol, the Volstead Act enacted in 1920, legislation following passage of the Eighteenth Amendment to the Constitution. Prohibition inaugurated a now legendary era in American social history, when Americans thirsty for a good drink were easily satisfied with the availability of bootleg. Mob boss Johnny Torrio had just decamped from Chicago to New York, leaving Al Capone and his Chicago Outfit to run the city's lucrative bootleg liquor market from his headquarters at the Lexington Hotel on Michigan Avenue. Speakeasies selling bootleg were hidden in funeral parlors and tailor shops, basements and office buildings all over town, admitting entry to anyone with a "membership card" and a password. The city was awash in liquor from Canada, but also Mexico, the Caribbean, and the hidden stills of resourceful country folk in hills and hollers across America.

I like to imagine Jack and Peggy, dressed in an evening dress and tuxedo (the expected dress at swankier establishments), wrapped against the Chicago cold and giggling conspiratorially at the door of a speakeasy while the bouncer inside slid open a little window to hear the password before opening the door. I imagine them hearing the laughter on the other side of the door, and perhaps the sound of tap shoes, a torch singer, or rolling dice at a gambling table, thrilling at the adventure of it all.

On his first day in Chicago, Jack reported a night out with the Sneiders, *a knock-out couple – with Dinty and Jane Stafford – also a peach. We went to see Irene Bondini in "Little Miss Bluebeard" (wonderful) and then to the Tent...They really are quite nice, but a bit too free about spending. Sneider got slightly tight, hence the generosity about sleeping on his comfortable floor.*

He continued, *The Tent was just like all those places – exclusive crowd and really wonderful music. Did I tell you the Sneiders have a large open (top down) Pierce-Arrow – in which we almost froze driving around.*

In contrast, Jack prepared for his first day of work, laying out long underwear, rough pants and woolen shirts, and oiling his shoes and gloves. In the routine that he established, he would rise at 6:30 AM, get his breakfast with the Duffys and Miss Bandolini and head for the work site. Jack's hard won degree notwithstanding, the McNultys started him out as a laborer, working outside in chill winter winds off Lake Michigan. The McNultys, tough Irish Chicagoans, probably wanted to see how well the college boy, with all his connections, would do standing on a construction scaffolding wearing a tool belt in the bitter winter weather. Here is Jack's report of his first day of work, on

Monday, January 6, 1925.
Peggy darlingest,

I'm just dead, and I've got an ache in every muscle and bone – and to make it worse, there wasn't any letter from you waiting for me, and I was sure there would be. I rose at 6:30, and put in a day

of hard labor and no joke about it. I hate to think of it tomorrow, and till I get over this soreness and exhaustion. I was extravagant, too. I spent 60 cents for lunch. I'm going to see if Miss Lyons won't make me a couple of sandwiches and I'll buy a little thermos bottle. I tottered straight to a hot bath when I got back here, and now I'm waiting for the dinner bell. And believe me, darling girl, I'm going straight to bed after dinner – no reading or writing or anything. And the way I feel just makes the ache for you worse too, my darling. Give my love to everybody. You know it's all yours anyway...

The next day didn't feel much better, except for the prospect of a paycheck, which he miscalculated here at a rate of eighty-two and a half cents an hour.

Your letters are the only things that give me a new lease on life, when the working day is over, and I'm dead on my feet. You see, darling, it's real labor, carrying and lifting heavy lumber, wheeling concrete briqques, etc. Don't worry, I'm enthusiastic enough, because I'm working for us. But it isn't exactly fun – yet. As to the "beeg brass" watching me, I don't know. It was "How're things today, Jack?" – "Fine, Bill" today...

Feeling at least able to move tonight, I think I'll call on the Brackens, and return the dress vest I borrowed Saturday. I can't remember whether I told you I started (last Saturday) a checking-savings account at the National Bank of the Republic (with a $10 deposit). Darling, I've earned $19.80 for us already, at 82 ½ cents an hour. When I get more accustomed to it I can work overtime, and get paid for time and a half, and double for Saturday afternoon and Sunday. Speaking of work, I'm afraid I'll have to get another pair of shoes. The ill-fitting and stiff ones I have almost kill my feet.

Jack was disappointed to discover later that he would not be paid a laborer's wage at first, but would start at 62 cents an hour. For his work, Jack started out at a salary of $36.30 per week, on the weeks when the Chicago weather permitted a full work schedule.

Luckily for the McNultys and Jack, Chicago was, according to newspaper accounts, experiencing a building boom, with a record of more than $311 million in building permits for the first ten months of 1925. That meant there was a promise of steady construction work ahead. Jack bought himself a book on building costs, and reported that he was doing his best to learn all about the business.

Uncle Ed was looking out for Jack, too. In early February, he wrote to Jack's father in Biloxi, *Jack is looking perfectly splendid and is contented for the time being, but of course is rather anxious to know from the McNultys just what they have in mind for him. He feels it is rather too early yet to discuss the matter, but intends doing so in about a month. I again called on Mr. Fallon, the V.P. and chief engineer of the Chicago Elevated Lines, and he told me he would be very glad to have me bring Jack in any time he's contemplating making a change...*

Once Peggy arrived in Chicago, around the 15th of January, and moved into Mrs. Lyons' boarding house, she must have captured the landlady's heart – a very young, pretty wife just beginning to show her pregnancy. Mrs. Lyons, it turned out, spent the winter inviting Peggy downstairs for a nourishing lunch every day, even though the extra meal wasn't covered in their weekly board.

Jack reported to his father that *for amusement we sometimes take walks in the evening, or rides on the bus, but generally, since we have such a late dinner, we go early to bed, and I'm always ready for it.* On weekends they had dinner and played bridge with friends, looked for apartments, and splurged on a big night out.

By June, in time for the arrival of their baby, Jack and Peggy had their own first floor apartment at Hampden Court, at $65 per month, and a new car they named "Clo," a 1925 Ford Model T Roadster with four cylinders. Perhaps in the end they did have to sell the Ford runabout Jack had bought at Cornell the year before. The average cost of a used car that year was $250, but they bought the new $345 car with a down payment of $136 and monthly payments of $26.50. A grocery bill saved from that year indicates that they were able to buy a half pound of liver for twenty five cents, and a half pound of bacon for another twenty-eight cents. Movies cost about 20 cents a ticket, a good restaurant meal 75 cents (a speakeasy cocktail could cost as much as four dollars) and gas cost about 12 cents a gallon.

But tragedy was just around the corner. On July 11, 1925, Peggy gave birth to her first child, my brother John Joseph Fleming III. His birth certificate, imprinted with two fat wrinkled footprints, indicates that he weighed a little over seven pounds. He was, according to family history, a robust, pretty, healthy baby, save a small complication – he was born "tongue tied," a condition not uncommon among newborns. Tongue-tied babies are those whose frenulum, the tissue connecting the tongue to the floor of the mouth, is too tight, or too near the front of the tongue, limiting the movement of the tongue. To free little John Joseph's tongue, the doctor clipped the attaching tissue with what must have been an unsterile instrument. The baby developed a swelling in his mouth that grew into a systemic staph infection, and he died of septicemia a week later.

It was a breathtaking blow. Mother Fleming provided details in a letter to Peggy's mother.

Sunday, July 20, 1925
Written on stationery of the Presbyterian Hospital of the City of Chicago
My dearest Mrs. Talbot,

When Jack telegraphed yesterday that the baby was very sick but not to come up, I came anyway on the afternoon train and straight to the hospital, where I found the baby still living – but the doctor had given very little hope – and at eleven o'clock he died. I did not know until I got here to the hospital this morning – and had been hoping – praying. Poor Peggy and Jack are heartbroken. He was the most beautiful baby and Peggy had gotten through so well and the baby so big and wonderful. But the little swelling of the throat came and the infection went through his system. The doctors said they hardly knew of a case like it. Everything that humanly could be done was done. All the doctors were the best that could be had and Jack and Peggy say everyone was interested – nurses – all. It is a great shock and loss to all of us but the grief to these two is heart rending. They have been looking forward with such joy to this little son and were so happy when he came. Peggy is showing the greatest courage. She mourns for Jack's loss and Jack's every thought is for her and her grief – and that is our hope – that for each other's sakes they will try to overcome their grief and look forward again. It is a blow and I know how grieved you will be. Peggy will go home tomorrow and have her nurse and I think that will help her to be away from here. I will stay for a few days until she is settled. We will have the dear and precious little body placed in a vault in the cemetery until later – when they can decide on whether to bury him here or in Burlington. I am so ashamed of not writing before. I waited at first until Peggy had written. Be assured that everything was done.

My love to you and Mr. Talbot.
Yours faithfully, Mary B. Fleming

Though the two mothers had corresponded in the last year, in this gentle and thoughtful letter to Mother Talbot, Mother Fleming was writing to someone she may have never met. This letter and the one that followed are generous in the recognition of their shared sorrow for this grieving young couple.

Back in Burlington later that week, Mother Fleming wrote a further description of Peggy's strength in this adversity that clearly made a positive impression on her. It is possible that Peggy's mother found it surprising and moving, too, that her daughter, who had been such a difficult child, such a *prima donna*, could stand tall in the face of such a devastating turn of events. Peggy's strength disintegrated as the summer wore on, but she tried very hard to be brave at first.

July 25, 1925, from Burlington, Iowa
My dear Mrs. Talbot,

I came home yesterday and feel rested today, but my thoughts are with Peggy and Jack all the time. It is merciful that nature will not permit suffering beyond a certain point and numbness comes – because they could not have continued as they felt all that Saturday and Sunday. Monday Peggy was brought back to their little apartment – and Miss Walsh the nurse is very kind and warm hearted. Peggy looks very well – and is most anxious to be well and does everything to help...Jack and Peggy loved that little baby with their whole hearts, they might miss an older child more but they both say they could not have loved one more. He was the most beautiful baby I ever saw. Everyone's heart goes out to them. Peggy has borne the sorrow in the highest way. There is sorrow but no bitterness, no questioning. She says she wants 'Thy will be done' on the little tombstone, and to my mind that is the perfection of Christian resignation – to accept the Divine Will.

On one of the rare occasions we talked about this baby, my mother told me with undiminished bitterness that the priest who delivered last rites to the baby assured her that it must have been God's will to take him. He might otherwise have become a thief or murderer, the priest concluded. I used to believe that Peggy just never got around to joining the Catholic Church, as she had promised in the first flush of their marriage. I wonder now if there was a moment when Peggy consciously decided not to become a Catholic, and if this was the moment.

I was young when I first learned from Mary Vaughan, who cooked and cleaned for us, that I had had another brother. Stunned by this information, I rushed to ask my mother if it were true, and she confirmed Mary's story but warned that I was never to mention it to my father. I don't think I ever did. Thus the fact of my baby older brother was a taboo subject in my family, too painful a memory to touch – ever. My brother Tommy knew about the baby but did not remember how or when he learned about him. How Mary Vaughan knew, and why she told me, a little girl in her charge, is also a mystery. My older cousins also recall that the subject was taboo in their families – they too knew about the baby, but no one talked about it.

It is difficult to imagine the enormity of the loss of that baby to my young, hopeful parents, or the cruelty (surely unintended) of that priest. The church's clumsy version of grief counseling stands in stark contrast to what would be available to Jack and Peggy now. Contemporary grief literature encourages parents to acknowledge the loss rather than bury the memory. They would have been encouraged to share the lonely burden of grief together. Surely, the nurse who attended to Peggy's post-partum physical needs also offered some emotional comfort. No doubt my parents did what they could bear to do at the time.

But it is hard to believe that the loss of that baby didn't have long term psychological consequences for Jack and Peggy, affecting Tommy's childhood in particular. That Tommy was a cherished child, undiluted Talbot in the tradition of Harry and his forbears, all boy, self-confident, courageous and heroic in the eyes of his parents was undisputed by anyone, including Tommy. All his life, Tommy shouldered not only the adulation of his family but the responsibility, during perennial family crises, for keeping them solvent, for keeping Jack employed even into old age, for paying their bills when they couldn't, just as Jack's parents had done. Jack's pattern of profligacy had been established very early. But can Tommy's overly developed sense of responsibility for his parents have begun with the loss of little John Joseph Fleming III, and the arrival, a year and a half later, of another beautiful little boy who *lived*, who for sixteen years was the only child on whom all the lost love was lavished?

Jack's 1925 letters began again in September, six weeks after the death of their baby, when Jack and Peggy went to Philadelphia, and perhaps to the cottage in Spray Beach, New Jersey, for a vacation. Peggy, still recovering from her pregnancy and the loss of the baby, and perhaps encouraged by a worried family, stayed in Philadelphia for the month of September. Fanny and in particular Ninny would have ached for Peggy, and even Harry would have felt her loss. They might have been alarmed at her physical condition. Peggy was already a thin girl and she became gaunt and frail after the baby's death. No doubt Fanny, and Harry, too, tried to be a comfort to their daughter.

Jack was left to go back alone to Chicago, to an apartment in apparent disorder, and to work. He described his trip home to Chicago, armed with the gift of a radio from Peggy's brother Tom, to replace the crystal set a Cornell friend had made them the year before.

Special Delivery, September 10, 1925, to Peggy in Glenside
Peggy sweetheart,
Here I am in this lonesome apartment just aching for you. Darling, I didn't know such a small place could be so empty. Having made a clearing in the debris about me, I can now tell you why it's so late, and why it's still a mess here. You'd never guess where I've been this evening – to dinner with Mr. and Mrs. J.P. McNulty.

After taxiing out to our empty messy little nest here, I decided to get the Ford ready for the morrow, buy a radio battery, and possibly straighten things up. Well, darlingest, I found poor Clo (the car) had been shamefully mistreated. Boss had passed the buck to the janitor, who had left the Ford at the little garage next to the building. After much fussing around and waking people up, I got the keys, and then I tried *to start it, to find the battery down, the fan belt broken, and several other minor details. Isn't that infuriating? Well, darling, I worked till eleven before I got her started, and I'm glad to say no serious damage was done, because she runs all right now.*

To continue, I went forth and bought a "B" battery, came back to the apartment (it was like an oven, by the way), and set up the radio at once. It works fine, although we are still limited to the Chicago stations, but of course it is much clearer and more selective than the crystal set. Then to bed, and oh, precious, what a fitful lonesome sleep it was, and up in the nick of time to go to the office where I spent the entire day at desultory work. Of course it was a rush to get smoothed up for dinner – and the rest I've told you.

Now I'm going to bed and read till I can't keep my eyes open, or fiddle with the radio, or anything to make it more bearable.

Nothing about the baby. Because Peggy's letters from 1925 have not survived, I can only guess at her physical and mental condition that fall. She had been so strong, so philosophical, in the face of Jack's troubles and their disappointments a year earlier. Now I wonder if her emotional resolve had cracked with the loss of her baby. The Peggy I knew was always emotionally fragile. This must have been very, very hard for her, and it does not surprise me that she retreated from such sadness. It only saddens me that she left Jack, who had shown himself to be vulnerable to depression, alone with his loss. He wrote:

193

I was so damn glad to get your letter today, and I'm so glad you could go swimming. I'll bet you all had fun, I'm glad if you did. I know you're getting strong and well already. And, sweetheart, your disposition couldn't be improved on. Whenever you were upset, it was just nerves, and it's your nervous system, mainly, that needs strength. I am glad you are going to see Wilfred and Polly again, because I know you love it there. Will you think lots of me, and breathe lots of that wonderful country air for me?

Physically, at least, Peggy was well enough to go to Baltimore to visit Jack's sister Polly and her husband Wilfred while she was in the east. But Jack was obviously worried about her.

Now that they had their own apartment, with no generous boarding house meals awaiting him, Jack was available for invitations to dinner during the month alone. Some nights, he disciplined himself to stay at home, save for a trip to Walgreens for a malted milk. On those nights he found comfort in the radio. *Such a quiet lonesome evening at home,* he lamented to Peggy,...*this radio is a Godsend – I'd be frantic without it. I've been listening to your old friend 'the 85-pound tenor' and a new r.h.*(for "red hot") *mama at the Edgewater Beach who sang and played 'Sister Kate.'*

But he didn't spend many nights at home. He took care of his mental state in his usual way by distracting himself with all the entertainments Chicago had to offer, whatever it cost. There were plenty of people to keep Jack company, including "Chi," a Cornell friend with whom he grabbed lunch at the Drake Hotel grill, the Seeleys, who the year before had offered to help Jack find a job, and Emily Clary, a Burlington girl who now lived with her mother in Chicago. Emily was a readily available companion Jack could call at the last minute, with whom Jack indulged himself, however guiltily, in restaurant meals and dancing the Charleston at the Rendezvous or the Marigold or the Ivanhoe. To an unaccountably un-jealous Peggy he reported on several excursions with Emily.

194

...I am going out to dinner tonight...It's a good thing – the exchequer is getting low, and I squandered well near a dollar last night with Emily. You see, sweetheart, just for fun, we went out to the Marigold Ballroom (remember it?) with all the toughies. It was fun dancing – but I wanted you so badly, Peggy, I can't enjoy anything without you.

We had a lot of fun trying to learn the Charleston, and had plenty of far-from-backward instructions in the gentle art. I got pretty good, much better than Emily, we both agreed. It's a lovely dance, the basic stance being a knock-kneed, pigeon-toed position, from which all the steps originate. Doesn't it sound pretty, precious? Then of course on returning, Mrs. Clary was there for a good hour's talk (wouldn't you know it?).

It was nice being at the Seeleys' Thursday night, Jack reports in another letter. *They're both pretty well.* Jack was funny – he's crazy to learn the Charleston, perfectly serious about it. He says *he is not going to be the last to learn, and everybody will soon be doing it (which I doubt very much).*

Jack was wrong about the Charleston – everyone *was* doing it

A little ungraciously for a guy who was looking hard for free dinners, he reported of his co-worker in the office at McNulty's, *Well, I drove Curtis home after work, at his request, and in return he asked me to stay for supper. His wife and sister-in-law were there. They're all terrible – somewhat Wilson Avenue. The apartment is like a million others; beflowered lamps and a bird cage. The only reading matter in sight was 'Hollywood Scandals' – and the 'girls' rushed for the paper (American) to read the latest of the 'Jazz Bride' – so much for the Curtises.*

Jack went on to describe the coda of the evening. *I left there about 8:30 and stopped at the Clary's on the way home, where they were entertaining – or being entertained by – a Roy Braunberger, a former Burlingtonian who is now a Chicago financier and cabaret hound. He talked continually, about cabarets, entertainers, influential friends, and millions, and "that Florida real estate deal." It was indeed a rare treat to sit and listen, and ask for more. He left at twelve, at which time I also started but was forcibly held back. Emily and Mrs. C wanted to talk about him...*

And Emily again...

I had had coffee and a roll on Saturday, and by 4:30, with the little money I had (I had paid next month's Ford), I got desperate, went to the Ivanhoe, ate a large meal and got a pint of gin, some of which I drugged myself with, to the extent I got home at 5:30 and fell asleep, waking mussed and muzzy at ten after a dream-troubled sleep. Then, more nervous and restless than ever, I went over and got Emily and we went to the Rendezvous and danced till four, and spent the rest of this week's money (with exactly $3 in the bank). Darling girl of mine, that was very bad of me to spend that money – I know it was – but I just had to do something. I'm just lost without you, darling girl. I need you more and more all the time. Then, this morning, adorable, I woke up at eleven with a hell of a cold (to add to my troubles), went to Mass at St. Patrick's, got the usual coffee and roll, and went to the office for the afternoon. I borrowed $5 from Curtis, went to the Drake and got a sandwich at five – more extravagance. But it did taste good for a change after all this hectic eating.

In Peggy's absence, Jack was drifting back into his old bad habits. He didn't have enough money to entertain himself like this, of course. And there were Peggy's and the baby's medical bills hanging over them. Some form of disability insurance had existed in the U.S. since the Civil War, and some hospitals were just beginning to offer services on a pre-paid basis – a kind of insurance – but there would be no group health insurance plans until 1929, no Blue Cross until 1932, and no employer-provided insurance until the 1940s. So Jack and Peggy carried a heavier than usual financial burden that fall. He wrote Peggy reporting some considerable juggling and borrowing, including cashing in another Liberty Bond, in order to keep them solvent. He wanted to show Peggy he was making a good faith effort wrestle down their ever-present money issues.

Darling, I made my financial plan today, and by borrowing $200 and being frugal, I can get everything paid, including next month's regular bills (except Dr. Heaney's) by September 22. That budget, however, doesn't include a Burlington trip – but now I am worrying you again, and I mustn't. And you mustn't worry – just try to be happy, like I'm trying...

The unspecified Burlington trip would be the trip they must take to bury their baby in the Fleming family plot. A week later, Jack reported further progress: *Dad gave me $20 and loaned me $100, as Mr. McCabe is away for a week (I found out Saturday, when I cashed the Liberty Bond – I hated so to do it, darling, but I had to, didn't I?) So, this afternoon and tonight I've been busy with my accounts, little sweetheart. After depositing $120 in the bank, I paid this month's rent and garage, Dr. Powellie, Dr. McCarty, last month's telephone, gas and light – so that's a start... And I straightened out my office account, and I owed them $9, which I will pay tomorrow.*

Then, predictably, *I did a dumb thing today. After having a malted milk in the morning, I completely forgot to eat lunch. You see I was rushing every minute after getting off the train. And tonight, when starting out to eat, my eye fell upon the Rudegrous, so I ate there, just to be different, and got a pretty good dinner for $1.50, to the accompaniment of pretty fair music.*

It's not hard to figure out that they were living beyond their means. Assuming Jack was, in September, still getting his starting salary of $36.30 per week (though perhaps by fall he was getting something closer to the salary he had expected from the McNultys at the beginning of the year – $62 per week), his annual salary would have been close to $1,900 per year, below the national average earnings, $2,200, in 1925, but not bad for a young man just beginning a career .If it was still the lesser salary, then they were paying almost two weeks' salary for rent (at $65 per month) and almost one week's salary for the car (at $26 per month). Incredibly, they apparently had a laundress for their clothes.

Darling, at an early hour this morning, to my great surprise (I had forgotten) Lena arrived, like an angel from heaven. I gave her carte blanche, and on returning tonight, I found everything washed and ironed – suits hung up and all, and it was a great relief.

Peggy was not very domestic nor much interested in cooking in her forties and fifties, so it's safe to assume that she was not particularly interested in cooking or cleaning or washing in her twenties. While lower class women might work for others in order to contribute to the family income, and middle class women might learn to do their own housework, Peggy saw herself in a more privileged class. Jack, too, assumed a social status that demanded he would be the breadwinner, the provider. Trapped by their class aspirations, Jack and Peggy were maintaining a lifestyle they couldn't afford.

Fortunately, Jack was recognized at work. In mid-September, he reported with some ambivalence on his new circumstances that may have included a change in pay, though a raise is not mentioned:

I got a piece of news from Curtis yesterday. He said that Bill is planning to have me in the office most of the time from now on. Curtis had told Bill he needed help at the office, then Bill told him the above. Curtis said we'd probably move into larger offices where Bill and Jack could each have a private office, and Curtis and I have an office. Darling, I don't know just what to think about it – whether it means a raise or a rut; whether it means they are satisfied with my work, and think I've served enough outside apprenticeship, or whether they think I'm not so good on the jobs themselves.

Jack had a heartrending task to take care of – a job he found himself undertaking alone, before Peggy returned from the east – to bury his son. Why? Had Peggy asked him to take care of this without her, or was he worried about her emotional stability? The baby's body had been left in a vault in the Colroy Cemetery in Chicago, pending my parents' decision about his final disposition. If this seems very odd, not to mention unkind to Jack (I think it does), it is also unsurprising to me. Peggy was either too unstable to participate at this point, or she was hiding behind her fragile state in order to avoid doing something very hard. She had just lost her baby – but it was always hard to know whether she was sick or just phenomenally selfish. Perhaps she couldn't bring herself to witness the internment of her baby. In any case, she left Jack alone with this awful undertaking.

Jack narrated his unhappy trip to Burlington in the letters that follow. On Saturday, September 13, he wrote:

Precious, I went to Colroy Cemetery this morning and made all arrangements for my sorrowful trip. I'm going on the night train tonight, getting into Burlington Sunday morning. Darling, I'm taking him where the air is cleaner, and it's quieter, and we always know that he is happy, sweetheart. He is an angel. I adore you so, darling. We mustn't feel too badly.

Then I'll be back here Monday morning, in time for work…

On Monday, the 15th, he told Peggy about the trip:

I hope you are feeling well, and that your eyes won't bother you anymore (and that maybe you can write to me). It's raining here again – it's always raining – and it's so still here in the apartment.

Precious, I took Johnny's little body to Burlington Saturday night. I rode on the day coach, just as near as I could possibly be. The train got in at five Sunday morning. It was raining terribly hard, and Dad, Mother, and Warren (Jack's childhood friend) *were there to meet me – mighty nice of Warren, wasn't it? Then, sweetest, after taking the little box to the chapel, we went to six o'clock Mass, and I went to communion, for us darling. Then, about nine o'clock, the rain stopped a little bit, and we went to the cemetery, and Mary* (Jack's sister) *and Father Gallagan were there. And in a little while, I laid our little boy to rest – oh, it hurts so, darling – no one can know but you and I. But he couldn't be in a quieter, prettier spot, darling. I am glad of that, aren't you, precious? I want so for us to be there together. Then I went back to the house, and after dinner, slept for a little while. Then I went over to Mary and Henry's. They sent their love to you – everyone did – and everyone was so sorry that you weren't there too.*

Jack seemed to accept Peggy's absence, but I wonder what his family thought.

The baby now lies buried in a small Catholic cemetery in Burlington, in the shade of old tulip poplar trees on a bluff overlooking the Mississippi River. His grave lies alongside our grandparents, John Joseph and Mary Bracken Fleming, and our great grandparents, Michael and Bridget Fleming. His small marble headstone reads "Thy will be done," as Peggy wished.

Jack spent the rest of September writing increasingly anxious and miserable letters, urging Peggy to come back home to Chicago. At the end of the week following the trip to Burlington, he wrote:

I can't help it if it is selfish to tell you, but this week has been like a year. Oh darling, I miss you so much. Precious, do you think you ought to stay 'till your father gets back? Do you think he would be hurt if you didn't? October 5th – lord, I don't see how I could stand it, honestly I don't, Peggy, but I do want to just think of what's best for you, and if you are getting a rest... When do you go to Polly's? I think that will be better for you than anything. But, my little sweetheart, don't stay away from me very long, because I need you so.

200

What, indeed, was Peggy doing at home? She apparently didn't write Jack much. Her mother, or perhaps her father, had asked her to stay in Philadelphia until his return from his annual fall hunting trip, and she could see her childhood friends, who now were having babies themselves. But it was time for Peggy to come home to Jack. On September 23, Jack wrote,

...I'm just unbearably lonely for you. I just have to have you. Get ready to start just as soon as you get this letter, if you haven't done so before, because you've been away so long. I don't want to be selfish, but it has done a lot of good already, hasn't it, sweetest, and you do love me and want to come back, don't you?

Finally, on September 30,

Your letter last night gave me the most glorious news yet, that you are really coming back to me, and maybe (make it surely) by the end of this week...Took Emily to the Radio Show last night – dumb thing – but Bill gave me some free tickets. But, precious, I can't have any fun with anybody but you, my adorable...

Peggy came home in early October, and Jack and Peggy remained in Chicago until the spring of 1927. Jack continued to work for the McNultys in increasingly responsible jobs, while he and Peggy led an urban life, working and playing under the affectionate watchful eye of Jack's uncles.

In January, 1927, Peggy gave birth to another healthy baby boy who was also tongue tied. For several days, she would not let the doctors touch the baby's tongue, but they finally prevailed and the baby, Thomas Talbot Fleming, left the hospital with a loosened tongue, as healthy as he arrived.

1927

Working on the River

Ballad

In the winter of '27
We wuz holin' up in Chi.
It was somewhere east of Clark St.,
Crummy pad, but warm and dry.
Old lady hollers, "Jack – these pains
Is mean – we'd better go!
They's comin' pretty often
And that tourin' car is slow!"…
So we put on all the clothes we had,
And I packed my 44 gun,
And we climbed into that Model A
For the ride to Evanston…

This "ballad" written by Jack provides the detail for me to imagine Jack and Peggy on January 18, 1927, the day of my brother Thomas Talbot Fleming's birth, jumping into their Model A Ford for the trip to a hospital in Evanston, a Chicago suburb just up Lake Shore Drive from their apartment at The Brewster on the North Side – *not* the Presbyterian Hospital in Chicago, where little John Joseph was born and died 18 months earlier. Peggy was now 23 years old, and Jack would soon have his 26th birthday.

The letters begin again in the spring of 1927, when Jack embarked on his second job, working as an engineer for a utility company building dams and bridges along the great American rivers, and Peggy and Baby Tommy went to Philadelphia.

They both must have been terrified when Tommy was born, sick with anxiety that they might go through the same agony of loss again, only to discover that Tommy had exactly the same condition. Once again they were faced with a tongue tied baby, whose frenum would have to be cut. She would suffer this anxiety one more time when I was born with the same condition seventeen years later. Now, of course, the surgery to sever the frenum is regarded as less urgent, depending on the severity of the condition. A tongue tied baby can have trouble sucking, and its speech development is sometimes complicated by a tight frenum. In any case, it would probably be managed with laser surgery, and modern pediatricians would want to avoid such surgery for at least six months, to avoid putting such tiny little systems under general anesthesia. Even in 1925, an infection never should have happened. And though it caused a few frantic days; it didn't happen again with Tommy.

Tommy was born in the year that Charles Lindbergh made his solo flight across the Atlantic – a story that absolutely consumed the American psyche. But the biggest story of the year was the Great 1927 Flood on the Ohio, Mississippi, Arkansas, Missouri, Illinois, Tennessee, St. Francis, and Red Rivers, a flood that put the downtowns of Pittsburgh and Cincinnati under water, and by the end left 500 hundred people dead and 600,000 thousand more displaced, in the care of the Red Cross. The Mississippi and Arkansas Rivers flooded millions of acres in the south, especially in the state of Mississippi, destroying $160 million in crops. The flood captured the headlines in major newspapers around the country and sent state legislatures, the U.S. government and the U.S. Army Corps of Engineers, into frantic arguments about river management policy, with politically risky consequences for leaders from President Calvin Coolidge to the mayor of New Orleans. Jack would soon be an eyewitness to the flood and its consequences.

By April 1927, now supporting a family of three and after more than two years of employment with no real advancement, Jack decided to leave the McNulty Brothers' construction company to find new work. The Fleming family was thrilled. They had heard from Burlington friends with Chicago connections that the McNultys were "ignorant vulgarians not fit to wipe Jack's shoes." Nevertheless, with the help of a generous "To whom it may concern" letter of recommendation from the McNultys and the influence of one of Mother Fleming's cousins, Frank Bracken, Jack was hired by the United Gas Improvement Company (UGI) to work as an engineer on large dam, bridge, and railroad construction projects around the country.

It was a job at the heart of the great engine of growth in America, and an exciting opportunity for Jack at a time when the country was experiencing a soaring economy, rapid industrialization, and life altering transformation – beginning to change the lives of even rural Americans with the help of electrification. But the job would take Peggy and Jack and now Tommy away from Chicago in the spring of 1927, right into flood country. This was to be the beginning of a vagabond life in which Jack, Peggy and Tommy would travel from job site to job site on the Ohio and Mississippi Rivers for the next four years.

As it happens, however, Jack started on this adventure alone, beginning in May, 1927, in Newburgh, Indiana. In his summer letters, Jack made a reference to Peggy's health – *I want you to get strong and well. I should say stronger, because you are well now. I couldn't have left you if you weren't.* Peggy reported several times during the summer that her health was improving, that she'd been to the doctor, who had completed "my obstetrical work." And she mentioned her weight – she was up to 112 pounds, though Jack wanted her to get (back?) to 125.

Almost certainly, they were especially anxious about the baby's wellbeing – the loss of their first baby was still a fresh pain for both of them. Peggy wrote that she wanted them to do "what's best for Tommy," and it's understandable that she would feel especially protective of the baby's health, though it's not clear what, exactly, she was worried would threaten Tommy's wellbeing in Newburgh.

Money and bills were, as usual, a factor in their decision, and this is a rationale that makes sense. They had leftover doctor's bills from Tommy's birth and they were still carrying some old debts that resurfaced in the summer's correspondence – a bank note for $500 renewed and cosigned by his father, and an old note for $100 left unpaid from the winter of 1923 in Ithaca.

But something else happened between Jack and Peggy as they prepared to move into the next chapter of their lives. A late summer letter hints that there had been a big confrontation in the spring, almost too painful for Peggy to remember. *I hope you'll never again misunderstand me like you did this spring,* she wrote in August. *It hurts me every time I think of it.* I think my father must have assumed, reasonably, that he and Peggy would go to Newburgh together, and Peggy flatly refused to go. I think he didn't trust that she was telling the whole truth about her resistance to joining him (Tommy's safety, her physical recovery, money) and, for once in his life, he fought back. I am suspicious, too. Though I, in her shoes, would have been anxious about my baby, I suspect Peggy was also fearful of the unknown, and resistant to a plan that didn't fit her ambition for their life together. Living in a little river town in Indiana was not her idea of moving up in the world, I'm guessing. Keeping house and cooking for her hard working husband must have sounded so domestic and ordinary after a heady couple of years of apartment life in Chicago, with restaurants and concerts and palatial gilded movie theatres nearby. So, using all the manipulative behavior she could muster, Peggy insisted on going home to Glenside and familiar territory. She'd done nearly the same thing two years before when she left Jack in Chicago to bury their baby while she retreated to her parents' house. Peggy knew what she was doing, and she probably felt guilty about it, understanding, as she said in one letter, that *I have Tommy and am here with my family and friends, and you are just a stranger in a strange place.*

Jack was ready for his new assignment and eager to start. UGI, the oldest public utility holding company in the United States, held interests in forty-five gas, electric, and railway service companies across the country, including the Philadelphia Gas Works, a connection that would be a matter of significance for Jack and Peggy later. In 1920, the company diversified for a time into heavy construction projects, and by 1928 had become the largest general engineering and construction firm in the United States. The Army Corps of Engineers, which held responsibility for the improvement of navigation along the nation's rivers, hired UGI to undertake the construction of dams and bridges along the Ohio and Mississippi. As it happens, Jack's brother Phil, now an officer in the Corps, was closely involved in contract negotiations with UGI.

Jack's first assignment was to work as one of three engineers on the construction of Dam 47, at Newburgh, Indiana, just east of the larger town of Evansville on the Ohio River. The dam was part of a chain of 50 dams with navigation locks commissioned by the Army Corps of Engineers to create a reliable "slackwater" system, damming the river to provide pools of at least nine-foot depths in stages. This made it possible for large river boats to carry freight along the 968 miles between Pittsburgh, Pennsylvania, where the Allegheny and Monongahela Rivers join to create the Ohio, and

Cairo, Illinois, where the Ohio joins the Mississippi River. According to "The UGI Circle," the company newsletter from August 1928, "The big shippers are now building modern towboats and steel barges, ready to take advantage of cheaper freight rates and relieve the congestion."

The UGI writer added imaginatively "If one of the giants of myth and legend, one of extreme stature, could stand on the bar at Cairo, and look upstream on the Ohio River, far in the distance, 968 miles, he would see Pittsburgh, 426 feet higher than his feet; he would see the completed slackwater system of the Ohio River, a succession of dams, rising one above the other like a gigantic flight of steps."

For Jack it must have been especially exciting to work on a project commissioned by the Army Corps of Engineers, in which his brother played an important role. He wrote his brother about his assignment, and got the following response: *I'm glad you find the Ohio River work so interesting. One of my first jobs was on Dam No. 28 near Huntington, West Virginia...you may be interested in knowing that I helped to draw up the contract with UGI for #47, recommended the award and OK'd the final contract for the Chief's signature. Do you ever see Col. Spalding or any of the other officers from the Louisville District Office? If so, please introduce yourself.*

To this day, the railroads and the river freight industry compete to be the best, cheapest, and most efficient mode of freight transportation in the U.S. A longstanding rivalry between Chicago and St. Louis as centers of commerce was also a rivalry between river transport and railroads. The Mississippi River valley provides the country with a bigger basin, and thus a bigger engine of industry and transport, than most of the river basins of the world. Encompassing 31 states of the United States, it has a larger basin than that of the Nile, the Ganges, or the Rhine Rivers. Only the Amazon and Congo Rivers have larger drainage basins.

Put in that context, the events of the spring of 1927 were all the more dramatic, when the Mississippi River experienced a catastrophic, historic flood from Cairo, where the Ohio met the Mississippi, all the way to the Gulf of Mexico.

Persistent rains were flooding the Midwest beginning in August 1926, when Jack and Peggy were still in Chicago, washing out bridges and railroads. By the end of the year, gauge readings on the rivers showed the highest volume of water ever recorded. Pittsburgh flooded on January 23, 1927, and on April 15 the *New York Times* reported flood stage on the Ohio at Evansville. Jack would arrive in Evansville to begin work little more than a month later, about the 20th of May, when the rain was still coming relentlessly down.

Jack and Peggy's physical separation provides a summer of correspondence that narrates the details of their lives in 1927. By May, Jack had installed Peggy and Tommy at home with the Talbots in Glenside while he went by train to Indiana to begin his job. It was a separation that would last four months, until mid-September.

After the mysterious "misunderstanding" that took place in the spring, they settled on a plan in which Jack would live alone in Newburgh, sending home most of his pay, and Peggy would pay their debts from Glenside until they had sufficient cash to buy train tickets for Peggy and Tommy and they could afford to rent a house. He opened a checking account at an Evansville bank after checking out the bank in Newburgh with pre-Depression, pre-FDIC caution: *Newburgh has a bank, but as it is a small town bank, probably dependent on farmers, I'm afraid of it, even for the little bit we will have.*

Father Fleming, now chairman of the Burlington Savings Bank, had no doubt endured more than enough worry about Jack's profligacy and offered gentle advice:

Naturally I am pleased to know that you have opened a bank account and I hope you are going to be able to build it up by laying by a little from your earnings every week. No matter how small the deposit, it means an addition to your savings, and it will get you into a mighty desirable habit of putting by a little from time to time, for the traditional rainy day. Evidently you picked a good bank. I don't happen to know any of the officers or in fact any bankers in Evansville, but looking over the Bankers Register I find the Citizens to be the biggest and strongest bank in Evansville.

Peggy said she was flattered that Jack trusted her with the responsibility for paying their bills. *I guess it's best we just make the best of it,* she wrote, *and get these damn bills paid...It makes me feel very important and businesslike to have you trust me with our money.* The truth was, she was beginning not to trust Jack with the bills. She wrote somewhat obliquely, *Darling I think you have been so good about the money. I'm awfully proud of you. And I can't explain at all about you not knowing how to handle money. I think we both have learned how to handle it, though, don't you Jack. Let's teach Tommy that when he's young. We can do it by giving him as generous an allowance as we feel we can afford and is good for him – and then make him account for it.*

Jack didn't miss the reference and took some umbrage at that. *I want you to feel that money is safe in my hands – it would hurt very much to think that you didn't feel that way.*

Paying the bills was a responsibility that in later years Peggy held with an iron grip, sequestering the checkbook and fat envelopes of cash in her capacious handbag, which never left her side, and not trusting Jack with any more money than he would need to buy gas and lunch.

Jack's first correspondence is a postcard written en route to Newburgh from "The American," a Pennsylvania Railroad train making a daily run from New York to St. Louis. He mentioned that *all the little streams and brooks are terribly swollen – will this deluge never cease?* When he arrived in Newburgh and got settled, he wrote:

Sweetheart, I've got so much to tell you, so many impressions to transcribe, I hardly know where to begin. I'm a bit tired, too, so I'll just give a jumble of facts and impressions now, and go into more detail tomorrow. Here goes, darling. I am now living at the home of the Boyers family – (young mechanic, wife and female child – they are what you might expect) – in the spare room, of course, small but airy, neat, clean and really quite attractive, formerly occupied by Cadet engineer West, (Ralph West, a colleague on the job at Dam 47) *who is a nice boy, now living in Newburgh with mother - $3.50 per week (the room, I mean). Board – the one and only place – German woman, stacks and countless varieties of plain good German food - $7 a week. Evansville – Burlington multiplied by three. Newburgh no suburb at all – just a funny little Southern town – 1200 pop – corner store loafers and all – either be amusing or deadly. Country – not bad, lots of foliage, occasional coalmines. Heat – terrific – 85 all day – I've perspired away two pounds. Job – looks interesting but darn hard work – 7 days a week – laugh that off. And 7 am starting time! All this is slack season – the river is still too high for regular work. However, I understand that one works nine hours a day so often that two hours or so suffices on Sunday – let us give thanks. Company cars – a myth – car will be absolute necessity for us.* ["Clo" had evidently been sold when they left Chicago] *West took me to Evansville for supplies in his Ford... went to movie – good D. Gish in "London" – came out at 9:15 to go home – discovered next and last car to Newburgh at 11:15 – so had to alternate between sitting in terminal and walking the main street amid the hatless, coatless, aimless Saturday nighters. This Uncle Joe style of mine was to condense facts, but they seem to have spread out anyway. My own precious – can you get a picture of the place now?*

211

As usual, Jack made a socio-cultural study of Newburgh and Evansville, sketching quick impressions and amusing details that would entertain Peggy, reinforcing the image they shared of themselves as better than "common people." In doing so, Jack presents a telling snapshot of a 1927 river town in Indiana,

The fellow boarders – West and his mother – a young preacher with a Polish name – a young fellow that runs a grocery store – two small town engineers on the government pay, as well as inspectors, and occasionally others. The people at Mass this morning – perfect farmer types – sun burned gaunt men with drawls, trick haircuts, suspenders, celluloid collars with or without neckties, and awkward women. I introduced myself to the young priest – Father Winterhalen, I think – a big good natured and earnest young man – his first parish, I think. His sermon on prayer was lofty and quite well delivered – but not close enough to realities.

It's surprising, being accustomed to the glassy stares of city folk, to find people so friendly. Everyone says "morning" or "howdy." I don't understand, tho, why homeliness is so much more prevalent in the country. It certainly is, however. I wish you could have seen me bringing my trunk from the interurban station to the house. I commandeered the town delivery wagon, a ramshackle affair owned by an old negro, and hauled by a spavined horse! He is an old fellow who has a wonderful system – he has a little negro boy, small and slight, that does all the work. His strength is amazing. I was invited to accompany the trunk, so I sat on the seat in state with the little driver, while the old man sat in the back as we ambled up the shady tar-soaked main street.

Evansville, as I said, darling, is an overgrown Burlington – the same kind of people plodding the streets and loafing on all corners. I saw some quite pretty houses in the outer edges – and some big ugly ones in the town, too. I gather there is the same sort of "society" in the background – the "old families" – owners of factories, stores and the like. An occasional swanky roadster – probably country club – proves that. Quite an elaborate movie theatre, too, with vaudeville thrown in –In one vaudeville act there was a big, fat blonde – à la Sophie Tucker – raucous voice and everything – whom you would have loved – she was really amusing. One of the song titles,   "She used to be a soldier's sweetheart, but now she's an officer's mess!"

I learned something today – the government is building a tennis court near the dam – heaven be praised!

Do you get a picture of your future home, now darling? If Newburgh isn't anything else, it's a wonderful place to save money, get strong – rest – and learn about the genus Americanus rural. And if you can forget about gleaming city pavement and architecture, and sophistication, and modern methods and conveniences, it really should be pleasant. In a lifetime, unthinkable, but for a few months, a change, and not bad at all. I'm going native already and shedding articles of wearing apparel one by one.

Peggy responded as he must have hoped: *I've read your letter about Newburgh over and over and just pictured everything. It sounds like an attractive little place, and cheap, certainly, and thank goodness for that. We'd love it Jack. You know what a kick I get out of things like that, when I'm with you and Tommy. It just makes everything seem romantic. I'm just sorry you have to work so terribly hard. Is it because they have to make up time on the job? Gee I hope that doesn't increase correspondingly as the season advances...I'm just glad about the tennis court. Have you met any attractive men that are there with the co? Anyone congenial, I mean?* Was she asking if there were any people that were "our kind?" Peggy wanted to be enthusiastic, to find the prospect of life in Newburgh "romantic," but this sounds tentative to me.

213

In his daily correspondence, Jack outlined the rhythms of his days – breakfast, then a long day's work, followed by a sumptuous supper – *chicken, mashed potatoes, stuffing, string beans, carrots, cornbread, coffee, strawberries, and what not. All the meals, except breakfast, are like that* – followed by a vigorous tennis game (an activity that became a central part of his life that summer) with West and other acquaintances he met on the newly built courts in Newburgh, followed by reading, letter writing, and bed. At least two evenings a week he went into Evansville to do errands and go to the movies at the grand theatre there – a better option than the theatre in Newburgh, which Jack described as *"a little narrow hall with a machine that has to stop between reels and an orthophonic victrola to furnish the music."* Talking pictures were introduced by the motion picture industry in 1927, but Newburgh and Evansville were probably not ready to show them. He even worked at the dam for a couple of hours before Mass on Sundays.

Jack had no trouble – ever – making friends, and he soon was invited to play tennis, have dinner, play bridge, or dance outdoors with co-workers and their families at Rambo Gardens. He called on a couple of Evansville families for whom he had introductions (including the family of Peggy's boarding school roommate Alice Ashby, who had grown up in Evansville, and whose mother still spent part of the year there), and these visits generated more invitations.

The best, most exciting outing would come within a week of Jack's arrival in Newburgh – a trip with Ralph West to the Indy 500 auto race at Indianapolis. Both men were able to get a couple of days off from work at the dam to go watch the "thundering Duesenbergs."

This adventure generated a letter rich with atmospheric details,

I was pretty tired last night... You see darling, West and I left in his Ford coupe Sunday about 9 am, and drove up by way of

French Lick, Bedford, and Bloomington. The roads weren't so good that way, but it's really lovely country – hilly and woody. French Lick and West Baden, you know, are big resorts – large hotels, golf courses, etc, and not much else! Bedford is the place where nearly all the limestone comes from, and we stopped to look into the enormous quarries – hundreds of feet deep, with huge blocks of stone piled about carelessly, like the ruins of a colossal temple. Bloomington's claim to fame is Indiana University, and a very pretty campus they have, too. The country is lovely, but barren and the houses throughout are mostly tumble down shacks. And the water is six inches over the highways in many places and all the lowlands covered over. The famed gardens at West Baden were inundated.

We reached Indianapolis about 5:30 (200 miles from here) and it's really a city – the city of the state, of course. The streets were crowded to the grounds, and hotel rooms unavailable, of course. So West conceived the idea of applying at the "Y" and they gave us an address of a so-called "private home." After traversing the colored district we found it – by the children on the doorstep. They gave us a choice of three unmade beds, so we left immediately, bedless. So this was my idea – we picked a good street, stopped at a nice small apartment building, asked the old lady on the porch if a room was available, and sure enough, we were given two nice little cots in a big living room – after some hesitation, of course (it evidently not being customary)! The daughter of the household was a school teacher, and insisted on guiding us on a tour of the city after supper – was, in fact, all for calling up another girl till told it wasn't at all necessary. They were nice, though – let us use their garage, and the place was very clean.

We left early in the morning for the track, taking our things with us, so we could start immediately after the race. Traffic was terrific, of course, and when we got there, grandstand seats were at a premium, so we went inside the track, near the pits. The crowd

215

was enormous, about 175,000, all around the 2 ½ mile brick track. Airplanes overhead, bands, and all the trimmings. The start was wonderful – it's a big kick seeing 33 cars going 100 miles per hour. But five hours is a pretty long time to stand up and walk around. After a while, it's just a procession of roaring engines and bright colors flashing by, and the stops in the pits for tires, gas, etc, are exciting – everything is done so quickly. We didn't see any spills, and you know the results of course – all the old timers had trouble and all the new were in the front at the finish. When you and Tommy and I go, we'll have box seats and cushions...

Jack was a natural writer. He made every experience sound interesting, turning his observations into entertaining scenes, sketching characters that brought the scenes alive. But it was important to Jack, always, to dress up his experiences (with box seats and cushions) to paint a rosier future for Peggy. He must have felt a lot of pressure to promise her a future that would be grander than the present.

At home in Glenside, Peggy's days were filled, first, with the care of Tommy, who was installed with her in her old bedroom. *Jack it's the sweetest thing,* she wrote, *to see him all tucked up in his little bassinette (he is still using it). His crib is so near me I can reach out and touch his little hands whenever I want to. I love him so.*

Peggy was besotted with her baby, who was four months old when she went to Philadelphia. Her daily descriptions of his progress show, in touching, good humored detail, the growing love affair between mother and son. In May she reported, *Tommy has learned two new things. He puts his hands out to be lifted up when you say come to him. And he pulled himself up to a sitting position in his carriage. He gained his six oz .and now weighs 14.14 – very nearly fifteen pounds.* In June, Tommy was saying "da-da." By July, when he was six months old, she sent this news: *Tommy I see has gone to sleep after raising quite a row. I don't mean crying*

– he's really darling, Jack. I put him in his crib and then he just wears himself out kicking, throwing himself around grabbing the bars of the crib and cooing. He makes all kinds of funny little noises now, and you can distinguish different syllables and letters in his gibberish. In August she reported, *The little bunny can nearly climb out of his carriage. He gets up on his knees and hangs over – then he takes his toys and throws them out one at a time, and when they are all on the floor he looks up at me and down at the toys and then screams at the top of his lungs.*

Then when I fix him he will burst into a great big smile.

These details both delighted Jack and caused him pain. All these milestones were happening in his absence. He was thrilled with the news that Tommy was calling "his" name, Dada, but he begged: *Don't let Tommy grow too fast. Hold him back a little now, and then let him just burst forth like a little bud when I have you again -* to which Peggy responded, *I told him what you said about growing, but it doesn't seem to make any difference, he just insists upon learning things..."*

With Tommy at her side, Peggy, too, fell into a domestic rhythm at home. For a girl who never liked her mother and was embarrassed by her father, she seemed surprisingly content to fall back into her old life. She paid visits to her childhood friends Lottie, Marty and Mary, who now had babies themselves, or were about to. She was invited to bridge games and went shopping for new rompers and toys for Tommy. She became the principal driver in the family, taking her mother and her aunt Ninny on errands or to "church sociables." The household, which also included her father, when he was home from New York on weekends, and a servant, Bridie Murphy (who no doubt helped with the babysitting when Peggy went out), was considerably animated by the return of her younger brother Tom from his junior year at Dartmouth, and the reappearance of his old friends. When Tom got a summer job at a local country club, Peggy took him to work and picked him up.

On weekends, Peggy would join Harry on a Sunday drive in the Philadelphia countryside.

On the 4th of July, while Jack watched boat races and fireworks on the Ohio River, Peggy had her own adventure – a brief flight with her brother on a Pitcairn Aviation bi-plane. *It was very thrilling and I loved it, but it would have been so much more fun if you had been with us. Tom has the bug. Simply suggested we go. I didn't really intend to go with him, but finally persuaded myself it would be fun – Jack you would love it.* The "bug" was no doubt inspired by the enormous excitement generated by Lindbergh's solo flight across the Atlantic to Le Bourget Airport in Paris in May. Peggy was consumed with the Lindbergh story, as was Harry, who went to the ticker tape parade for Lindbergh in New York City on June 13, and reported that he had never seen anything like it. *We haven't been doing anything exciting,* Peggy wrote, *except reading about Lindbergh, our latest hero. Red Grange* (a college and professional football star)*, the Prince of Wales and even* (handsome British actor) *Dennis King have become lesser stars in comparison – weren't you thrilled about him?*

Perhaps the most interesting person in Peggy's life that summer was Mrs. Gates, who turned up regularly in her letters, while her mother and Ninny were barely mentioned. Mrs. Gates was an older neighbor with whom she had always had a very good relationship – no doubt a lucky circumstance for Peggy, who wanted so to be smart and well read, and had, at the same time, such an unsuccessful relationship with her own mother. While Mrs. Gates, who was childless, probably didn't have much interest in Tommy – Peggy reported to Jack that she had called the baby "a comical little chap" – she seemed to have a great deal of interest in Peggy's mind. The two had their own private reading group, trading books and magazines, which Peggy promptly sent on to Jack. It was a signature part of Peggy and Jack's relationship that they were both avid readers, and they reported on their reading in almost every letter (as the summer began, Peggy was reading Hemingway's *The Sun Also Rises*, and Jack was reading Edith Wharton). Peggy sent weekly packages of magazines – Vanity Fair, Harpers, and their main staple, the Saturday Evening Post – along with a regular package of fudge. Peggy must have had a lot of help with the baby in Glenside – she seems to have had plenty of free time.

The fudge was the product of one of Peggy's rare encounters with a kitchen stove. She remained disdainful of "domestic" work, though she reported once during the summer that she had given a luncheon party – *You should have been there. I was very domestic and cooked the luncheon myself.* But she was nervous about all the invitations Jack was getting that would have to be repaid when she got to Newburgh – *I certainly will have some social obligations in Newburgh – returning all the entertaining you are enjoying. Good meals I gather. I'm afraid I won't be much of a competition for the local talent. I suppose they all make flawless apple pies – and have never even heard of good old unfailing "Aunt Mary's"* (a prepackaged pie, like "Mrs. Smith's?"). *But I shall do my best by you darling, and meeting all the friends you've made.*

Jack reported that the endless rain made work on the dam difficult at the beginning of the summer. He wrote in early June that the river was 24 feet deep at the dam site, and construction work could not proceed until it had receded to 18 feet. Dam construction began with pile driving and the building of a coffer dam, a temporary wooden structure filled with sand and water, enclosing the area that would, at the right time, be "unwatered" by pumping boats so that the permanent dam, built of concrete and steel, could be constructed under dry conditions. While the river continued rising, Jack reported.

All but the most valuable firemen at the job have been laid off, and it is ridiculous to see them, high priced men, unloading cars of rock, and such labor, just to keep them more or less busy. And the repairs – all the "fleet" (pump boats, derrick boats, barges, scows, etc) has been repaired so much, for something to do, that it should be like new. If the working season (governed by low water) doesn't last way into December, it will look like Christmas in Newburgh for us – ho hum – such is the life of tramps, isn't it, lover?

Jack's own work was not in jeopardy. The Home Office, he explained, *has two branches in the field: the Engineering – represented by Lamphere, the erecting engineer; West, acting as cost engineer, and myself; and the treasurer's dept, represented by two field auditors... the above are all that are on the Home Office payroll. Other office help, such as timekeepers, clerks, stenographers, first aid man and construction superintendent, foremen and on down the line are all hired in the field and paid on a weekly basis. Do you follow? ...we are checking up on equipment – quantities etc, and the new work on the dam, unless there is a great change, won't start for two weeks.*

Jack threw himself into his new life, but not without nightly bouts of deep loneliness for Peggy and Tommy. By July he'd had enough of missing her company and the baby's development. After almost two months of admirable fiscal discipline, Jack was *"so pleased about the bills. Our goal of financial independence seems appreciably closer, doesn't it? More so than for months, years, almost.* And he had good news to report – the prospect of a free trip for Peggy and Tommy to Newburgh: *Mrs. Lamphere* (the wife of Jack's boss) *is now driving to her house in Baltimore and will be driving back about the end of the month. Mr. Lamphere suggested that you and Tommy might come along. How does that strike you, sweetest?*

Surprisingly, the idea didn't strike Peggy particularly well. *That was such an interesting letter today all about the fish fry and the Lampheres,* she wrote. *It sounded like so much fun. To tell you the truth Jack you haven't told me much about the Lampheres...I would love going back with Mrs. Lamphere but am afraid it would be rather hard for Tommy. Anyway so much depends on whether it is very hot or not. He has been such a good baby I don't want to do anything that might be tiring for him.*

So Jack went back to the original plan, asked for a reckoning on their remaining bills, and made a stab at setting a definite date, *And you can figure on about $70 on July 16, and the rest as soon as I can get it there – about Aug. 3 – on which date, if you can't afford to leave before, I want you to climb in the old train and come to me, please, my adorable.*

Still Peggy demurred, *Whew – such heat – 90 all day – the bills are gradually diminishing – thank goodness – which brings me to the point. Darling I've been thinking about coming out to you – you know how much I want and need you. But Jack, if it's as hot as this, I don't see how I could take Tommy on such a trip, until it's cooler do you? And I don't believe that will be till later than we had counted on. What do you think, Jack? I want to come the minute our bills are paid. I am so terribly lonesome for you. But darling, Tommy is so little and dependent and I hate to risk his health, don't you? Not that I think it could be hotter there than it is here. It's just the difference in the milk and the atmosphere...*

She was running out of excuses, but still Peggy dug in her heels. I suspect she was more worried about herself than she was about Tommy, but I don't know why.

Jack had spent a good part of his free time looking at housing possibilities in both Newburgh and Evansville, reporting his finds to Peggy in several letters. Now he pursued the issue of housing in earnest, and as one more carrot reported,

Now for some news – maybe – we have a house! It is only a possibility, but such a possibility that I didn't want to miss it. And I know you, knowing the circumstances here, wouldn't either, darling. The house is about a 4-room one story frame house in Newburgh, painted white, nice little yard, "central location," – furnishing only passable, but Frigidaire and electric stove (if

221

Peggy had been more interested in domestic work, this could have been a huge selling point. These very contemporary conveniences came into common use only in the 1920s) *bathroom, living room, bedroom, and a sort of tiny bedroom. Rent $45 a month. The man that has it now works in the store room on the job, and thinks he is going away with his family. He will let me know definitely in about three days. You know I want you to choose for yourself, darling, but I'll take no lease, of course, and we needn't stay longer than a month. Then – my job is such that I have to be here, which would be difficult from Evansville – and make me late at night, too. Again, Newburgh is cooler and that's important. It isn't much, but it's good for Newburgh, and if you think it will be all right, I hope it goes through. I'm prepared to be pleased about it. And I hope you will be, sweetheart. There – that is news, isn't it?*

Still Peggy found reasons to worry: *Are the rooms very tiny? The thing that interests me most about it is the heating. Is there a furnace? Darling can you come home to luncheon? Then you could fix the furnace for us. They are rather hard to get to understand, I've heard. That will be a new expense, darling, doing our own heating – such an added expense, too. Are electricity and gas high in Newburgh? Do they have telephones – I don't mean to be impudent or also to take any credit that's due Newburgh from it. I am just looking for information. You see you haven't told me so much about the place except that it is quite rural and pretty. From what I understand it is more or less a typical little river town...*

Jack reported that the house was heated with coal, which reassured her – she was frightened of oil furnaces – and that he would be home for lunch and be able to help her. He learned some romantic history about Newburgh that he hoped would interest her, *I spent about an hour tonight talking to one of my fellow boarders, who raises flowers – a man, usually taciturn and silent, who I find is an expert botanist. Knows Newburgh and its territory, and*

222

through his flowers, knows many prominent people. He did keep me interested. He told me of the time when Newburgh was the trade center – when all roads were crowded with wagons loaded with tobacco, corn, wheat – loading the boats that lined the river (then) for shipment everywhere – when Newburgh was dotted with tobacco warehouses and little hotels for the traders – when the Newburgh man chartered a ship and took a load of tobacco to London, only to have the price fall before he got there – ruining him. And of the old families, and then illustrious sons and daughters, now residing in New York, Florida or the continent. But isn't it remarkable, darling, of the interest, romance, almost, that fills lives everywhere – the stories that are behind almost every surface that one scratches? I'm getting my metaphors all mixed – but you understand, don't you precious...

It breaks my heart to read this. Jack was trying so hard to woo her there, pulling out every piece of information that would elevate this little town in Peggy's imagination He shouldn't have had to work this hard.

And he had more to add, *it isn't exactly a typical river town – years ago, in Indian times, before Evansville existed, it was quite a trading center – but it died as a rising town long since – and has become a place with practically no business – where some of the people live because their families have always lived here – and where a good many Evansville people have homes to get away from the heat, rush and bustle of the city (?). The dam, of course, has given it new life – temporarily – and, for that reason, people like the Humphries, who come here for quiet – aren't so fond of it – the dam, I mean. And Newburgh was, of course, totally unprepared for such an inrush of inhabitants –and now, in the frowsy rooming houses, they sleep as they work, i.e. in three shifts – as some of the boys say "it don't even give the bed a chance to git cool." All that, of course, will pass – and Newburgh will return to its former status of a town with a past. The chief local, or*

223

nearby industries (also?) are the coal mines, the Thornton Home for retired Presbyterian Ministers and Families, a couple large fruit farms, and a somewhat shady establishment, ensconced in a beautiful old stone house that seems to be a sanitarium for dopes or drunks or something – I've never seen the inmates. It takes about half an hour to get to Evansville – either driving (on good roads) – or on the Traction (the trolley).

He even sweetened the picture with an account of some local entertainment offered by a passing showboat – a form of entertainment that in 1927 was almost gone. He described a visit from the Cotton Blossom, and the sound of the dogs that would no doubt chase Little Eva through town as part of their performance of "Uncle Tom's Cabin."

Still no luck. Near the end of July, Jack decided to apply some real pressure: *Called on Mrs. Ashby* (mother of Peggy's friend Alice) *last night and she is perfectly charming isn't she – I liked her so much. She is awfully disappointed that you and Tommy aren't here – and thinks (we talked it over) that you ought to come. And that's what I want to talk about. I know how you feel, darling, about traveling with Tommy, but really, the weather here is better than Philadelphia – and you would just be putting it off – and the milk will have to be changed anyway (though cows is cows the world over) – and besides I need you so badly. I don't want to be selfish, you know that, Peggy darling, and of course I wouldn't want you to start the trip in tremendous heat. But if it's just enduring summer weather, you wouldn't mind the trip a bit I don't believe, darling...*

Peggy knew how to push back, and in doing so used the best weapon she had in her arsenal – guilt, about that confrontation in the spring:

Darling I haven't written you for several days because I have been thinking and thinking and trying to decide what to do – and Jack I have come to the conclusion while your letter sounds most

224

enticing, Tommy is our first consideration. That much difference in the time won't make much difference in handling him on the train. Really Jack, while it isn't any farther where you are, it is the trip that counts. I would have to put him on canned milk because his milk would most likely sour with all the juggling on the train. Then again he had prickly heat badly and it would be hard to keep him comfortable on the train – and I would much rather wait until it is cooler. Of course, darling, his milk has to be changed but it is easier to do in cooler weather. I know Jack it is because you don't understand how delicate their little stomachs are that you suggest it. The least little thing upsets them in hot weather. I consulted Dr. Faris and he said if it were cooler in the middle of August and I didn't start in a hot spell it would be all right so Jack will you just let me use my judgment and not be hurt at me – or get too lonesome because that will just make me feel so badly, darling.

And here comes her biggest weapon:

Jack, nothing hurts me so much as for you not to understand and I hope you'll never again misunderstand me like you did this spring – it hurts me every time I think of it. You see Jack I have always thought that you were as nearly perfect as anyone could be... Darling I have spent the whole summer trying to get over my nervousness and the silly prejudices I had – and I have pretty well succeeded. And darling I realize that the first step is in being secure to your own self because darling no matter how much you love anyone, if you haven't convictions and the strength of your own convictions you won't or can't be happy – and while we can guide and help each other we can't control each other and I think Jack we will be much happier just facing that don't you, darling? And I am saying sincerely Jack that I never want you to do anything for me that is against your own convictions. It was silly and weak for me to let myself be so emotional and it must have been very hard for you darling and it has done me a lot of good to think it all out without talking about it. That's why I never wrote you how I was because the best way to get over it was just not to discuss it at all. And darling while I am still not a Mrs. Hercules – it's not my constitution to be – I have a much better hold on myself and as my state of mind improves my strength will come back – and the first thing you know I'll be your big strong mama!! I love you so much anyway that in itself would make me feel strong.

It seems important to me to try to understand what Peggy was saying in this letter. In a moment of clarity and candor, she seems to have recognized her own weakness and fragility. She did not, I conclude, have the *courage* to go to Newburgh with Jack. I assume the "silly prejudices" were prejudices against a small Midwestern town, and I think she felt that though she was not emotionally strong, she considered her stubborn resistance to Jack's entreaties to be a kind of strength. Above all, even as she wished she were his "big strong mama," she wanted him to back off.

Was her illness in fact an emotional illness? Or postpartum depression? Perhaps Tommy's birth generated a kind of post-traumatic stress disorder, recalling the death of their first baby. Whatever it was, when I read it I feel more anger than sympathy.

Jack did what Peggy wanted him to do – he retreated: *I do appreciate and understand what you have gone through and how you have felt – and my first consideration is the welfare of you and Tommy. I know that you know best – and if you feel that you shouldn't come out here now, I know that's right, and I understand perfectly. Precious little Tommy. He is so healthy now, we can't afford to take the least little chance of upsetting him, can we darling Darling girl, I'm so glad you feel you are on the road to better health and strength – just feeling that way will help. Don't think I don't know how discouraging any kind of sickness or condition that seems to continue indefinitely can be.*

Nevertheless, as July rolled into August, Jack continued to talk about his hopes that Peggy and Tommy would come soon, and he sent a precise itinerary for their train trip, including costs for each leg, and instructions for them to get a hotel room in Terre Haute for a few hours to "rest." He asked Peggy to keep this information in her purse for reference and so it would not get lost. But it was clear that he was becoming depressed. He was upset when one of the workers on the dam fell into the construction site and lost a leg. And Jack had an accident himself. He fell off the coffer, lighting on a timber in the river and bruising his side rather painfully. His maternal grandmother, Gran Bracken, who had been a fixture of the Burlington household through his childhood, had been fading all summer and died in early August, and it must have been heartbreaking to Jack that he was unable to go to Burlington to join his family for her funeral. Gran had been a benign presence throughout his childhood, and an active support to Jack and Peggy when they upset everyone by marrying so precipitously.

Peggy noticed and felt a little guilty herself. *...you do sound a little depressed and lonely and that makes me feel so badly, when I want to do the best thing for all of us – and Jack more than anything in the world I want to be with you. Newburgh sounds awfully interesting. I shall love having you show me all the funny interesting little places and meeting all the friends you have made.*

Jack must have been surprised, then, when Peggy wrote soon after that the whole Talbot family would go to Ocean City for a two-week vacation during the last half of August. *Darling the idea is that we go down the shore for two weeks and come home for a day and straight out to you – what do you think precious? I don't give a hang about the shore except for the change – and the air is so bracing – and then a summer away from the water. Although it hasn't been so bad, just a couple of weeks of hot weather...and darling don't you think it's a good idea to get about $160 ahead so we can buy a little car and pay it off on our note...Jack tell me what you think – will you get a day off Labor Day so we can have a holiday? I want to dance...and go to a fish fry, and on a riverboat...*

Jack did not raise any objection to this idea, but he wasn't happy, *You speak of a couple weeks at the sea shore – that would be lovely I know, but darling my heart does sink a little bit every time I think of you being away a little longer. But you know best...and I'd like to know that you are comfortable and happy and being benefitted by the sea air. And whatever you decide I'll know that's best. But I'm awfully lonesome for my darling wife and darling baby.*

The Talbots did go to Ocean City for two weeks, where they shopped and went to the beach and rolled on the boardwalk in roller chairs, and Peggy did go back to Glenside at the end of August to do her laundry and pack. The trip, however, was delayed an additional week, because her brother Tom had an emergency tonsillectomy, for which Peggy said her father asked her to stay. She arrived in Newburgh around the 10th of September. It's hard for me to believe that he wasn't angry at her for her delay.

Early in the summer, Peggy had written Jack, about their future on the American rivers: *Isn't it fun meeting people and becoming accustomed to different modes of living. Aren't you glad we have the same reactions to things and can be interested in almost anything? We must always keep our senses of humor – then we can enjoy being gypsies and make moving around seem like a big adventure.* She talked a good game and knew the right things to say. Was she telling the truth, or did she just wish she felt this way? I can't shake the feeling that my mother was thinking of herself and her own comfort, and that all the rest, all the excuses, all the "sympathy" for Jack were little lies.

Nevertheless, I hope that Jack, Peggy, and Tommy did enjoy being gypsies. From Newburgh, Indiana, they would go on to Cape Girardeau, Missouri, Golconda, Illinois, Bessemer, Alabama, and McKeesport, Pennsylvania. Though there are letters from this period, mostly to other members of the family, Jack and Peggy were not separated from each other for extended periods of time.

Knowing that the Depression was around the corner, I wonder if this was the last period when they still believed in their dreams, when they still thought the house, the social status, the life they sought was possible.

1928 to 1930

Vagabond Years

From the UGI Circle, August 1928

...It seems a long while since the pioneer of the west came with his family from the east over the mountains, through dense forest, following the trail of the deer and Indian, and settling along the banks of the Ohio to make a home in a vast unbroken wilderness. Soon came others... [who], abandoning the dangerous pack horse trail found going easier and less dangerous by water, and so came down the Ohio in canoe, flat boat or raft. The New Orleans, the first steamer on the Ohio, in 1811 awakened the people, and there followed an urgent demand for river improvement...

From the perspective provided by this excerpt from Jack's company newsletter, Jack and Peggy's life on the rivers in the late 1920s had a romance to it. They were participating in the last hopeful growth spurt in the engine of American progress, before the economy crashed and things fell apart for the world – and for them. Because Jack and Peggy were rarely separated during the next fourteen years, I rely on fragments – letters between Jack and his mother, a 1929 journal written by Peggy with entries for January and April, company newsletters, childhood memories of my brother Tommy, who was a growing boy in these years, and recorded history of this troubled period in American life. From the written fragments I have enough to piece together the facts of their life during these years. For the emotional context, I need to read between the lines.

Jack and Peggy were on the road at least through 1930, while Jack continued to work as a vagabond engineer for United Engineers. After several months together in Newburgh, they were sent in early 1928 to Cape Girardeau, Missouri, a city that was once a settlement and trading post occupied by French Canadian traders at a bend in the Mississippi River. United Engineers had a contract to build the substructure for a Mississippi River highway bridge, replacing a ferry between the Missouri and Illinois sides – a bridge that was itself replaced in 2003 with a new four-lane bridge. The company newsletter, the *UGI Circle,* reported that workers on the bridge job were once again fighting against mighty waters, which threatened to flood the cofferdam (the same kind of preliminary structure used for Dam 47 in Newburgh) at Pier 8 of the proposed bridge. The UGI newsletter notes that the crisis prompted *"even workers in the office to go out on the river and assist with work on the pier."* Perhaps Jack, too, was out there at Pier 8 working to complete the job of pouring concrete into the cofferdam before the river overwhelmed their efforts. He was cost engineer (in charge of estimating the project's component costs) for this and future projects (a kind of irony, given his personal failures at cost control). He must have been concerned about the cost of a delay in construction on the bridge substructure, estimated at $10,000.

Of their life in Cape Girardeau, Jack reported to his father, *we are comfortably settled now – having our meals in our apartment – a pleasant change from the monotonous hotel food served hereabouts. Tommy is thriving and while his words are limited to "bye bye, pussy, dada, ball" and the like, he is remarkably active – walks and climbs everywhere – even up and down the stairs – and yesterday, for the first time, he ran away from the yard – to where some boys were playing ball a block away. We found him looking on wistfully, his face pressed to the wicker fence.*

This is a frightening thought, given that Tommy was about eighteen months old at the time. For a very protective mother, Peggy was more than a little casual about this active toddler's whereabouts.

Jack and Peggy were in Cape Girardeau for about six months. By August they were settled in Golconda, Illinois, back on the Ohio River, not far from Cairo. The UGI Circle notes that "Golconda, [once] a settlement in the wilderness...[is] where...products from the north and south will be unloaded from modern river craft and shipped by rail and by automobile trucks in all directions..." There Jack was a field engineer for Lock and Dam 51, responsible for lines, grades, and dimensions on the last of the movable dams to be built as part of the slackwatering project.

While Jack was hard at work, Peggy was feeling restless and bored with her life. And who could blame her? She hated housework, she wasn't interested in cooking, she was in a town that probably did not offer an abundance of entertainment, she knew no one but Jack, and she had no impulse to find a community for herself, as they would move in a matter of months. And apparently she did not consider minding Tommy to be a full time job. The following letter, written in the old petulant voice of her teenage years that Peggy, then 25, still allowed herself with her parents, confirms her hunger for a more significant life. She had written her parents asking for money to start a dress shop in her rented house in Golconda, and not surprisingly, they refused to provide the money. I can understand why. It seems a stunningly impractical scheme.

Peggy to her parents, August 10, 1928
Dear Mother and Daddy,

I'm not to be daunted so easily – although I really didn't expect Harry to be very enthusiastic about my plan. My housework consists of getting breakfast made and bed – sweeping two rooms and bathing and dressing Tommy – and fixing my luncheon. It's all complete at 9 am, since I get up at six. So if I had a dress shop I might have it right here at home. Business wouldn't be simply wishing you know and I would have plenty of time to do all I have to. Jack has built Tommy a sandbox and fenced in a yard for him so he runs around all day. Jack is working awfully hard – from 6 am to 6 and sometimes in the evening – never later than 8 o'clock however. That's too much time to mope. I do think everyone needs something to interest them - not just housework. And I find that my friends that are doing something are the ones that are happy.

This begins to sound like the discontent that came to a head at the beginning of the women's movement in the 1960s. By the late 1920s, with the advent of electrified houses and modern conveniences like refrigerators, washing machines, vacuum cleaners and gas or electric stoves, women were free of daily shopping, hand washing, daily floor scrubbing, hauling wood, and all the dawn-to-dusk work of keeping a household going. Yet women of a certain class were not encouraged to work outside the home – in fact, Jack explicitly didn't want Peggy to work. He wanted to be the breadwinner who provided for all of his family's needs. Peggy had willfully neglected her studies and now she wished she had done more. She went on,

I wish more and more every day that I had had two years at the "Le Gay" conservatory and had that much artistic training. It's what I love. Alice is keeping up with her acting, and Marge is

writing and Gladys has a position – it's old fashioned to think you have to grow old just because you're married – and you tend to grow old if you haven't anything to think about. It was quite plain to me at home among the girls – so many of them had nothing to do and they were just stale. That's that. Can't you tell I'm getting back a little of my pep?

Tommy is growing wilder every minute. Honestly he simply tears all over the place and is saying more all the time. Every time he sees an ant he yells "bug, bug" and tries to catch it. I caught him up on the table the other day buttering himself a piece of bread...

...I have ordered myself a typewriter and am going to take a couple of courses in Columbia...

It's unclear exactly what artistic training Peggy was pining for – piano? She had been interested in her piano lessons as a child. And did she think of getting a secretarial job after her typing courses? It does seem that she was feeling more like her old self. So can we gather that she was in fact frail, either physically or emotionally (or both) the summer before, when she was in Glenside and Jack was in Newburgh?

Peggy was not a natural nester. In fact, she seemed to be naïve about what it took to care for a toddler. That she believed Tommy, at 20 months, could amuse himself in the back yard while she ran a dress shop in the house is a little startling, particularly with a toddler capable of disappearing down the street to watch boys play ball through a wicker fence.

I wonder if "Le Gay Conservatory," whatever that was, would have sent her off into the glamorous occupations she continued to yearn for. In different circumstances, might she have written this book? There is ample evidence, in the form of notes to herself among the letters that she wanted to. Poor Peggy, her ambitions were to remain forever beyond her reach.

Peggy's letter to her parents, with its imperious tone, seems a reflection of her father's, who wrote, in what must have been a continuing contest of wills between them through the fall of 1928.

Harry to Peggy

Dear Peg,

I enclose your check for $25. I do not know what you want it for, but I suspect for some other reason than stated by you. In other words, I think you are putting over a fast one on father. Why you can't live on the salary of Jack's $80 a week, and out in the country at that.

When you know where you are going let us know at once. I hope it is to some good place where you will not have to pay too much there. I guess I will send you money for Xmas – I'd not know what to get you. What you asked for is out of the question. Why did you not ask for a house and lot?

I am going down to North Carolina to hunt, and am leaving on Thanksgiving Day. Will not be back until Xmas so will have no chance to buy Xmas presents after I leave.

Write us soon. Love to all, dad

Harry's hope was realized, as a consequence of his own hospitality. By Christmas 1928, Jack, Peggy, and Tommy were back in Philadelphia, camping in her parents' house in Glenside, where they had no rent to pay at all. That was lucky for Jack who, between assignments, earned no salary for the month of December.

Shortly after Christmas, Jack's father suddenly died. This must have been a complicated loss for Jack, who was forever trying and failing to prove to his father that he could be responsible with money. While his most abiding and intense relationship was with his mother, his father seemed a gentle enough soul, and Jack must have felt the loss of him keenly.

Jack and Peggy joined the whole Fleming family, driving to Burlington, Iowa through winter weather for a grand funeral service at St. Paul's Catholic Church, with four priests and a cardinal's personal representative in attendance. Jack's father was buried in the little Catholic cemetery adjacent to *his* parents, Michael and Bridget Fleming, and Jack and Peggy's baby, little John Joseph.

Peggy, who was keeping a journal in January 1929, noted the comings and goings of family and visitors bearing gifts at the Fleming household in Burlington – flowers, an orange cake – and she joined a group effort writing thank you notes and greeting callers. Jack, Peggy, and Tommy left on January 7, armed with sandwiches and coffee and the gift of a pint of whiskey for the trip home, through traffic and minus-ten-degree weather. *Jack has had word to report at once for duty in Philadelphia,* Peggy noted in her journal, *which is a relief as we have had no pay for a month now. The only drawback is that Jack's salary is to be cut by one third, which is rather discouraging. Especially when we were just beginning to pay off our notes. Such is the life of an engineer,* she added, with just a hint of pride at the romance of it.

The car trip took the three of them through Chicago; Freemont, Indiana; Akron and Youngstown, Ohio, where fortunately they found lodging with college friends and family, as *our finances are very low – a dollar something.* The price for free lodging was sometimes an evening of boredom. At Cousin Michael Bracken's house in Johnstown, Pennsylvania, they were treated to *an evening looking at stereopticon views of their trip to the Yellowstone – not very exciting.* They reached home – Glenside – through the Alleghenies, *by far the prettiest part of the trip, except for the little mining towns, which are horrible.*

They were at home with the Talbots in Glenside for the first three months of 1929, that fateful year in the history of the American economy, when investors and stock speculators were still optimistic, running on the energy of the 1920s boom, and the markets were careening toward their peak. That peak would be reached on September 3, the crash on October 29.

Jack went to work every day at the home office of UGI, working on estimates for the Pennsylvania Railroad's Philadelphia improvements, including the beautiful 30th Street Station, while Peggy resumed an active social life with her childhood friends. Jack and Peggy went to the Keswick Movie Theatre – *very advanced for Glenside,* Peggy noted in her journal, *with vaudeville and all the garnishes...* In 1929, movie houses were still showing silent movies along with the more technically advanced talkies.

In February Jack and Peggy went to New York City and saw the *old crowd from Cornell,* with whom they went to a nightclub and a couple of speakeasies. Incredibly, Peggy reported having tea with Dr. and Mrs. Sophian – who must be the same Mrs. Sophian, longtime "companion" of her father's salad days, and that Mrs. Sophian gave her *a lovely luncheon set.* If Peggy was smart, she didn't mention this gift to her mother.

They went to the auto show and decided they *would like a LaSalle, a Graham Paige, a Jordan or a baby Packard,* Peggy wrote. *To be conservative, the LaSalle salesman advises that we stick to what we have till we can afford one.* What a wise, restrained car salesman! LaSalles in particular were fancy cars for the age, a short step down from Cadillacs, and Graham Paiges were very stylish looking, if less fancy. Jordans and baby Packards may have been closer to their price range, but for the time being, they stuck with their trusty Ford.

They even looked for houses and apartments in Philadelphia, which they found expensive and probably impractical given the uncertainty that Jack's work would keep them there.

Given Peggy's difficult history with her mother, it is a testament to both of them that they were able to live together off and on through these years. *We are having a rather hard time as usual getting accustomed to each other's ways – mother not*

238

approving of ours, it always takes us a little while to become acclimated, so to speak. Nevertheless, Jack and Peggy apparently felt free to install themselves in Glenside when they needed to.

By March 1929, Jack, Peggy, and Tommy were on the move again to another assignment, in Bessemer, Alabama, where United Engineers had the contract to build a plant for the Pullman Car and Manufacturing Corporation. The United Engineers crew would build three groups of buildings for a steel shop, a wood shop, and a paint shop, all intended to support the eventual manufacture of 25 freight and refrigerator cars a day for the railroads crisscrossing the southern United States. From Jack's letter to his mother in the spring of 1929, it is easy to imagine this handsome young family rattling down dusty country roads in their Ford, probably closed by now with a roof, as 80 percent of cars were by that time. But I see Peggy sitting in a fetching cloche hat while Jack drove, perhaps shading his eyes with a slouching fedora, Tommy snuggled in his mother's lap or found a spot for himself among the bags and baskets in the back. Jack wrote his mother:

...I rather expected to be placed on some job in Philadelphia – when I was told that I was to be placed in the cost division, and was to report to this (Bessemer) job immediately as cost engineer – no warning as usual. Again, as usual, we made frantic preparations for leaving – packing, crating and shipping – getting my final instructions, getting the car in shape, and finally, getting off.

Their route took them south through Baltimore and Washington, where they saw Jack's sister's Polly, in the Green Spring Valley north of Baltimore, and his sister Esther in Washington. *We had a flying but pleasant visit the first day,* he wrote his mother. *Dinner with Polly, bed and breakfast with Esther... The next day trip was down the Shenandoah Valley through Lexington to Roanoke – the following day into Tennessee and Knoxville, still following the Allegheny ranges into the Great*

239

Smokies – and how lovely that part of the country is. The fourth day of the trip brought us into the flooded districts – through Chattanooga, where high water detained us, to Rome Georgia, still over a hundred miles from Birmingham, which we made about noon the fifth day. The whole trip was like driving into spring. Each day, each hour, almost, brought us to greener, warmer districts – each mile showed us more blossoms and flowers after we crossed the Tennessee lines – and it might have been midsummer here in Alabama, what with the cotton and barefoot negroes and dusty roads.

Jack had a talent for providing just the perfect nuggets of information that made all his work locations seem out of the ordinary, interesting places in themselves: *We came right to Bessemer, which is a mill town of about 20,000 population, 15 miles west of Birmingham. The whole district, you may know, is the steel center of the south – being situated in the tip end of the Appalachians – between a mountain of ore and a mountain of coal. Our job is a large plant for the Pullman Company – a car manufacturing works, which is to be completed by the middle of August, if possible. I might add that the job had been going 40 days when I got here – which meant 40 days work for me to catch up with – and it's given me some busy days. We stayed at the local hotel, an old but clean place, for a week, during which Peggy was house hunting.*

On this assignment, Peggy found a really nice place for them to live, one in which they could settle and feel comfortable and at home as a family. Jack continued:

We finally got a little cottage just outside Bessemer, really a summer place, in a little swimming and fishing resort known as West Lake. We have living room, dining room, kitchen, two bedrooms and a bath – really quite palatial for us. The furniture is sparse to say the least, and it took two days cleaning to make it look respectable, but for $25 a month, we can't complain. And, we

*have a lovely big yard for Tommy – and a little garden, and rose
bushes, plants, and what not and a fig tree, our pride. The lake is
about a hundred yards from us, and we have a grove of towering
pines on one side. Our trunks and boxes came today and we're just
settled. We have a Negro girl that makes biscuits or corn bread for
every meal. So I think we'll like it if it doesn't get too awfully hot –
the country around here is very pretty, hilly and wooded.
Birmingham is a real city – and has some of the loveliest suburbs
I've ever seen (on the other side, of course). However, we think
we're nicely fixed.*

Their life quickly settled into a routine, and though this comes
from Jack's perspective, I sense a more cheerful, less anxious Jack
and a more settled, contented family in this picture he creates,
*We're about two miles from the job – and Peggy drives me in and
out twice a day. Tommy is perfectly contented here, the heartless
little wretch makes his home where his cap is – and has no regrets
about leaving any place. He has so many things to see here and
sees everything vocally now – "See a bug? See a fower? See a
bird?" and so on. He was crazy about his bunny you sent him and
plays with it by the hour. And he still clings to the battered choo
choo. Easter morning we had his bunny cart loaded with candy
under the bed and when we awakened he had eaten all the candy
and was engrossed with the rabbit...*

Peggy's journal description of their life seems happy enough.
In addition to slogging through Sigrid Undset's *Kristin
Lavransdottir* that summer, she wrote:

*Our chief amusement has been the stock company, where we
saw several plays – all Broadway successes – so it has been a
weekly pilgrimage to the Alabama [Theatre] to have all the first
run talkies, or a ride out to Fair Park to give Tommy a ride on the
ponies. We go swimming every day. Our neighbors are very nice
and invite us to their parties and it is nice to meet people even if
we didn't have very much in common. We go to Roberts Field, the*

local airport and watch the planes – saw some fire stunting and parachute jumping. We would both like to learn to fly but, I confess that I wish that planes had been a little more perfect. There are still so many accidents even among the best pilots. But I feel that this is the time to learn while we are still young enough to be a little rash and still have all our faculties.

As always, Peggy was very interested in the social environment of her temporary home, and the possibilities for social contact. She noted about Bessemer in her journal, *"the people who live here are comparatively poor, although they live very comfortably...there are no aristocratic families here. Our neighbors are all pleasant, although we have made no close or really congenial friends. Tommy,* (who was almost two and a half) *however, has done better and has a regular gang of his own consisting of about seven little boys ranging between the ages of two and seven...I would like to meet a really representative southern family...*which I take to mean a representative socially prominent family – perhaps descendents of families who once owned plantations framed by languid willow trees and tended by docile servants. In fact, even among the simpler people she met she found she had her own social handicap. West Lake may well have been the setting for a story Peggy told of those years, about a neighbor who came to call, asking what church Jack and Peggy would be attending. When Peggy mentioned that Jack was a Catholic, the woman promptly stood up, stammered an excuse and abruptly departed. It was an era of rabid anti-Catholicism (the resurgent Ku Klux Klan in the 1920s was as explicitly opposed to Catholics as they were to blacks and Jews). Peggy must have had at least an inkling that Jack's Catholicism was going to be a problem for her in some circles.

Harry Talbot's health was beginning to fail. Taking control of life with his usual determination, Harry decided to check himself into the Battle Creek Sanitarium in Michigan, in order to make a frontal assault on his declining condition. Harry was mean, but he could also be funny. This letter is one of my favorites,

Dear Peggy and Jack,

Maybe you would like to know what I think of this place. I would call it a very beautiful Hell full of cripples and cranks. I do not know which class I belong to, maybe both. I would like it if it were not for the food. I am only allowed 1,000 calories a day, even bran is taboo, no meats, no butter, no milk except buttermilk, no tea and no coffee. Mainly fruits and vegetables, and most of this I do not like. I will stick if I can, but I would like a nice juicy steak right now. I lost 7 lbs from Tuesday until yesterday. I get up about 6 a.m. At 7 I have ½ hour of sitting up exercise, breakfast at 7:30. At nine there is dumbbell exercise and a march of 1 ½ miles. I then go down to the room where all the electric vibrating machines are. Horses, jiggling straps etc etc. I then go to the massage room for massage. That takes ½ hour then down to the room where they sweat you with hot packs, cabinet baths etc. After that a swim in the pool. Then you go to see your Dr. By this time it is dinner. After dinner I go out into the open air gym for sun. All we wear there is a heat cloth, and we lie in the sun on cots until we get tanned red. While we are there we get more sitting with exercise, also play volleyball, and swim in a very long and beautiful crystal pool. This outdoor gym is certainly very attractive, beautiful trees, green grass and flowers. After supper, we have club swinging exercise on the roof and a march of about 3 miles to visit men and women. Then we sit around on one of the handsomest verandahs I have ever seen where I have marked the cross (on a drawing of the sanitarium at the top of stationery), and go to bed early. What do you think of it? How are you getting along and how is Tommy? Give him my love and love to you both. Dad

A large, willful and stubbornly overweight man, Harry must have been a challenge to the staff at Battle Creek. It's also interesting to note that spas have not changed much. The

243

equipment evolves, but the message remains the same: good health will only be achieved with a good diet and exercise, exercise, exercise.

Jack went on to a brief assignment, on his own, at Port Chester, New York, working as a cost engineer on construction of an extension of the Boston and West Chester Railroad. His next – and probably last – on-site assignment for UGI's United Engineers was back on the Ohio in McKeesport, Pennsylvania, just downriver from Pittsburgh. There he supervised engineering details for the electrification of rolling mills of the National Tube Company. Those rolling mills produced tubes used to carry water that converted to the steam that powered railroad steam engines. One of several steel manufacturing companies in a steelworker's town, National Tube was eventually sold to U.S. Steel.

Jack began his work in McKeesport about six weeks after the stock market crashed, on October 29, and though few people felt the effects of the crash so soon – and few thought the economic crisis would be long term – construction companies like United Engineers felt an impact almost immediately. By 1933 the company would be operating in the red, and by 1938, with its stock values wiped out, the company would be sold by its parent company, UGI.

Peggy and Tommy were back in Glenside getting ready for Christmas while Jack settled into his work in McKeesport and tried to get some idea of housing possibilities. Away from Peggy, he wrote daily letters about his new job. His letters contain no hint of any economic fears beyond their usual close-to-the-bone family finances.

Jack, from the Penn McKee Hotel in McKeesport, PA to Peggy in Glenside
December 12, 1929
My precious darling,

...Things went as scheduled this morning. I arrived in a dark and rainy Pittsburgh, came right out here, and right to this establishment where Middleton was waiting for me. I have a room here (without) at $2 – and it isn't at all bad – the hotel, in fact, is rather surprisingly good considering the town. McKeesport itself is bigger than you would imagine. It gives rather the impression of Johnstown – you know, many bright cheery stores and rather dirty streets – unlovely – and depending entirely on the steel mills, which are enormous. It is fifteen miles – a half hour ride by train – from P. It's been a dark, rainy, miserable day – but I might as well get used to them, because I'm told we won't see the sun until April. Sol, in other words, retires practically with the groundhog in this verdant valley where a tree is a sickly thing clutching to a rocky hillside... Jack was not sugarcoating the charms of McKeesport to entice Peggy to join him, as he had of Newburgh, Indiana in the summer of 1927. In fact, he seemed more than a little gloomy and weighed down with their personal financial circumstances. A day later he wrote:

I was very busy today, getting caught up with the things they always have waiting for the luckless cost engineer. I am, for all practical purposes, the accountant – and have a nice young chap by the name of Taffy Williams who is a sort of timekeeper, cub accountant, and assistant to me.

I'm still here at the hotel, as you see, at $12 a week. The only other place seems to be the YMCA, which is cheaper, but you have to join. I'll have to do something – or quit eating – or walk to Philadelphia Christmas Eve. Speaking of that, I think, as you suggested, I can get a train bringing me in about 11:30 and we can go to midnight mass – how would that be?

And four days later:

... Peggy for the last two solid hours I've been wrestling with figures, and my head is going round. It's maddening – this cutting and paring – but I reached some conclusions,   if I

Move to the Y tomorrow

Mother sends me the money present

We spend only $5 while I am in Philadelphia

We can get through. That isn't a very pleasant prospect for you, my precious, just at Christmas time – but my Christmas will be getting home to you and Tommy and I don't want anything else – except to be able to give you two something nice. It's discouraging – makes me want to get a job in one city and be able to stay there and get somewhere. I do wish we were together so we could talk about it. I'm sunk, precious. I just wish I had you here – close to me, and I could forget about all these damnable worries....

The special agony of Christmas was to be a theme throughout the country as families began to feel the effects of the crash. No one wanted to disappoint the children, who hoped against hope that Santa Claus would leave an abundance of toys under the Christmas tree. For my parents, providing for Tommy's Christmas wishes became a paramount concern over the next ten years. It saddens me to read how much they wanted to please him, and how hard it was to pull off.

Sometime in 1930 Jack was reassigned to the home office in Philadelphia with, regrettably, not much work to do. The three of them, Jack, Peggy, and Tommy, were together again, finally settled in one place, building a life.

As it turns out, life didn't get easier for them. The world economy was collapsing around them, but most people, including Jack and Peggy, who were always in crisis, were still unaware that they were living at the beginning of a great economic depression.

1931 to 1940

The Depression

December 15, 1931, Jack to his mother

Mother dearest,

Please excuse the paper, but I'm writing from the office, where I am not as busy as I might be. Things just aren't picking up, and I still expect to be off in January and March. Cousin Frank sent me to a Vice President of the Philadelphia Gas Works Co. – another U.G.I. company – in the hope that he might find me employment to fill in, but nothing has come of it yet, and I doubt if anything will, since there are too many without any work at all. However, we have been getting along all right, and I'm sure can continue to do so. It just means, as you pointed out, getting along without things that aren't necessary to physical wellbeing. The difficult thing is catching up on the checks that were caught in the bank failure, but we are gradually doing that, and when the bank finally makes a payment, it will be just so much extra.

By the end of 1931, everyone knew that the country was in crisis. In the fall, more than 300 banks had closed and10 million

247

people – 17 percent of the working population – were unemployed. Salaries were cut, shops were empty, factories were running at 20 percent of capacity, breadlines, soup kitchens, panhandlers, freight car transients and Hoovervilles, makeshift shacks huddled together under bridges, were increasingly common sights.

Beginning in 1931, the first of years of vicious drought hit Kansas, Arkansas, Texas and Colorado, draining wells and leaving vast desolate fields of withered crops. The drought and the ensuing clouds of dust, caused by years of intensive farming (following World War I, when demand mushroomed for American agricultural products) removed thousands of acres of topsoil in the Midwest. This was another blow to the American economy, another reason it took so long to recover.

Jack was mistaken about two things in this letter home to his mother: the failed bank never repaid them for the checks they had been unable to honor, but with Cousin Frank Bracken's help, Jack *did* find a job at the Philadelphia Gas Works – an hourly (rather than salaried) job as a cadet engineer and supervisor in the distribution department – a job that sent him out on city streets at night checking gas leaks. He was probably able to transfer directly from UGI to the gas company without a period of unemployment.

Peggy's voice is completely absent from this piece of their history, which is too bad, because it is during this period that a fundamental shift occurred in her attitude toward Jack and the stability of their relationship. I am left to guess the nature of that change.

From the letters I have – mostly Jack's to his mother – I glean the following about Jack and Peggy's circumstances in the early 30s. They had settled on Philadelphia for their permanent home. By 1931 they were in a rented house (*"our miniature country place"* Jack called it in a letter to his mother) in Flourtown, not far from the Talbot parents in Glenside and Peggy's brother Tom Talbot, now a lawyer married to Gladys Damon, a wealthy woman from Cleveland, Ohio, and living in Philadelphia. Peggy had stationery made, with some irony and a bit of grandeur giving the house a name, "Crow's Nest."

Jack had a steady job and a salary, though it was significantly smaller than his salary at UGI. That was a common circumstance of the Depression. By 1932, average earnings in the U.S. were a bit more than half - 54 percent – of average earnings before the crash in 1929. Though 75 percent of Americans kept their jobs, even during the worst of the Depression, they were forced to accept reduced salaries and reduced work hours.

Jack, on the other hand, was working long hours with very little time off, even on weekends. *I've been working literally like a dog – you remember telling me I would have to live and breathe "gas"?* Jack wrote to his mother. *I've been doing just that from 6:30 in the morning till I stagger home at, often, 8 or later at night.*

Still, he noted hopefully, *Next month, I believe I get an indefinite assignment as supervisor of about 15 complaint men – it will be a startup, at least, and I do hope it will pay me a little more.*

In addition to working punishing hours for less money, Jack had surely suffered a loss in status with his new job. If his mother had worried that in his new job, he would "live and breathe gas," Peggy must have smelled it, perhaps on a uniform, when he came home at night. In November 1932, just after Franklin Roosevelt's first election, Jack wrote his mother,

I particularly remember how I enjoyed having lunch in the kitchen of the Union League Club, with the chef, on Election Day – me, practically the only Democrat in Montgomery County. I was looked on as a semi-Bolshevik before election, but since, some of my Republican friends have condescendingly admitted that Frank may turn out all right, after all.

"Frank" had promised a "new deal for the American people," a program that would provide "relief, recovery and reform." Surely Jack, who was politically progressive, would find comfort in Roosevelt's platform.

President Hoover hadn't helped. Noting the rugged grit of the American people in the first years of the Depression, he resisted any legislation that would provide relief to newly indigent Americans. He exhorted Americans to remember the value of industry and individual initiative, noting that with hard work Americans always had pulled themselves up to a higher standard of living. The problem was that during the Depression, the economy provided insurmountable obstacles to individual initiative. The result was that the poor were victim to feelings of shame and inadequacy for their failure to live up to the American dream, a shame to which Jack was susceptible.

There must also have been some sting for him in the distance between the social status he came from and aspired to and the status defined by their current life. Their closest relatives and friends were faring better. Jack's brother Phil was moving up the ladder of the Army Corps of Engineers where he would ultimately achieve the rank of Major General, and traveling in powerful political circles; Mary and Polly were living with their husbands in suburban Maryland, riding horses, hunting and fishing with the local gentry. Agnes and her husband were ranching in Wyoming, and Esther and her husband were living a comfortable life in the Army Officer Corps. Jack's best friends from Burlington were thriving. Henry and Maureen Ringgold were living in Scarsdale, New York while Henry found success in the New York advertising scene. The Stevens had a very glamorous life in their New York penthouse. And Tom Talbot had a respectable start on his career as a Philadelphia lawyer.

There is no doubt that their status bothered Peggy. While Jack tried hard to be stoical about their circumstances, she put up a fierce fight against them. Her first project was to get Tommy into a good private school, tuition be damned, with children from "good" families. Jack went along with this, though not without some good humored skepticism. He explained her efforts to his mother,

Tommy is going to Nursery School in Flourtown and a very grand one, too. To give you the name, I must explain. In Flourtown is the "Corson College for Orphan Girls," a highly endowed and "exclusive" institution which has many acres of valuable property, and buildings that look and are like a group of country houses. The Nursery School is separate, of course, has a building of its own, fine teachers for twenty children, who are mostly of wealthy families and chauffeur driven. The tuition is rather high, we found on inquiry, but the head teacher, anxious to have Tommy, dug up a half-rate "scholarship" – and so he is entered, and loves it. Such a business – entering – medical examinations and long questionnaires – and they are cracked on the subject of child psychology. We have already attended a parent-teacher meeting (held in the evening so the fathers can attend) and I was afraid I was going to laugh aloud – they take it all so seriously. The teachers, it seems, eavesdrop and write down verbatim conversations – then read them to us as "sheer poetry." I think I'll write an article called "Our child's got rhythm." But they have marvelous equipment, and awfully nice children attend, and I really think it will be fine for Tommy...

The nursery school was Tommy's introduction to a good education, and it was Peggy's introduction to the real Philadelphia society, the one that had been invisible to her when she grew up in a parallel universe just a few miles down the road in Glenside. I am surprised that Peggy's ambition for social status manifested itself so early, and with such accurate focus. She was right. In Philadelphia, nursery schools represented an important first step in making the connections that would maintain the old social order, and because of that, they were often run by society women.

Writers and sociologists who have studied its aristocracy agree that Philadelphia is unique among American cities in the durability and impenetrability of the upper class. In *Philadelphia Gentleman,* sociologist Digby Baltzell said that of the Social Register cities (Boston, New York, Philadelphia, Cincinnati, St. Louis, San Francisco, Washington, DC, among others) the first three provide an interesting perspective on social status; in Boston, education can elevate social status; in New York, financial success will carry you into an upper class; in Philadelphia, the only determinant is family and social connections. Nathaniel Burt, in *The Perennial Philadelphians,* noted that in Philadelphia inherited position is better than self-made position, and inherited money is better than made money. Self-made men like the fictional Horatio Alger were of no interest to Old Philadelphians. In Philadelphia, Burt wrote, it was not so important to be rich as to be part of a family that has held its social station for several generations. These families all knew each other, in part, because their grandparents had known each other. And they all came from Protestant, northern European families who had earned their wealth and status in medicine, law, insurance and banking in the early days of the country. Later, some of those families were involved in the development of steel, railroads, and coal.

In other words, Peggy and Jack never had a chance of penetrating this social group, even if Jack had not been an Irish Catholic, and even if he had been financially successful. In retrospect, it's too bad that Peggy set her sights on it. In the end, it only made her unhappy.

They had, during the 1930s, expanded their social circle beyond the "old gang" in Glenside and the more glamorous Burlington friends in New York to include some of Jack's better heeled associates from the gas company, and now, notwithstanding their financial circumstances, through Tommy they had friends in more aristocratic circles.

Jack and Peggy's social life wasn't all bad – friends and family swept them up in their fun. In Jack's 1934 Christmas letter to his mother, he reported,

Strangely enough, after many weeks, months even, without a trip, we spent the two weekends preceding this one in New York. The first, we went on a long promised visit to the Stevens, who now, by the way, have a weeks old baby girl in their penthouse. It was lots of fun – the high spot being a matinee of "At Home Abroad," with Bea Lillie and Eleanor Powell. Last weekend, Sunday rather, we drove over for the day with Newt Ryerson and a girl of his, and took Tommy for his first glimpse of New York. And a full and interesting day we had – doing nothing, incidentally, that cost anything – except eating, that is. Our itinerary was something like this, early start – ferry across the Hudson with a good look at a couple of big liners – 11 o'clock mass at St. Paul's with the Paulist choir, the Van Gogh exhibition at the Museum of Modern Art, the RCA broadcast called the "Magic Key" at Radio City, with Rose Bampton of the Met, and the Dan Cossack Russian Singles, dinner at a little French restaurant which offered escargots and frogs legs to Tommy's disgust, the Columbia broadcast of the Bond Bread hour with Julia Sanderson and Frank Commit – then through the tunnel and home. Which reminds me, did we tell you that we disposed of our two cars, and got one 1934 Ford phaeton? It runs beautifully, looks very snappy, has four tires on it, and doesn't have to be repaired every ten days – which is why we got it.

We are going to a dance in Bryn Mawr tomorrow night – given by the Tuttles, who are inlaws of Don Wilbur, a friend and associate of mine. It's one of those annual, family parties such as they used to have in Burlington – and will be a lot of fun, I think. As for New Year's – instead of going over to the Ringgolds, we have asked them here.

253

If most of the foregoing sounds like a whirl, it partly just happened, and partly is due to the holidays. Generally, recreation is limited to the movies, bridge, or squash. My job is just about the same – still lots of work, and no change of any kind, yet.

When I look at their lives in the context of the Depression, I think Jack and Peggy were lucky. While unemployment would go to 25 percent during the worst years, Jack had a job – and influential friends, including Cousin Frank Bracken, a successful Philadelphia lawyer, in high places. They had more fortunate friends who swept them up in their social life, and brother Phil always made sure they had good seats at Army football games in Philadelphia and New York.

But they didn't feel lucky. Almost everyone suffered at least some reverses from the collapsed economy in the 1930s. Children of the wealthy were pulled out of private school; prosperous family businesses collapsed, leaving extended families to move in together to save money; doctors and lawyers accepted produce and chickens in lieu of money for services rendered and luckier families left instructions in the kitchen to provide suppers to hungry travelers appearing at the kitchen door. But the Depression years did not produce a sense of community, as it might have – a shared comfort that "we are all in this together." Instead, it left most Americans, my parents included, isolated with their own sense of failure.

"Failure" was exactly the word Peggy came to use as a whipsaw against Jack. Despite the acknowledged universal effect of the Depression on most people, Peggy had come to be bitterly disappointed with Jack's ability to earn a living, and Tommy later recalled that she took every opportunity to drive home the point that Tommy had to do better. He told a story of being given twenty-five cents to go to the Flourtown Fair, an annual hurdy-gurdy event in McCloskey's coal yard down the street from Crow's Nest, to raise money for the local fire department. Tommy used the money on a candy apple game and, wanting to do more, went home and broke into his piggy bank for another quarter. When Peggy found out, she raged at Tommy, shouting that he was just as irresponsible as his father and that, like his father, he would be a failure. "I felt like John Dillinger," Tommy said. These were cruel words from a woman so beloved by her husband. By the mid-1930s, Peggy had lost faith in Jack and was eager to punish him for disappointing her.

The highlights Jack wanted his mother to know about, in his letters, were annual family reunions at Army Navy games, with box tickets provided by Phil, and social outings that no doubt reassured Mother Fleming.

We are looking forward to Christmas on Tommy's account – it's such a happy time for him. The thing he wants most of all is an electric train, so we have joined forces here, the Talbots, Tom, and ourselves, and bought him one. Aside from that, we are just not going to try to give Christmas presents, and I hope you won't either. Christmas is so full of memories for us, isn't it? I would give anything to be with you. And really, I have secretly had a half formed plan to do so all year. But I just can't, as you know. Henry and Maureen (the Ringgolds) are driving to Chicago in a friend's car on the 19th, and wanted us to go along. It was awfully tempting, but impossible, of course. I couldn't take the time off, in the first place.

We certainly had a grand time the latter part of November, what with the Penn-Cornell game here, and the Army-Notre Dame game in New York. Phil gave us perfectly wonderful seats (we took the Egon Quittners with us), and it was a great game.

There were trips to the Talbot beach cottage in New Jersey and holiday plans, generally centering around Tommy, the senior Talbots, and Uncle Tom, who stayed home to be with Tommy at Christmastime, while his wife went home to Cleveland. Uncle Tom's proximity and availability would be an enormous comfort to Jack, Peggy, and especially Tommy. With no children of his own at that time, Tom became a devoted uncle. For Jack and Peggy he was a chief advocate and advisor, whom they consulted for almost every big decision they made. Peggy, in particular, leaned heavily on Tom's support.

Though Jack didn't write about it, they were surely gripped by the dramas of the time, the kidnapping of the Lindbergh baby, the love affair between the King of England, Edward VIII and the Baltimore divorcee Wallis Simpson; the tragic story of the zeppelin airship the Hindenburg, which erupted into a hydrogen fireball while attempting to dock at the Naval airfield in Lakehurst, New Jersey; and the inexorable march of Hitler and the Nazis across Europe.

Peggy's father, Harry, died at 58, in 1933. The following letter to Fanny from a sympathetic physician is an interesting outsider's perspective on Harry's difficult personality. It leaves no doubt that he was a terror on the way out.

My dear Mrs. Talbot,

It has frequently been in my mind and heart to write to you since the passing of Mr. Talbot. With his nature as it was it was perfectly evident to me from the day that I first saw him when he was, supposedly, perfectly well that his life would not in all probability be long as measured by years.

Even then, unless his entire nature could have changed, which change would have rendered him perfectly miserable, I doubt if much more than a few months could have been added to his length of days...He had those qualities of, so termed, successful men and he suffered those defects of inner vision that such men are all too commonly affected with, but that does not make us love them less but rather makes us study their personalities and heredity to explain their natures. You and those who loved him with you used such excellent judgment in his care that even those last trying weeks, always a martyrdom to such a nature, were made endurable.

Dr. Faris was a tower of strength because he not only thoroughly understood the illness but, more important still, he understood the patient through and through. You are too near to the tragedy to see clearly, as I unfortunately do, how much more wretched and unhappy Mr. Talbot could have been made by attempts to alter his nature by suggestions, advice, etc, etc.

If a consciousness of duty performed with graciousness and kindness and no trifle left undone can make for your contentment of mind then you are indeed happy. Thru most trying illness your husband had the most loving and understanding care by all about him. Any unhappiness that was present came from within and was due to causes that could not, in this life, be remedied.

With admiration and respect I am

Sincerely yours always, John Beardsley

I can only think that Dr. Beardsley witnessed an extremely difficult patient in Harry, and that he pitied Fanny, who was no doubt the chief recipient of Harry's abuse. Losing control of his life must have been a bitter pill for my grandfather, of all people, to swallow.

Harry had lost much of his money in the stock market crash, but was able to provide sufficient funds to care for Peggy's mother (modestly) for the rest of her life. Harry may have left a small inheritance to Peggy, which would have come in handy, because Jack remained an hourly employee of the gas company until the spring of 1936. That meant that for those years he had four days of vacation a year, to occur in late September. If he were to ask for more time, he would have to take it without pay, and if he had to miss work because of illness, his pay was docked. It wasn't until 1938, with the passage of the Fair Labor Standards Act, that 40-hour work weeks, with overtime pay for more hours, and the concept of paid vacations were introduced in the American workplace.

He was always on the lookout for other opportunities. In 1935, newspapers around the country announced that his brother Phil had been named chief engineer of the Roosevelt project to harness the energy of the Passamaquoddy River with the construction of a hydroelectric dam on the border between Maine and Canada. *It has been in the back of my mind to write him ever since I heard about it – with a job for myself in mind,* Jack wrote his mother. *But even if he were in a position to make me a good offer – I think I should consider carefully before giving up something that, while slow, is apparently very, very sure – and good for a lifetime – for 4 years and then a question mark.* It's a good thing he didn't pursue this – the Dam proposal never got through Congress.

In 1935, Jack was surprised by a request from the Tennessee Valley Authority (TVA) that he send a resume and application for employment on its by then famous rural development project. The TVA, one of the first inventions of Roosevelt's New Deal, was signed into law on May 18, 1933, a mere two months into President Roosevelt's first term in office. The Authority was created to aid navigation and flood control in the Tennessee River and at the same time provide electricity (initially through hydroelectric dams) and economic development to the Tennessee Valley, one of the areas of the country hardest hit by the Depression. (The TVA covers most of Tennessee, Alabama, Mississippi, Kentucky and pieces of Georgia, North Carolina, and Virginia.) In the end, Jack did not pursue this avenue. As he wrote his mother, *The TVA application which you mention I sent in at TVA's request. I don't know yet who gave them my name. I simply sent it in so as not to miss any bets. Phil, apparently, also received a questionnaire – I had given his name as a reference – and wrote me advising against going with TVA.* Jack's family would not have approved if he took a TVA job – Roosevelt's relief programs were regarded by many as just a step above welfare.

Jack and Peggy even considered an unidentified job in the Philippines (possibly with the Army Corps of Engineers, at Phil's recommendation). And, in another attempt to improve his lot, Jack went to see a psychiatrist to seek a cure for his stutter, thinking that it might be inhibiting his career growth. His doctor referred Jack to an expert at Bellevue Hospital in New York, in the following letter, a copy of which, surprisingly, survives in the files:

A patient who has been under our care in the clinic, Mr. John Fleming, has been troubled with mild stuttering since childhood and feels now that it interferes with his vocational success. It has been impossible for us here to employ methods of deep psychotherapy which might or might not be of benefit to him. He has learned from various sources about you and your work and is very anxious to interview you personally to find out whether or not hypnosis or some other method of psychotherapy might be of benefit to him. I am sure that you will find him a very engaging and attractive kind of patient to deal with and hope that you will be so kind as to give him a few moments at least of your valuable time.

The letter is one of many external assessments of Jack giving evidence of his personal appeal. Jack's easy popularity was to be a constant irritant to Peggy, who came to feel that he didn't earn it. She was no doubt jealous, too, that Jack could fail her so miserably, but at the same time engender such affection among all who knew him, while for her it was not so easy to win the popularity and affection she sought.

The Philadelphia Gas Works came through with a salaried job in March 1936 – at $90 per two-week pay period – after Jack had been employed by the utility for more than five years. Seven years earlier, he was earning $80 per week as an engineer in Golconda. He wrote his mother the good news on St. Patrick's Day:

The last months have been very hectic – the severe weather caused a repetition of the gas main troubles we experienced two years ago, when you were here (Mother Fleming came to stay with Jack and Peggy in the winter of 1934) *– and till a week ago I was working up to 15 hours a day and only home long enough to sleep. But a very good thing, personally, has come of it. And I know how glad you will be to hear it. I have been transferred to the Street Division, which has to do with the distribution of gas – that is street mains and house service pipes, I am to go on salary shortly; as soon as I can qualify – possibly within three of four months – I am to be made a supervising foreman, with a moderate increase in salary. Naturally we are pleased – it's not exactly a windfall, but it certainly is a betterment. Advantages – salary and all that goes with it – a vacation and no loss for days absent; also, I will probably be required to take a company car home at night. Disadvantages – for two or three months a year, during the worst of winter, I will probably have no time to call my own; during two weeks out of every month for the remainder of the year, I will be subject to call at night for emergency work - hence the company car. But it is, I feel, a distinct step ahead...*

It was. But it didn't make their life any easier. During Christmas week, 1936, Jack wrote:

I'm snatching an hour now at the office in the middle of the day. I am very, very busy, but I can take the time now better than at night, because this week (worse luck) is my week on leak duty, which means that during the off-business hours (nights, holidays, and Sundays) I am solely responsible for troubles which occur in the gas distribution system. And leaks recognize no holiday. It means that I am "on call," so to speak at all hours, and must be available for advice, and usually direct supervision of the work. I have one week out of five like this, then a second week "on reserve" – that is, holding myself available, but called only if things get too hot for the man on duty. Of course I have the company car with me at all times. The weather, of course, hasn't been severe enough yet to cause a general emergency such as we had when you were here during February, and which I took part in as a special assignment only. But it is interesting work. I've recently gotten a small raise – nothing spectacular yet, however – but we can keep going on it. As a matter of economy (and because of my work) we have forsworn all trips to New York and that kind of thing.

Jack and Peggy were living on a shoestring, as they always had. In September 1936, using an estimate sheet from work, Jack created a detailed household budget outlining the expenses to be paid from an annual salary of $2,340, in 26 pay periods of $90 per two week period. Included in the budget were the following monthly expenses (not accounting for income taxes or Social Security, first enacted in 1935),

Rent for Crow's Nest – $36 per month

Utilities – coal, gas, electric, oil – $32

Telephone – $3.50

Food – butcher, milkman, groceries – $41.50

Maid – $20

Laundry and yard – $8

A mysterious monthly bill for "Dr. Mayer" – $6

School – $10

Entertainment and wine – $7

...and other necessaries adding up to $82.50 per pay period. That left $7.50 per pay period, or $15 per month, as a cushion. Tri-monthly bills – insurance and water – were additional expenses, and "not specifically covered" in Jack's careful accounting were car, medical, clothing, trips, taxes and, also mysteriously, club dues. Perhaps this is when Peggy decided to get a job teaching in a nursery school.

Though "Crow's Nest" was "miniature," the budget shows that Peggy had a maid doing inside work, a laundress, and someone to maintain the outside of the property. She was not giving up on what she felt was due her. Of "Dr. Mayer," who was part of the monthly budget, I wonder if he was a psychiatrist, and if she had already begun getting psychiatric care as far back as 1936. She was to see several doctors during my childhood. And perhaps the "club dues" were for the Philadelphia Cricket Club, a social club to which Peggy belonged (as a single member) during my childhood and until the end of her life.

Thanks to Mother Fleming's interest in saving Jack's letters, we can hear Jack's voice in the 1930s. Jack mentioned Peggy only in passing in his letters, so it's frustrating not to hear her voice during this crucial period. According to Jack, she wrote regularly to her mother in law, some of which Mother Fleming saved. One begins, *Dear Mother Fleming, I too am sorry the past has been so stormy. I expect it is because we are fundamentally so different, and neither of us can help what we sincerely believe...I am glad you don't feel badly toward Jack for not writing whatever his reason...If it will be any comfort I shall try to write every couple of weeks...*

The saved letters include a number of seemingly affectionate letters from Mother Fleming to Peggy, and a few newsy letters from Peggy to her mother-in-law that were saved by Mother Fleming. But it's clear, at least from Peggy's perspective, that she and Mother Fleming did not have a comfortable relationship. So what on earth made Peggy even consider writing the following to her mother-in-law?

...I feel terribly that Jack doesn't write as I know you do. The only way I can explain it is that he has no sense of responsibility toward anything or anybody, which I think is tragic, since he has such potentiality – if you questioned his love he would be amazed. I hope you don't resent this coming from me but I do feel the whole thing is inexcusable – and it is hard for me to write you the kind of letters I know you want to get because we have not always been the

best of friends – and I know that you probably think it is my fault Jack does not write – which is not true. I do not pretend to be as close to my mother as Jack is to you and I never missed a week writing to her when I was away and would be broken hearted if Tommy didn't write to me – and would blame him entirely whether I liked his wife or not. It is very sad to think that anyone who is fond of Jack – sweet as he is – must suffer from his neglect, rather than other things he does to be mean.

It seems to me this letter was a bad idea, showing Peggy's poor judgment on so many levels. But it gives voice, in a period when we have only hearsay reports, to her profound anger at Jack, and her willingness to condemn him even to his most ardent fan and support. I have no idea what ground Peggy hoped to gain by writing the letter, except to exonerate herself from responsibility for Jack's poor communication. But I can't imagine that it was well received in Burlington, or that it improved Peggy's relationship with her mother-in-law.

Peggy managed to get Tommy into not just one, but a succession of private schools, all with generous scholarships. After the nursery school described by Jack in his letter to his mother, Tommy went to Plymouth Meeting Friends School, a sweet Quaker school that ended after Grade 6. Tommy then went on to two very good boys' schools, Chestnut Hill Academy, which ended after Grade 9, and Penn Charter School another highly regarded Philadelphia Quaker school, for the rest of his high school years. In these schools, Tommy met children from upper class Philadelphia families, and by age twelve, he was attending the dances organized by "Old Philadelphia" to winnow the wheat from the chaff of Philadelphia society between seventh grade and debutante year. In a 1939 Christmas letter (when Tommy was almost thirteen), Jack reported to his mother,

Tommy is having a gay vacation – Bill Wister, Ralph Starr and some of his other associates who had been at boarding school are

home and the phone rings constantly for him. He is going to his first dinner party on the 29th (I think) – preceding his semimonthly dancing evening, and is all prepared with a (cut down) dinner coat, black tie, etc.

Peggy had begun to earn money, too, as a kindergarten teacher in a nursery school, Pennybryn, run by one of her new friends, Mopsy Fox. And she began to run a summer camp in the back yard at Crow's Nest. A career was certainly not a part of Peggy's grand scheme for her life (though she had had those early fantasies of a creative life). Jack, who yearned so to be an adequate provider for the family, must have had mixed feelings about the job. But teaching in one of these little nursery schools was certainly regarded as genteel work. And the most interesting part is that Peggy was *good* at it. She loved the children, she admired their well-connected parents, and she was able to bring out her best self, in a gentle humor and patient advocacy, teaching the little minds and hands in her care to use scissors and crayons. Of the camp I know nothing, except that Tommy helped her. But I admire her enterprise in undertaking it.

It's interesting to try to imagine Peggy, so silent here, during these years. In a photo, I see a slim pretty woman of medium height (5'6") with brown hair styled with a permanent wave, wearing a cotton shirt dress with shoulder pads and nipped in at her trim waist, silver earrings and a silver pin at her throat. She looks youthful and capable and stylish enough. She didn't have to do much around the house, and probably didn't cook, but perhaps she took Tommy to school in the morning, talked to her friends on the phone, went to Mr. Hatch's grocery store, where she had a monthly tab, to do a little shopping, take care of some errands for her mother, now bedridden. I think of her going from task to task, at the same time ruminating about her life, dipping into the ever deepening well of resentment she felt. Was she ready for a fight when Jack came home at night, after a 12-hour day, with Tommy already fed and ready for bed? I wonder if she was still able to look at this tired, burdened, hapless man who had swept her off her feet in 1923, and feel some tenderness, some comfort.

Tommy's memories from the Depression years are very helpful. From both Jack and Peggy's letters, I know that he was a friendly, forthright, active, sunny little boy. I know that he was in an American Legion bugle corps with a handsome uniform complete with brass buttons and plumes. I know what he wanted for Christmas for several years – an electric train set, a Kaster Kit, for casting his own soldiers, a telescope. And I know he had the devoted attention of his Uncle Tom.

Tommy remembered a childhood filled with friends and sports – football, wrestling, and baseball – at school. His friends, who called themselves the "sewing circle," were good students, upper class, athletic, popular, and generally well behaved. After school, Tommy went home with his best friends Ralph Starr or Joe Fox, who lived in elegant, orderly, quiet households (unlike Crow's Nest). Ralph's father, a kind but reserved man, told Tommy that ordinarily he would want Ralph to stay away from Catholics, whose Pope wanted to take over the country. But he liked Tommy, and Tommy didn't feel any sting of discrimination. Most of the boys in the sewing circle went to boarding school, but always called Tommy as soon as they were home on vacation. Tommy liked the social milieu in which his friends lived, and I don't think he ever lacked confidence in his friendship with these boys.

Outside of school, Tommy found his greatest pleasure with his Irish setter, Sean O'Day, and with Uncle Tom. He recalled that because Jack was always working, it was Uncle Tom who was a constant adult companion. It was Unc, as he liked to be called, who gave Tommy a rifle and taught him how to shoot it, who took him hunting and fishing, and who stood at the edge of the school playing fields watching Tommy's games and cheering him on. Looking back, Tommy felt that Jack was notably absent from his life, physically and emotionally, and that Uncle Tom filled that void. Though he thought his mother was relentlessly mean to his father, Tommy had adopted some of her disappointment in Jack. If Jack had felt Tommy's disappointment, it would have made him very sad. His letters show a tremendous affection for and pride in his boy that his endless work may have kept him from demonstrating.

Every Saturday, without fail, Tommy was sent to his grandparents' house for the night. He remembered the gloomy setting of the house in Glenside, with a moose head, one of Harry's hunting trophies, prominently displayed in the windowless front hall and the heavy Victorian furniture in the parlor. It was in that parlor that Harry's body lay in an open casket after he died, in 1933. Tommy remembered that he, at age six, was assigned to sit next to the open casket alone while the family waited for guests to come pay their respects. It was a terrifying memory. Surely the Talbot house was not a particularly cheerful household, with the armed truce between Fanny, who was an unhappy woman, and Harry who, however entertaining he could be, must have been a frightening gruff presence to a little boy. Ninny, always a sweet leavening presence, was gone.

Tommy felt poor by contrast with his friends and he didn't like that, but he was not daunted or embittered by his circumstances. "When I couldn't afford to do something with my friends, I'd just say 'I can't do that.' It was just part of life," he remembered. In his own effort to help, Tommy earned money mowing lawns, delivering papers, and babysitting. And he helped Peggy with the camp.

At home, his life was dominated by Peggy who, mimicking her mother, attempted to keep an iron control over his activities. The Peggy he described was by this time bitter about her lot in life. He remembered a lot of arguments about money in the household. They were beginning to realize that they were only going to be able to grab at the edges of their dreams, aided by the generosity of friends and family.

Maybe it was all preordained in their relationship from the beginning. Maybe Peggy didn't love Jack as much as he loved her. Maybe when they met in 1923, Peggy, ever practical, saw this handsome, well read, besotted college boy as a ticket to a glamorous life, while Jack saw a pretty girl with molten brown eyes who believed, unlike his family, that he would *be* something. There is plenty of incriminating evidence in the early letters (thanks to her heavier handed archivist, Fanny) that Peggy could be a petulant, selfish, grandiose girl. Jack, at the same time, seemed to have learned early to live with the low expectations of his family, to accept the disappointments in his career. It is as if he didn't really expect to win. Peggy was both his salvation and his doom. While he bathed in her early adoration, he was also by early training vulnerable to her disappointment. No matter how hard he tried, he was always disappointing somebody, and was always abject about it. Jack was, for sure, irresponsible about money in the early days, but then Peggy expected so much. Now there was no less passionate engagement in their relations, but it was a passion turning bitter.

By the end of the 1930s, one piece of their dream was about to come true. With a combination of good luck and ingenuity, they would come upon an opportunity that would allow them, at extraordinary savings, to build a house of their own, a house whose design would echo the one they imagined in their first year of marriage.

1940 – 1942

Qualm Springs

February 10, 1940, Jack to his mother
Mother dearest,

...It's your birthday, but I'm going to talk about me, or rather us, because I have some news items for you. A, I got a raise; B, I bought a new(er) car, a Ford Station wagon, and C, most interesting, we are going to build – or rather rebuild – a house...

With this startling announcement, Jack laid out for his mother the serendipitous circumstances under which he and Peggy came into possession of two disassembled one-story frame structures they would use to build a house of their own. These structures would yield lumber, doors, windows, plumbing fixtures (though no tubs), heating boilers, radiators, and wiring – materials for the house in which I grew up. Jack explained to his mother how it happened:

On a large government low rent housing job, the Tusker Housing Project, the general contractor had two large field offices – one for the firm, one for the government men. They were one

269

story frame structures, 16' x 80' and 16' x 40', lined with wall board, and equipped with heating plants and plumbing systems. At the close of the job, after about 18 months use, it was necessary that they be removed from the site of the project, in order to complete the final landscaping. I knew the superintendent through business contacts, and he suggested in an offhand way that I buy them, setting the price, in place, at $500. I was interested, and Peggy and I, with Tom Talbot, discussed it at great length. We decided (as we discussed with you before) that now, if ever, is the time to get a house of our own, and this seemed a fortunate, if somewhat screwy, opportunity.

After 17 years of marriage, many temporary lodgings made personal with the accumulation of pictures, knick knacks, curtains, and the treasured wedding presents – and many dreams deferred – it *still* must have taken a great deal of courage for Jack and Peggy to grab at this windfall. Though war in Europe was helping, the country was not yet rescued from the doldrums of the Depression, and Jack was not on sure financial footing. They were living in a period when only four in ten families owned their own homes – the United States was a nation of renters. Nevertheless, this windfall gave Jack a chance to be the provider of house and home that he wanted to be. Perhaps he would also win back Peggy's admiration and good will. Jack was eager, too, to use his engineering skills and experience, this time for a project of his own imagining. He continued his report to his mother:

Well, I started on estimates, and got the advice of architect friend Kaye Hunter, who also likes the idea. Then we went into financing, and Peggy's mother offered to invest $4,000 of the estate funds in the project, while we guaranteed her a return equal to that now being received. Rather, let me say, Peggy, Tom and I worked out our ideas first, set $4,000 as the top figure, and presented the idea to Mother T, who readily agreed.

By that time my friend the superintendent had orders to get rid of his buildings by the end of January – so with pressure on I beat him down to $250. I then found a firm to dismantle and move the material to Flourtown for $350, and arranged with McCloskey, the local coal dealer, to store the material in his yard. I gave the orders to go ahead, and we now have the material for a house 16' x 120' in great piles in the coal yard. The least you can say is that the value, as is, is well in excess of the $600 invested.

Jack had hoped they would begin building in the spring of 1940 and be finished by the following September, but finding a piece of property that they liked and could afford proved to be a challenge:

The next step is a place to put the house, and I'm leaving that to Peggy, with certain restrictions as to locations. What we want, generally, is about an acre, in this area, for not over $1,000. When the lot is secured, we will proceed to plan. What we'll build will be one story and 16' wide, but the 120' length will be distributed any way that works out best. I think there will be room for living and dining room, kitchen, recreation room, one large and three small bedrooms and two baths. Kay Hunter will help us with the layout. I hope to start building in May or June – do as much as possible ourselves and be completed by September. The remaining $2,400 will have to be spread very thin to cover foundations and basement, water and electric supply, sewage disposal, erection of old and new material, plumbing, heating, new roof (the original was roll paper), interior finish, painting, rewiring and the thousand other things that must be done.

So we are just now in the odd position of having bought a house with no place to put it. But we are all extremely enthusiastic and getting more so all the time...

Their plans were delayed for a year, until the summer of 1941. In fact, for the next 16 months, there were more letters to Mother Fleming reporting on life as usual,   the gas work during an exceptionally cold winter, holiday visits with the Ringgolds and other friends, and more job feelers. In December 1940, Jack sent an application to Gamp Shipbuilding Company, which was reopening in Philadelphia with defense work. Though the United States was not yet involved in the War, Hitler had been trampling all over Europe since 1939. By the fall of 1940 Germany had invaded Poland, Moravia, Bohemia, Norway and Denmark, Holland, Belgium, and Luxembourg. Britain and France had declared war on Germany in September 1939, but by the fall of 1940, France had been overtaken by the Germans, and Britain was under heavy air attack in the Blitz. Americans were jittery, but on the positive side, the defense industry had been booming with orders from Europe for arms and war machinery. There was a giant lift in the American economy.

It wasn't until July 1941 that Jack wrote again about plans for the house. In the intervening year and four months, they had been struggling, with a couple of false starts, to find a piece of property they liked. I imagine this was a time of tension and conflict, along with the anticipation of a new start. In the midst of their more than busy lives – Tommy's at school and on the football field, (he was in ninth grade at Chestnut Hill Academy in 1941), Jack's at work in a utility gearing up for war, Peggy's in her kindergarten classroom – I imagine that the house plans provided a constant subtext, a kind of hum, surely of hope and just as surely of frustration, below the daily noise of their life. Jack's excitement about the project was palpable. He finally reported,

We are about to get under way with the house – at long last. You have no doubt heard of the agony we went through making up our minds what lot we wanted, but we finally did, and the deed should be in our hands the end of the week. Kaye Hunter is drawing up the plans for us, and next week should see the well driller start his search for water. We expect to get an ample supply at 80'. In memory of our mental waverings, I've about decided to name the place "Qualm Springs."

Their final choice of property was about three-quarters of an acre in Flourtown, a mile or so from Crow's Nest, with a sloping rise that would provide a perfect site for the house, and with access to electricity, city water, and telephone service. While the property had no trees – it had been a pasture for a neighboring farm – Jack and Peggy had plenty of landscaping ideas.

This was the house of my childhood, so I hold every detail of it in my memory. What they were planning was the landscape I knew intimately, the forsythia bush in the back yard that was the first to bloom in the spring, a brilliant yellow, followed by the big magnolia tree with its pink and white blooms and the dogwood; the perimeter of prickly bushes, so hard to wiggle through without getting scratched, across the crest of the slope of lawn in front of the house, hiding the front terrace from view; the weeping willow that would move with the breeze outside my bedroom window; the vine covered bank where a ground cover created my secret hideout, impregnable to all but the bees and praying mantises that routinely sent me back into daylight. Just outside the kitchen door was a honeysuckle bush whose blossoms offered a June treat, before the summer heat dried everything up.

Best of all, the land was on a private lane away from traffic. A few years later the lane would be named Fleming Road, in honor of the first family to build on it – us. Jack threw himself into the planning for the house, and sent his mother plat plans and sketches of the property.

The elevation (a drawing of the façade of the house from the front) that Jack sent to his mother in 1941 is almost a duplicate of the drawing he sent Peggy in 1923, when they were dreaming of a house of their own, in Burlington. He had held on to that dream for almost 20 years.

The layout lives in my memory and in the dreams that take me back to childhood. The living room, a piece of that 16-foot-wide original structure, formed the center section of the house, with windows on both sides and French doors giving onto both the front and back terraces. From one end of that room I could turn right at the dresser with the antique clock on it and go down a set of stairs to the recreation room that had become Jack's office, or left up a few stairs to the bedroom wing. Sitting at the bottom of the bedroom steps, I could peek around to watch my parents and their friends at cocktail hour.

Jack wrote: *A good suggestion of Kaye Hunter's, too, was the suggestion to use three piers of field stone on the front of the living room wall – very little stone, but giving the effect of an entire stone wall. Kaye has been very helpful, and is giving his services for almost nothing. I can do the rough planning, but Kaye adds the touches that will make the house both more attractive and more saleable, if the necessity for the latter should ever arise. I'm terribly anxious to get started on the house itself.*

Exhausting as it must have been, in addition to his work, he seemed so excited by the prospect of building his house, and I find myself rooting for him and for the possibility that this would make Jack feel a more successful bread winner and, to Peggy, less like a failure. This would be the home Jack and Peggy had always imagined – the one she, at twenty, had furnished with heart shaped pillows, warming to Jack's description of the imagined kitchen nook and a view of the old fashioned garden, intended to sit just across from the Fleming house.

Peggy's voice is so frustratingly absent through this period that it seems unfair to make assumptions about her enthusiasm for the house. I hang my hopes on memories of her gardens – the vegetable garden, in which I remember her stooping, absorbed, in a summer dress, her hair pulled back with side combs at the temples, inspecting her produce, or the wildflower garden, or the little oval flower bed on the front terrace, the one I could see from the window seat in the living room where Jack kept his Victrola and stack of long playing records. I'd like to think of these marks of her own creativity as evidence of her enthusiasm, her investment in a brighter future before them. But I suspect that Peggy, ever practical and certainly experienced in disappointment where financial resources were concerned, may have shielded herself from the disappointment of another false start by exhibiting some skepticism, perhaps a determination to keep the dream at a distance. And maybe she withheld her enthusiasm as a kind of punishment for Jack for the years of struggle. This would not be unlike her. Perhaps it was she who injected the idea that the house could be sold when it was finished. I think, too, of Tommy, the only child, the adolescent boy who must have, in his own way, felt such a burden of responsibility for his perennially vulnerable parents and their dreams, even as the tangible possibility lay there with a pile of lumber at McCloskey's coal yard.

Not surprisingly, as plans firmed up and the work began, Jack had to take a more realistic look at the financing of the house. They had borrowed $4,000 from Mother Talbot, against Peggy's eventual inheritance, and they had already spent $700 on the building materials (including storage at McCloskey's coal yard), and $900 to purchase the lot. Now, he reported to his mother, he was beginning to think about borrowing $1,500 from the Federal Housing Administration, the FHA, the then seven-year-old agency created by Congress in 1934 to help support the housing industry after the massive bank failures at the outset of the Depression. *It may be the soundest thing to do,* Jack wrote his mother in early August, *because the finished job will look like eight or ten thousand dollars and will undoubtedly be worth it.*

Having dropped that hint, Jack went back to his mother a couple of weeks later with a request that she grease the wheels once again with Mr. Smiler for a loan from the Burlington Savings Bank, the family bank that had saved Jack many times over the years. This time, though, Jack showed that he had learned something about debt, and he was able to construct a more realistic financial plan.

I would like to borrow from the Burlington Savings Bank, with your endorsement, $1,500. Peggy's family is advancing $4,000, and that is the prearranged and absolute limit from that source. And I would like to handle the repayment in this manner. That the money be loaned me now for one year, with interest discounted in advance. At the end of the year, starting say Sept. 1, 1942, I would like an arrangement whereby I will pay an equal amount on the principal and interest monthly, say $25 to $30, so that the entire loan will be paid off in 5 to 6 years. The exact amount and time depends of course upon the rate of interest. The reason I want to handle it in such a manner is this, I am now paying an amount in excess of $40 a month on the station wagon, which payments will be complete in August 1942. If you are agreeable, Mother (and I only ask because of your offer when we first discussed building a house) – will you either show this to Mr. Smiler, or discuss it with him and advise me as to what steps I should take?

By Labor Day, 1941, Jack had the $1,500 check from the Burlington Savings Bank in hand. This would not be the last time he would ask Mother Fleming for help with the house.

Meanwhile, life went on in the Fleming household at Crow's Nest. Tommy had spent the summer busy with tennis, golf, and swimming, when he wasn't earning money cutting grass and babysitting. He had grown into a string bean. At 14, he was six feet tall and weighed 148 pounds. He was invited to Maine for two weeks with a friend, and Jack and Peggy drove him up, grabbing a few days with friends who had a summer cottage on Deer Isle. They came home to spend the last few days of their vacation working on plans for the house. Traveling vacations were getting to be a luxury anyway, as the Roosevelt Administration was starting to ask Americans to conserve gas, and turn in their extra rubber tires in anticipation of war. Jack wrote,

We have been taking advantage of the long (3 day) weekend to work on our own affairs – I've been surveying, estimating and planning details for the house, and Peggy making her plans for moving, furnishing, and planting. It seems that nearly everyone else with a vehicle has gone out of town – disregarding all gasoline economy pleas. Probably all taking a last fling before the expected rationing starts. Apparently there is plenty of oil in the west – the difficulty is in the getting it East in sufficient quantities.

Throughout the period when the house was under construction, the probability increased that the Americans would enter the war. Jack and Uncle Tom were there working on the house on Sunday, December 7, 1941, the radio playing somewhere in the background, when the announcer interrupted the Sunday music to report that the Japanese had bombed Pearl Harbor. Unc, who had signed up for the Navy Reserve, left Jack holding the hammers and went to report for duty. I wonder how Jack must have felt at that moment, watching Tom prepare to go to war, while he had no plans to do anything but remain on the home front. I wonder if he thought about those afternoons on the campus of Georgetown University in 1917, watching the young recruits in their puttees and campaign hats drilling on the university quadrangle in preparation for World War I, the war that ended before Jack was old enough to volunteer.

Work on the house continued through the winter of 1942, and by spring, Jack had run through the available funds for the construction. He wrote his mother asking for another loan, $1,500 of her own funds, which she promptly supplied. On April Fool's Day, 1942, while they were still living in Crow's Nest, Jack wrote her:

I seem at last to have a found a little time to do what I want – I'm taking off these few days before Easter as part of my vacation – and the thing I want most to do is to thank you for helping me out *of a bad spot. I can't tell you how much I appreciate your sending me the $1500, and so quickly. And it is so nice to feel that you are not only a mother whom I love, but a friend in need, too. The matter of financing a house, I have found, is a complicated thing – thinking of that, plus the daily physical construction details and management of the various trades, plus my regular job – it really had my head whirling. However, this week I am able to give all my time to the house, and I feel that we are making real progress. The plastering is finished, the carpenters are installing the interior wood trim, the hardwood floors are being laid, the heating system is operating, and we have started painting. We have given notice to our present landlord that we will have vacated this house by May 1st, so, as you can see, the end is in sight. If the weather only holds now – we had, to my dismay, a freak snowstorm Sunday, but all traces of it are gone now. Peggy, Tommy, and* (Tommy's school friend) *Sonny Lukens all have vacations this week, too, and they form my squad of general workmen and painters. My chief difficulty is the stream of casual visitors who come to inspect, must be guided around, and take entirely too long enthusing – thus wasting the precious daylight hours.*

We're not planning anything for Easter – Tommy and I will go to 9 o'clock mass and receive Holy Communion, of course. Mother T wanted us all to go out to dinner in the middle of the day, but I really feel it's important that we spend all our time on the house.....I am certainly luxuriating in this time to myself – I'm beginning to think the right way to take a vacation is to stay home – besides the saving in rubber and gas – I'm even going to get my photographic work done...

At some time in the late 1930s, Jack had taken up a new hobby, photography. After purchasing a Rolleiflex camera, he began taking photographs. Soon he was immersed in the whole process, from the subject he framed in his box lens to the chemical process of producing an image on paper. *I tend to look at the results in the*

278

light of physics, chemistry and the artistic concepts of light, shade, line and mass, he wrote his mother about his new hobby. At the new house, he would convert the small middle bedroom into a darkroom. *This room would be remade into my bedroom when I came along.*

By June, 1942, Jack, Peggy, and Tommy were finally in residence in the new house, having once again gotten themselves into a frightening financial box that they all must have found both depressingly familiar and, with so much at stake, utterly terrifying. On June 25, Jack wrote from the new address,

Note address above – actually it doesn't make any difference as we still call at the Flourtown P.O. for our mail. I'm writing this in my car, in South Philadelphia – I had to talk to you and I just haven't found the uninterrupted time in the office or at home – so I brought this pad with me today and am stealing half an hour between jobs. Please don't think I didn't think of you- you have been part of my thoughts every day. I didn't write because I had such a problem on my hands in the matter of financing the house, and I wanted to be ready before talking to you. I think I have it now, but I still need your help, as I will explain.

With a familiar rueful tone, Jack continued,

I won't go deeply into the excessive cost of the house – that's over the dam now – the money is either spent or owed. It was a cumulative thing. The total costs seemed to grow like a rolling snowball. It was too big and elaborately planned in the first place – my first estimates were far too low even for the semi-unfurnished house we first planned – and we were forced because of financing requirements to include such refinements as tile baths and hardwood floors, which were not in the original scheme at all. Add to this the rising costs of labor and material, and the difficulty of getting material, and you have a picture of the mountain that confronted me. There was of course no possibility of backing out at any stage. I was committed to finishing. Before we moved – the latter part of May – we discussed trying to sell at once – or to rent – but found that would preclude getting a reasonable mortgage, as it is obviously a house built to live in and not to sell. Besides, we had to live there so that we ourselves could finish it completely as to yard and planting and landscaping etc.

(Let me interpolate here that we are living in the house – it is 100% finished, which some people consider remarkable, that it is really a charming and beautiful and outstandingly individual place, and we love it, all three of us.)

So we moved – still without a mortgage commitment. Then FHA turned me down because the house is on a private lane, and they insist on dedicated streets. The FHA man, however, was so taken with the house, and became so interested that he sent a friend of his from the Western Savings Fund Society of Philadelphia. I won't go into the intermediate details, but Monday I was notified by the Western that they would take the mortgage – 20 years – at 4 ½ percent, which is very good. But the funds I will realize from this will just cover all my local obligations, leaving me still owing you $1500 and the Burlington Savings Bank $1500. So what I want to ask of you is this, will you let me give you a note for this 1500, renewable semi-annually or annually, at 5% interest, which I will pay you in monthly installments? Can you afford it? Also, can you prevail upon the Burlington Savings Bank to renew my note periodically without reduction of the principal for the present at least? I must ask you this, because at the present it is the only workable plan that I can devise. Luckily, I have gotten another increase in salary, and I can afford to carry the house by paying the following:

Interest and principal on mortgage (all paid off in 20 years)
Interest to Mother T. on Talbot Estate funds (part of Peggy's eventual inheritance)
Interest to you
Interest to Burlington Savings Bank

Taxes and insurance

As I say, this plan is workable. The only other plan is to sell the house, and the best way to do that is to make the whole place as attractive as possible and wait for a good offer, rather than just dumping it on the market and taking anything. That would probably be the sensible thing to do, but it would be heart breaking. I have put so much of myself into the place, and Peggy and Tommy have too, that I would like to feel that it is ours for the rest of our lives.

I would have liked that too, but it wasn't to be. During the summer of 1942, work on the house continued.

It's late of a Friday night, Jack reported to his mother, *but ahead of the first free weekend I've had in some time. You see, when the house was under construction, I not only took most of my vacation in occasional days, but I also traded off my periodical night and weekend duty, and I'm just getting through paying off for it all. Not that the work at home is ended – far from it – I still have screens to fit, closets to build and much yard work. I thought there would come a time when construction ended and maintenance began, but apparently there is just a gradual transition from one to the other...your help has made the difference between night and day. Things are pretty well straightened out now – and on a workable basis. The worry is gone from my mind, and I don't want you to worry. If it turns out the load is too heavy (and I don't believe it will) we'll just unload it, that's all.*

Despite all the attendant financial anxieties, I hope that Jack and Peggy and Tommy found new life in the new house, and not just a continued rough course in their little boat. The country was waking up to a new war that would profoundly alter the lives of all Americans, including my family. Jack was participating in his own way, but it would not be enough for him.

The war looms larger all the time, with more and more of my daily work done for war purposes – both in war production plants,

281

and with plans to protect our own system and plant in the event of the bombing that all of us feel is sure to come, sooner or later. Our practice raids and blackouts are becoming more frequent and seriously considered. Tom is still in the Philadelphia area but (secret) expecting to be sent elsewhere soon. By the way, we learn that John Bracken, who returned safely on the "Marblehead," the cruiser that miraculously returned, damaged, from Malay, is gone again, as Flag Lieutenant to an admiral.

On behalf of friends who wanted wartime assignments, Jack wrote his brother Phil, now administrator of the Federal Works Agency, and still an influential Army officer. He told himself – and his mother – that *his* civilian work was important to the defense of the country. *...I have been extremely busy – defense work has required us to expand our system tremendously. Gas, you see, is a most essential commodity, used in many ways by the large industries, the Navy Yard, and the Arsenals. It also turns out that I am a most essential operating man, and I couldn't possibly consider doing any other defense work than I am doing now – long hours every day. We are studying too, methods of protections, and methods of quick emergency repairs in case of sabotage or bombing. It looks like we're in it, doesn't it? And frankly, I say "What are we waiting for?"*

Peggy, meanwhile, was doing her part for the war effort. *Peggy completed her Red Cross First Aid course,* Jack wrote his mother. In World War II, Red Cross volunteers provided a variety of services, serving in understaffed hospitals, producing emergency medical supplies, running victory gardens and blood donor programs, participating in civil defense actions. I don't know what Peggy did for the Red Cross, but I remember her wood paneled station wagon with a Red Cross painted on the side, and somewhere I may still have her Red Cross uniform, a brown wool suit emblazoned with service pins. It made a very satisfying dress up costume for my daughters.

Jack continued in his letter to his mother, *Peggy is now taking a much more difficult course in training for the Red Cross Motor Corps. Tommy and I plan to let her change the next tire that goes flat.*

In the end, Jack couldn't convince himself that protecting the nation's gas supply was enough. He'd waited a long time to be in the uniform worn with pride by so many members of his family, and he couldn't let another opportunity pass him by. Against Peggy's wishes, but with Tommy's tacit support, he wrote his brother Phil again, this time on his own behalf.

September 17, 1942
To Brig. Gen. Philip B. Fleming
Administrator, Federal Works Agency, Washington
Dear Phil,

This time I am writing you to ask help, not for a friend, but for myself. To get to the point at once, I have made up my mind to apply for a commission in the Naval Reserve, Civil Engineer Corps. You may remember that I gave it some thought several years ago, but was finally deterred by the requirement which calls for a letter from the employer, stating that the applicant can be released in the event of mobilization.

At that time my employer refused to so state. Now, of course, an entirely different picture presents itself. First of all, I am not entirely happy in a civilian role, no matter how essential it may be considered; and I think I could make greater contribution as an engineer and as an officer. Second, the PGW Co. has recently adopted a policy granting a military leave of absence to all who enter the service, guaranteeing the old job back without loss of seniority. This is, for my part, in the nature of insurance. I feel the Navy might be an avenue into something permanently better. Third, I have been given to understand that the CEC, USNR, needs men with field experience, probably for work with the Seabees o to release men for such work. I believe I can qualify for 2 ½ stripes, perhaps 2, but in either case it would represent an increase in salary. And last, with a long war in prospect, there is no assurance that I might not eventually be taken into the service under much less happy circumstances. The foregoing makes sense, doesn't it?

Now I know that getting a commission in the naval reserve is a pretty difficult thing to do (even though they may have recently relaxed a little on the requirements) and that's why I want your help. And I naturally want to get as high a rank as possible. Before I take any steps, however, I would like to have you tell me the best way of going about it. You no doubt have Navy friends who could advise you, and who might possibly be willing to put in a word for me.

Peggy and Tommy are well, and about to start their fall activities, Peggy with her Nursery School and Tommy as a new boy at Penn Charter School, in the high school junior class. Chestnut Hill Academy's upper school closed this year, hence the change. Tommy has been attending preseason football practice, and hopes to be playing right tackle, at least as an alternate...

There is of course no tearing hurry on the USNR business (I understand it sometimes takes months after the initial application) and I won't do anything until I hear from you...

He would hear from Phil, and soon.

1943 to 1945
The War Years

January 10, 1943 – Jack to his mother

...I am now a lieutenant in the United States Naval Reserve – my orders arrived Friday. I was sworn in the same day, and am leaving Tuesday for Norfolk, Virginia. My commission reads "Assistant Civil Engineer with the rank of Lieutenant. I am in the Civil Engineering Corps, under the Bureau of Yards and Docks, and my training will be for duty with the Construction Battalions, generally known as the "Seabees." I have had the minimum time to do a tremendous number of things – so far, I have closed my affairs with the Gas Company (amicably, I might say, with a leave of absence for the duration) and ordered my uniforms, which will be ready the day I leave. Peggy and Tommy will carry on as is for the present – we will decide what the next step should be when I get a permanent station, or rather orders to permanent active duty. I don't need to tell you that I am pleased, excited and anxious to get on with it...

With the help of his brother Phil, Jack was at long last inducted into the Fleming family business – the military. He would be one of 17 children and grandchildren of Mother Fleming to participate in World War II, and though he was not one of the family's several graduates of West Point or the Naval Academy, he would be an officer – a leader, at long last, in an effort that matched his skills and experience.

For Jack it must have been a thrilling turn of events. This was an idea that may have lodged itself in Jack's imagination when Phil, his only brother, left home for West Point, when Jack was just a little boy. And we know his yearning for military service had been acute in 1917, during that last year at boarding school on a campus in a fever of war preparation.

Peggy must have been in a state of utter shock at this turn of events. Once again, I don't *know* how Peggy felt, because her voice is absent from the correspondence of this period – only one of her wartime letters remains – and I can only guess at her sputtering disbelief, her panic at the thought of being left alone with the responsibility for managing their life for God knows how long. Jack had been working on the possibility of joining the Navy partly in the hope that he could increase his income by going into the service. The Seabees were, felicitously, among the highest paid servicemen in the war.

But I know Peggy must have hoped that at age forty-two, Jack would not be accepted. Or even if he were accepted, she must have assumed that he would not in the end abandon his wife and son and brand new home for some old puerile dream of glory. At his age he would not be drafted and he could avoid service without shame. Surely he would not go against her wishes. He never had, in spite of her growing bitterness and disappointment, her wounding assaults on his self-image. Though Tommy remembered he wanted his father to show some courage, to stand up to Peggy just once, he too, at age fifteen must have been startled by Jack's resolve, even cheered, though he couldn't have known the burdens Jack's escape would put on him. I too am surprised that Jack was so willing to follow this dream of his. He would increase his earnings as an officer in the Navy, and this surely was a motivation he thought Peggy would appreciate. But even as he spoke of doing his part in defeating a ruthless enemy, it must have meant more than that to him. Jack surely wanted to wear a uniform, to be a hero for once, to stand up and fight for his country but also to bolster his own self esteem. It was an act of self-preservation.

By January 1943, the war in Europe had been going on for more than three years, with Germany and Italy spreading their aggression in all directions, north, as noted earlier, into Norway, Denmark, the Netherlands, Belgium and Luxembourg; west into France and England, south into North African and Middle Eastern countries – Egypt, Tunisia, Syria, Iraq; and east into Russia. With American entry into the war in December 1941, the Germans and Italians were, if not in retreat, certainly on the defensive.

While Jack was beginning his training in Virginia in January 1943, American planes were firebombing German cities and soldiers were fighting on the ground in North Africa. After a year of bloody sea battles and the loss of many American lives, American troops were beginning to turn the tide of war against Japan in the Pacific, and by January of 1943 were defeating the Japanese in Guadalcanal, the Gilbert Islands and New Guinea.

Jack could only hope that Peggy would pull herself together and carry on as millions of other wives were doing, fending for themselves in the absence of their warriors in this awful conflict. There were, by the end of the war, 11 million Americans in the armed forces, so Peggy was not alone with her circumstances. She may, however, have been alone among her friends in Philadelphia, all women in their late thirties whose husbands were beyond draft age.

Jack trusted Peggy and Tommy to manage their first winter in a new house, even if they didn't know whether the storm windows worked or if the rationed heating oil would be enough to keep them warm. He gave lip service to the idea that he might be assigned to a domestic construction site, and that the family might follow him around the U.S. for the duration of his Navy service. I doubt, though, if he really thought that would happen.

That everything happened so fast may reflect the depth of Uncle Phil's influence throughout the armed services, but I'd like to think that Jack was just what the Navy needed as the United States entered its second year of involvement in world war. The Navy construction battalions, CBs, or "Seabees," had been created at the end of 1941, after the Japanese bombing of Pearl Harbor made it clear that the Americans would be involved in two theatres of war, in Europe and in the Pacific.

William Bradford Huie, in his book *Can Do! The Story of the Seabees,* points out that since the American Revolution, the Navy had employed civilian contractors to build the necessary bases, and harbor facilities to support defensive military preparations, lest an enemy cross the ocean to attack the U.S. The first naval bases outside the U.S. were at Samoa in 1892 and at Pearl Harbor, Guantanamo Bay, and the Philippines, at the beginning of the 20th century. Now, with two theatres of war, a need for overseas construction work, it made sense to provide minimal military training to construction workers who would be sent to build forward bases in combat areas.

The men who enlisted were plumbers, carpenters, electricians, heavy machinery operators, mechanics, truck drivers, surveyors, draftsmen, and clerks who were, on average, in their thirties, married men with children who could have avoided military service, but who wanted to lend their experience to the war effort. Engineers, men like Jack who had been project managers in their civilian lives, were made officers. Jack's age was not unusual in the Seabees. As a lieutenant, he was a "two-striper." He had hoped for the two-and-a-half stripes of a lieutenant commander, with its larger paycheck, but counted on, and promised Peggy, a field promotion to bring that about. This was to become Jack's Holy Grail, an elusive goal for almost the entire duration of the war, and a source of tremendous frustration for him as Peggy's unhappiness increased.

On January 12, 1943, less than a week after receiving his orders, Jack was on a crowded overnight train from Philadelphia to Cape Charles, Virginia, on the tip of the Eastern Shore, and then a three-hour ferry ride jam packed with soldiers crossing Chesapeake Bay to the Naval Operations Base in Norfolk. He spent a brief 10 days at Camp Allen in Norfolk, bunking in with three other officers for an accelerated version of basic training in an appropriately Spartan setting. Perhaps it felt like a summer camp without the recreation. Jack said it was like military school. An average day began with "bugle" at 0600, then 15 minutes of physical training, breakfast, making bunks, a "colors" ceremony at the flagpole, five hours of classes, lunch, three hours of drill, supper, and two hours of study until "lights out" at 2300.

If I haven't conveyed the idea that it's tough – all business and war business, I haven't made my point, he wrote Peggy shortly after his arrival. *It's bleak, too – long wooden buildings, high wire fences, sand walks, cement roads.*

The officers were learning what the enlisted men in the battalion were learning, military discipline and the use of light arms, and later Marine training in the use of rifles and machine guns. But more importantly, they were learning about beach landings, jungle warfare, night maneuvers, and how to unload ships of vital materiel. This would come in handy later.

Jack soon learned he was to be assigned to the 76th construction battalion, as commander of the 240 men in Company C, now training at Camp Bradford, another camp in the Norfolk area. As they were short of officers at Bradford, Jack and his fellow officers rushed through their own training, then were transferred to the command of their own companies on January 22. So, just a couple of weeks after he ordered his uniforms, Jack was in a position of command. It must have been a dizzying transition.

Jack wrote Peggy explaining the structure of Seabee battalions:

Battalions are composed of about 1,200 men, and the officer in charge is a lieutenant commander. He has an executive staff including aides, supply corps officers, disbursing officer, medical officer, and chaplain. Then there is a headquarters company, and three regular companies, A, B, C and D. Each company is commanded by a lieutenant, who has as junior officers a lieutenant JG (junior grade), an ensign, and a warrant officer. I believe each company has chiefs, petty officers, yeomen, and skilled workers of various kinds. The men are generally enlisted before the officers, and undergo three or four weeks of detention and basic training at one of the CB camps.

Then Jack confirmed for Peggy that their future would include an extended separation. *I haven't found out much about it yet, but I must tell you, apparently overseas work is slated for all of us here. There just isn't any choice – you do what you are told, and find out things as best you can as you go along...*

That news surely did not improve Peggy's mood. She was punishing Jack with silence, by not writing him, and Tommy, a 16-year-old, was not much more reliable as a correspondent. Each of Jack's letters began with a plea for a letter from one of them. When Peggy did write, her letters were full of worries about bills and household concerns, to which Jack would write back careful instructions about how to approach each problem. Knowing full well what her mood was, he would end his letters with "*Keep your chin up,*" or "*Try not to be blue.*"

His mind never drifted too far from his own sense of failure at providing Peggy the life she wanted. While in Norfolk he ran into friends from Philadelphia and paid a visit to their beautiful beach house on Chesapeake Bay. *You would love their setup*, he wrote: *I don't know why I'm not the kind of a person that can provide such for you. I always seem to draw the tough assignments for both of us.*

Jack's mother was another story. Knowing this beloved son so well, she wrote: *I loved all the details of your work. The Seabees sound very thrilling and I know you love building things and would always have felt regret if you had not been in uniform in the service of your country in this greatest of all wars. I know there is danger but I will not think of that, only of the better world and life after you have won the war – and my prayers follow you daily.*

That she knew what this experience in the service meant to him must have been very comforting to Jack. He was about to have what was for him the experience of a lifetime, the experience of leadership, of command. He reflected on this in a letter to Peggy.

When I move to Camp Bradford on Sunday, I take over the command – military command – of about 240 men that I've never seen before, and I'm naturally somewhat nervous about it. However, they have had Navy drilled into them for five weeks, and are probably as curious about me as I am about them. Being a Navy officer – with men – is far different from being a boss in civil life. An officer is far more than a boss – and the Navy is an autocratic establishment. An officer has to be a leader, and guide, and example – he is respected and obeyed, and actually has the law in his hands. I can't describe the difference, really. But Navy custom and tradition is a far more powerful thing than you would imagine.

When he got to Camp Bradford, Jack wrote:

The most interesting thing of course was meeting the men – the enlisted personnel, and I think they are going to be a good, very good, gang. They are almost all from Texas, Oklahoma (Okies), Alabama, and California – a good many with oil field experience.

The names are largely English – American – and they all speak with a drawl. I have seven chief petty officers in Co. C – older men, formerly carpenter foremen, construction superintendents, and the like. And they were all lined up to greet me in the Co. headquarters hut. It was really affecting – obviously they wanted to like me and are anxious to please. They indicated they weren't much on military yet, but could really turn out the work. Actually I'm greener in Navy ways than they are, but I don't dare fully admit it. We still have a handful of training instructors handling the men, and this week we will gradually take over. Next Monday the Marines will take over giving us all advanced training which is pretty rough. The officers are a congenial group of better than average engineers.

Peggy went to Virginia to spend a weekend leave with Jack during the first weekend in February. By this time, my mother must have been in the first month of her pregnancy with me. The question that comes to my mind when I think of this is "What on earth were they thinking!!?" Can it possibly be that they intended to have another baby just at this stressful moment in their lives? I remember when I was a small child, someone looked at me and said to my mother, "This must be the little surprise!" Many years later, I made a wry comment to my mother about being an "accident," and she said, "Oh, no, when your father went to war, I said to him 'You never let me have that other baby.'" In any case, my mother was to add pregnancy, at 40, to her complicated life in 1943.

What was Peggy's life like? She paid the bills, managed the house, a teenaged son and the dogs, Phineas, a slobbery overgrown, long eared mutt, and Tommy's dignified setter, Sean O'Day. She called the repairmen when necessary, and went to work at her nursery school every day in her wood paneled station wagon using rationed gasoline. She visited her mother, who mostly stayed in bed in her Glenside house, with a house full of boarders in the other rooms. As a Red Cross volunteer, Peggy no doubt had weekly service responsibilities. And she had the tedious task of going to the local elementary school to get her monthly ration card so that she could buy groceries and gas.

Rationing had been instituted in the spring of 1942 with two purposes. The first was to assure the availability of valuable materials – metals, rubber, gasoline and fuel – for the war effort. The second was to assure that food, sugar, clothing, gasoline, paper and other supplies were fairly distributed to all citizens, and people with more money couldn't buy in bulk and hoard what they needed. Meat, butter, dairy products, fruit, canned goods, baby food and especially sugar were rationed. Tires on unused vehicles could be confiscated, while citizens who depended on their cars to get to work (including Peggy) were given a higher ration of gas. The government recommended that no one drive over 40 miles per hour, not so much to save gas as to save the tires. Americans were encouraged to turn in boots, bathing caps, raincoats, and garden hoses. As for clothes, the government got into the fashion business, suggesting the length of hems, the width of belts, and the presence of cuffs, in order to save clothing material.

To her credit, Peggy continued to run her summer camp for small children in the back yard of the new Flourtown house in the summer of 1943, when she must have been quite pregnant, and in the succeeding wartime summers. For a rest, she and Tommy went to her mother's house at Spray Beach, New Jersey when camp was over and before school started again.

Through the war, at Jack's request, Peggy wrote to other Seabee wives, met Jack's Navy colleagues on leave, if they were traveling through Philadelphia, and sent presents to new Navy babies, all at Jack's direction, behaving like a good naval officer's wife. At the same time, she relied heavily on her brother Tom for help with the responsibilities Jack had left her with, and she saw her old friends who, knowing Peggy, worried about her. Peggy reported to Jack, probably trying to make him feel guilty, that some had offered to take her and Tommy into their homes for the duration of the war, and Jack wrote back that she should do whatever felt right to her. She stayed at home.

Nevertheless, Peggy was frightened, alone in the house, and I think her circumstances during the war must have brought into full flower the instability that handicapped her for the rest of her life. The most disturbing evidence of that was that she somehow managed to coerce Tommy, a teenager, to sleep in the same room with her, with the bedroom door locked and the windows nailed shut, for the duration of Tommy's residence at home during the war. It was a terrible thing to ask of a teenaged boy, abusive, really. Peggy was blinded to everything but her own fear, her own need for reassurance. That Tommy accepted this shows the depth of his feelings of responsibility for her, not to mention her powers of manipulation. Tommy had an extraordinarily healthy adult ego, but he did suffer for years from nightmares of being buried alive – dreams that were so violent he actually broke through windows in his sleep. In that way, he was able to subvert whatever anger he may have felt towards his mother.

On March 10, with a Navy band playing "Anchors Aweigh" on the train platform, the 76th CB Battalion boarded a train for Camp Holliday, an advance training base in Gulfport, Mississippi, a town Jack and Peggy had visited during their summer in Bessemer, Alabama while Jack was still working for UGI. From Jack's description, it must have been quite a scene: *Wednesday the 10th, we left as scheduled – my train first – seven civil war coaches and two baggage cars. The loading went off without a hitch or a man missing – and we got quickly organized in the train with the 10 officers and mess attendants in the last – and dirtiest – car. Our first meal was a skimpy box supper taken on at a little N.C. town, on which the vendor must have made $200 on the U.S. meal ticket I gave him. Nightfall found half the cars without lights or water – a* *situation which we partially remedied at the first division stop. When time to try to sleep came, seat backs came off to form sort of continuous bumpy benches along the sides of the cars, with men stretched in every possible position. We picked up two southern RR diners during the night. I got very chummy with the Dining Car Steward, and was his special guest at dinner, at which we two had cocktails and super sirloins – to the dismay of the other officers.* Jack couldn't help himself. He made friends effortlessly. I imagine him striking up a conversation with the dining car steward on the way through the car, asking him where he was from, smiling his genial smile, and pretty soon he had a napkin tucked into his crisp new uniform and a cocktail in his hand.

The Battalion remained at the Advanced Base Depot in Gulfport only two weeks, long enough to pick up equipment and take a nine-day leave before they boarded a troop train again, bound for Port Hueneme, California. Jack used the leave to take a 1,000 mile train trip up the Mississippi River to Burlington to see his overjoyed mother.

He wired Peggy and Tommy to take a train across the country and meet him in Los Angeles. Though the window of time was very short, they did, staying with friends for a few days while the battalion went through further staging and outfitting just up the coast at Hueneme, the principal Seabees base. I suspect it was a briefer visit than they anticipated, and probably unsatisfying for all three of them.

His orders to go west meant for sure that the 76th Battalion would be deployed in the Pacific theater, with a prolonged absence from home. Huie, in his book, points out that since Roman times, war has been a fight for roads, for passage through territory. The work of the Navy Seabees was to create five military "roads," two across the Atlantic Ocean (North and South Atlantic roads) and three across the Pacific Ocean (North, Central, and South Pacific roads), building 400 advance bases for American troops. The mobility of troops in both theaters of war, but especially in the Pacific, depended on the availability, the number and the location of bases along their "road" to war. By the end of the war, Army, Marines, and Navy had literally built and fought their way to victory, with the Seabees contributing airstrips, piers, breakwaters, ammunition magazines, warehouses, hospitals, pipelines, petroleum facilities, and bases with housing for 1.5 million men.

They didn't know it when their transport, the U.S.S. Kenmore, set sail out of San Francisco Bay on April 8, with a dirigible following overhead, heading out to sea under the Golden Gate Bridge, but the 76th Battalion would help build the Central Pacific road, through Hawaii, the Marshall Islands, Gilbert Islands, and Mariana Islands, to the Ryukyu Islands, just off the Japanese coast. The Central Pacific road would, in fact, make the greatest contribution to the Pacific war effort, leading to the destruction of the Japanese perimeter and the beginning of the end of war with Japan.

In fact, during the eight days they were aboard ship, the Seabees didn't know where they were going as they made a zigzag course across the Pacific, their wake lit up with phosphorescent sea life, with the comforting sight of their little escort ship in the distance. It wasn't until they woke up to the sight of Diamond Head and shortly rounded into Pearl Harbor, with the wreckage of Navy ships still visible, that they learned their next station was on Oahu, in the Territory of Hawaii. Jack, as an officer, no doubt did know. He reported to Peggy that he had been given the assignment of *education advisor. We plan to give a series of courses on Island X and hope to get them organized on the way there.*

The 76th Battalion was assigned to build a camp at Lualualei, the location of a Navy ammunition dump, but Jack's company, Company C, was soon detached to Wahiawa, site of a radio station, to carve a camp, roads and services out of the surrounding taro, cane, and pineapple fields. *This, I suppose, is a garden spot*

296

as far as nature is concerned, Jack wrote Peggy. *Deep blue waters, white sand, coral, cloud draped mountains, pineapple and cane fields, bougainvillea, frangipani, tulip trees, bananas, papaya, mango, mongooses and mynah birds. All those things are here, but doing what we are doing, we see more of dry red clay dust, lava rock, cactus, and gnarled kiane trees. What we are building is necessary but quite commonplace construction.* These details were probably enough to make Peggy sick with jealousy. Jack learned soon enough that these positive reports were having a negative effect at home.

Jack was officer in charge at the Wahiawa base, and he felt proud of his responsibilities.   *I have full responsibility for practically the entire lives of all the men under me. I hold Captain's Mast* (on-the-spot trials) *and assign punishments to the transgressors; I supervise the housing, and inspect quarters. I have to give liberties, and furnish transportation for liberty parties – and of course I'm responsible to both the station C.O. and my own C.O. for the operations, and conduct of the entire group. Believe me it's a responsibility but I can't help but like it. I feel I'm doing something – and feel personally proud of the progress we make. And on top of that, another job I had was to act as senior member on a Summary Court Martial. It was not a pleasant duty – and I certainly wished I had Tom's legal help.* Jack was used to being a good guy, the one everyone loved. It no doubt took all the courage he could muster to court martial one of his men.

Because he couldn't really talk about the substance of his work – all letters were now censored by fellow officers – he talked about his free time,   hiking, swimming at the beach, playing tennis, going to the officer's club for cocktails, to Waikiki to see the outrigger canoe races, arranging dances with the Red Cross nurses at the local hospital. Almost immediately, Jack got in touch with a college classmate, Doc Cooper, who lived on the Big Island, Hawaii, but whose mother had a lovely house on Oahu. Though

Hawaii was not yet a state, there were a number of Americans in residence, making grand livings from the sugar and pineapple industry or providing civilian support to the American armed forces stationed there. Thanks to Mrs. Cooper, Jack was soon swept up into a wartime social life with elite Honolulu families, attending dinner parties at the Coopers and their friends the Gartleys, and even the home of a Navy Captain and his wife, the Grahams. *Capt. Graham was very complimentary about the Seabees in general and my group in particular,* Jack reported, *and about the way they have dug into the job here. We talked of the Coopers, of course. When Capt. G. asked me how we liked the station, I told him the one thing we missed was a radio. He promptly found and loaned me a peach. Long and short wave – we can even listen to the lies pouring in and out of Tokyo.*

Company C had built itself an outdoor movie theatre and everyone went to the movies every night. Movies were so central to the company's morale Jack wondered in one of his letters how wars had been fought before without entertainment courtesy of Hollywood. He wrote Peggy, *And did I tell you the officers have big comfortable lounge chairs and everybody smokes? Luxurious isn't it? But after all, we are a long way from home, where we want to be, where I want to be, and these are puny compensations...* This sounds hollow even to me, and I shudder to think of Peggy's reaction when she read it. He was having the time of his life and she knew it.

From Jack's responses to Peggy's letters, it seems clear that the contrast between Jack's fun and Peggy's responsibilities did not go down well at home. With letter after letter filled with lists of expensive problems at home, Peggy seems to have concluded that not only had Jack abandoned her, he had also stopped caring about her and her persistent troubles, and she wrote as much to him. Jack tried to explain himself. *Your very little, but very very welcome, letter came this morning, and I feel you're a little mad at me.*

Please don't be, Peggy darling – please don't ever be anymore. I love you and miss you and want you so much. I regret every cross word we ever had. Later in the summer of 1943 he wrote again, *I don't know why it is hard for you to write to me, darling, when you know I love every word you put down, and am vitally interested in every detail of your life at home, which I know isn't easy. I know the problems you have are terribly hard of solution, but please know, Peggy, that they are my problems too. You do me an injustice if you think they are not of primary importance to me too. Because we are in the armed service, and in a good location, things are easier for us. It doesn't seem fair, I know. But we are away from those whom we love, and when I say we I mean myself and many others of my own age and older...And when I write, as I usually do, of things that must seem inconsequential and unimportant – it is because they are the everyday things that I can write about, and because I think you will be interested and maybe amused a little.*

She was not amused. I wish that Peggy had been willing to trust his love and his concern for her. On the other hand, her burden must have felt overwhelming. I see her, six months pregnant, her damp hair pinned back, seeking shade and a breeze in her new, perhaps not quite finished, kitchen. She would have been wearing a maternity shift, reading the mail after all the younger mothers had picked up their children from camp. There would have been a stack of bills and this letter, asking her to have faith in his choice to go to war, when all she knew about were his tennis games and his dinners with Mrs. Cooper, not to mention the dances with Red Cross nurses to "boost the morale of the troops." What about her morale, she might have been thinking, ever ready tears starting at her eyes.

As the summer of 1943 drew to a close, Jack became increasingly anxious for news of the baby's – my – arrival. After talking to another father whose baby had just arrived, he suggested that Tommy notify him of the birth by Red Cross dispatch. Poor Tommy – it was he, of course, a boy in his senior year in high school, a defensive tackle on the school's varsity football team, who woke up to his mother in labor in the bed next to his. It was he who took her to the hospital, who waited, pacing, with the expectant fathers in the waiting room, and who sent the news, not heeding Jack's advice, via Western Union telegram.

Though I was born on October 5, Jack did not learn of my arrival until the 10th. He told the whole story in comic detail.

...The telegram, sent on the 5th, was mailed from San Francisco on the 6th. Our post office, you know, is at Lualualei. I was talking to the Skipper about 11 yesterday morning (the 9th – Saturday) on the phone, and he said, in passing, "by the way, there's a telegram here for you!" Well, I almost went nuts – because it seems the P.O. was locked up and they couldn't find the postal clerk. It was really funny, out of sheer sympathy, Pat, Don and Bob (Jack's fellow officers in C Company) *were as nervous and upset as I – couldn't sit still – couldn't eat lunch – just kept calling until we finally got John Kolesyn, who got into the P.O. and read it to me – about 1 pm. At the news, as you can imagine, all thought of work ended, and the celebrating began. The first thing was to get a message off to you – and that got into unbelievable complications...then in our travels, Don and I saw little girls' pinafores in a shop window, so went in and ordered some made for our daughters. By that time, nothing would do but that we go tell the Gartleys so we headed there, finding Dick and Gertrude. That of course turned into a party, with the addition of a couple of wandering soldiers from Gertrude's home town, Bob Babb with a bottle and some steaks we'd been hoarding and a 300 lb. half Hawaiian widowed neighbor who played the ukulele. It was a three-fold party – for the baby, whom we named Leilani (I didn't know for sure about Selby Anne until Tom's letter today) for Des' birthday (the 9th) and Gertrude's (the 8th). ...It ended up with five male guests sleeping*

around the house. We all went out to a USO restaurant for an "at cost" breakfast this morning – although we told the Gartleys they should hang a USO sign on their house. Baby still known as sweet Leilani "lei" flower, "lani" heavenly...I love you all so much I'm practically delirious...

It thrills me to read that Jack fell in love with his baby, sight unseen. For many months afterward, on the fifth of each month, Jack would celebrate my "month" birthday. He sent presents – a tiny hula skirt, a bracelet, a doll, little beaded moccasins – and he longed for news of me, turning bits of information over and over like pebbles in his hand, feeling their smooth comfort. *"I read avidly your stories of Selby and I love her aloofness. You mean she actually snubs, or ignores, certain individuals?"* It pained him to be away from me just as I was learning to say "bye bye" or taking my first steps. The details I know of my own infancy I know from these letters, and I have to confess, even at the beginning of old age, I feel treasured by my father. It was at about this time that Jack wrote me that first letter.

At home, life went on as usual, with the addition of a baby nurse, and after that, a live-in maid, Adelaide, who took care of me and the household while Peggy went back to work at the nursery school.

Tommy was chafing to get into the service himself as soon as he finished high school in June. The very idea that Tommy would go to war, too, must have made Peggy crazy. It was a subject of enormous concern, too, for Jack, who wanted him to apply for the Navy V-12 program, an officer training program that took place on college campuses. Tommy applied for the program as his father wished, but was rejected (a test revealed insufficient albumen in his liver, and that put a red flag on his application), and that was a severe disappointment to Jack. The alternative plan was for Tommy to go to college in the fall – his headmaster, a Quaker, chose Haverford, a Quaker college – and to try again for the V-12 later in the year.

Even as Jack worried about what was happening at home, he was earning the admiration of his colleagues in Oahu. He seemed always surprised and a little embarrassed to be recognized and praised by his peers. But it gave him comfort during the moments when he wondered if he was contributing enough to the war effort in this Garden of Eden. *Somehow, the things most prominent in my mind the last few days are the memories of planes and ships returning from the battle fronts. I have had occasion to see both come in and unload, and it made a deep impression on me. I can't of course tell you any details, but it has made me feel, paradoxically, close to the front, and also safe and soft and remote. And I talked to many very recently under fire – still fox hole conscious – and it makes me a little ashamed for our relatively placid life…*

In February 1944, a little over a year after he left home to serve in the Seabees, Jack was suddenly moved from Officer in Charge of Company C to Acting Executive Officer of the Battalion, and moved to Battalion Headquarters in what he called Camp A, back in the "desert" area. This meant that now, for the time being at least, Jack was second in command of the whole 76th Battalion, in a job ordinarily occupied by a lieutenant commander. As flattering as this was, clearly recognizing Jack's leadership abilities, it was also frustrating, because he was assigned to do a job without the promotion in rank, and the extra money that he desperately wanted to send home to Peggy. It was largely a desk job, away from the construction projects, but Jack had to have felt proud to be given the trust of his commander and the authority over 1,000 men.

Jack's departure didn't go unnoticed by the men in Company C. *The most touching thing that happened was a visitation – just before I left W. – from a delegation of my enlisted men there. The spokesman spoke of their feeling for me, and all that kind of business – then presented me with a really beautiful wrist watch, which I tried unsuccessfully to refuse. The card in the box read, "To Lt. John J. Fleming Jr. from the men of Co. C, in appreciation of the consideration shown us, please accept this token." Most embarrassing, strictly non-reg, and entirely out of order – but what could I do? They must have put the bite on the boys and acted in a hell of a hurry, because they didn't know until the day before that I was leaving.*

Tom Talbot, whom Peggy considered her anchor, got his deployment orders from the Navy in March 1944, and though he didn't go overseas until the following December, he was sent to a stateside Navy base. That meant that he was largely absent from Philadelphia. The thought of both Tom and Tommy leaving must have been almost unbearable to Peggy. Clearly, it fueled her resentment toward Jack, to whom she wrote increasingly punitive letters during the winter and spring of 1944. From Jack's responses, I know that she sent him a brief letter saying "she was not in the mood to write letters." In another she accused him of caring more about the war than the burdens he left behind; and in a third, in April 1944, that she and her welfare meant little to him – to which he responded, *Darling I wish with all my heart that you wouldn't feel that you and your welfare mean little to me, when as a matter of fact they mean everything. Surely you know that I am doing what I am, not for any personal pleasure or glory, but simply because I felt I had to? Certainly I feel the war is all important – you can't be here without seeing, feeling and living it – and it will be intensely more so for us in a matter of weeks. But at the same time, all I live for is the future – to get back to you and our children, whom I love. This is just an interlude, and that's the real life ahead.*

Good war news was coming in from Europe in June 1944 – the fall of Rome and the simultaneous invasion of Normandy in France. At the same time, Jack was beginning to sound depressed, concerned about Tommy's future, missing his baby's development, and guilty about the responsibilities he had left with Peggy, just as the 76th Seabee battalion was preparing for its next assignment – to construct an advance base in a combat zone. The entire battalion was ordered to move together again to Iroquois Point for intensive military training supervised by the Marines. Something big was about to happen. For Jack, who was still Exec of the Battalion, and would remain so, in his interim status, for the rest of the war, it meant organizing, reshuffling, moving and re-housing over 1,000 men. *It's like helping to run a city. Besides the main thing, running the work the men do, there are also all the necessary services, police, commissary, sanitation, clothing, entertainment...*

On June 18th, the 76th Battalion left Oahu on the USAT Hawaiian Shipper, part of a convoy of Navy ships bound for parts unknown, but not before Peggy got in a few more punches, adding that "no letter would be better" than the letters he wrote. Jack wrote Peggy that he was a "little scared," and in his last letter before embarking to an uncertain shore, he pleaded, *Peggy darling, my heart is so full of things that I want to say to you – that it seems there are not words for. Just to say I love you isn't enough. I want to be with you – to live our life together – in our own surroundings. To take the responsibilities that are mine – to solve the problems that are ours. I want to be a good husband, to be a father in the flesh to our two children, and not just ink marks on a piece of white paper. Please try to understand and believe in, and love me. ...This is it, darling, pray for me.*

Jack received Peggy's response to this parting plea two weeks later, while his ship was moored among an armada of Navy ships in the harbor at Eniwetok, a large, protective coral atoll in the Marshall Islands, recently recaptured from the Japanese. Her letter, though not available, was clearly not comforting. Jack responded, *Mail – I should be happy, but instead I am deeply hurt and utterly depressed. By a circumstance fortunate for the battalion, four bags* *of mail were intercepted, the first in 2 ½ weeks. I can't begin to tell you of the hope, and apprehension, that followed the sorting – then the agonizing anxiety at mail call, waiting and hoping for my name. Letters from you and Tommy postmarked the 14th, and Tommy's graduation invitation. I hardly know what to say, Peggy – I feel like a dog, who, looking for a pat and a kind word, has been kicked and cursed at. And the hurt remains – a deep ache inside me. What have I done Peggy that you should feel so bitterly toward me? Why do you doubt my love for you and our children? Why can't you believe me, darling when I tell you that I love you – that you and Tommy and Selby are all of life to me? You have twice quoted me as saying "you'll get along somehow," a phrase I don't remember saying – and if I did, I meant it in no sense as a disclaimer of responsibilities, but as an expression of confidence in your proven ability to do much with little money. Please Peggy, for God's sake, if you have any affection in your heart for me – don't deny it to me now. Do you miss me? Do you want me back? If you do, even a little – or even sometimes – couldn't you find it in your heart to tell me so? You are all important to me – am I nothing to you? You have made me feel like a lost soul, and in my present situation, that isn't good. I suppose this is all selfishness on my part, too.*

In fairness, my father's decision to join the war was not all about selfless duty. He needed the war as much as his country needed his service. And Peggy, like millions of other women but probably not many of her contemporaries, was left with awful responsibilities under trying circumstances. Even so, what in God's name was the matter with her? It seems unspeakably cruel to me that she would lash out at him just as he was explicitly asking for her support as he was about to go into real combat. I can imagine her latching onto his words, "you'll get along somehow," which I agree must have sounded callous, and used those words against him again and again. Knowing he would be farther away, in more remote circumstances, must have made her angrier and more frightened. And the timing…just as her brother had left her, and Tommy was getting restless and anxious to enlist. But once again I ask myself, was she unbalanced or just mean and selfish?

Jack's ship remained moored in the harbor at Eniwetok for a long, sweltering, boring, uncomfortable 30 days. The 76th was bound for Guam, in the Mariana Islands. Typically, the Seabees would go ashore at an island just after the Marines had captured it. The recapture of Guam from the Japanese took an unusual three weeks, from the first shelling on July 14 until August 4. Until then the battalion waited…and waited. While they waited the men mustered, practiced emergency "abandon ship" twice each day, read, played cards, ate K rations and watched movies on makeshift screens. Blackout requirements meant blocked portholes and no air circulation in the oppressive tropic heat, so many men, including Jack, slept on deck. Jack did not hear from Peggy but continued to write, though he said, *It's hard to keep writing without acknowledgement from you. It's like reaching for you in the dark and not finding you and I do so need the feel of your hand in mine…*He went on.

Being underway again, I am permitted to say I am at sea on a troop transport – in a combat area – and headed for a combat destination. I can't tell you how many long weeks we have spent aboard or where we have been, but I can tell you it hasn't been a holiday cruise…I'm writing now on a table in the troop officer's mess, our "wardroom" and the sweat is running off me in rivulets. There are portholes but the blackout screens effectively cut off air. It's a little cooler on deck and I've been sleeping these nights stretched out on a poncho. The only light out there is definitely not welcome – it being a half full and entirely too brilliant moon. Now and then, however, it shows the satisfactory silhouette of a deadly little escort vessel. The days and nights have been endless – the shipboard duties and routine becoming automatic and meaningless. But this phase is almost over — the next will be different —

Jack's ship left Eniwetok on July 25 and arrived at Guam on August 2, 1944, where they stayed near shore by day and were out at sea at night, watching the light of flares and gunfire on the island. Jack and his boss, Commander Frank Endebrock, debarked on August 5 with the first contingent of construction workers, those who would build the camp. Additional units would debark on August 6, and the remainder of the battalion on August 14. What they found was a devastated landscape with shorn treetops, stinking dead bodies, and mountains of rubble that had to be bulldozed out of the path of machines unloading rations, gas, ammunition, and rolling equipment from the ship's hold. And, it being the rainy season, they stepped off the ship into deep mud.

Guam, the largest island between Hawaii and the Philippines, had been an American possession since 1898, when it was won from the Spanish at the end of the Spanish American War. The U.S. had built a Navy base and air strip on the island in 1938, and most of the 20,000 Chamorros, the native people who lived on Guam, were employed by the American Navy. The island was captured by the Japanese in December 1941, just after the attack at Pearl Harbor. It was the first of American possessions to be taken by Japan when the war started. Within a short time after its recapture in August 1944, it would become the nerve center of the Pacific War, the advance headquarters of the Pacific fleet.

Almost right away, Commander Endebrock was felled by dengue fever, and Jack found himself in charge of the whole battalion. When he could write again, he painted a picture of the post-invasion scene at Guam.

I'm back on the ship at the moment and never thought that by comparison it would seem such a haven. Conditions ashore are indescribably chaotic. I can't give you any details now. Your feelings and desires become elemental — simply to keep a whole skin, to quench your thirst, to slake your hunger, to get a smoke, to get your body and clothes clean. And of course to do the job you are supposed to do. And the fact that the rainy season is getting a good start rounds out the picture. Our tents have been set in soupy mud – no lights except candles and flashlights (when any light is permitted) and trying to get off your damp and muddy clothes and get into a mosquito netted canvas cot without carrying 50 lbs of mud with you is a major problem. Then the bed has to be searched for little lizards and centipedes – big horny ones with a bite like fire.

Within a mere six weeks, all that rubble and mud had been turned into a camp for the 76th battalion – but not before Jack, too, had been felled by dengue fever. He described it – in a letter dictated to his yeoman, who had volunteered to come to his tent – as not very serious, *simply makes you feel lousy for something less than a week with temperature, back, head, and eye aches.* Because the men had accomplished a lot in a short time, Jack was in the relative luxury of a screened-in tent with a wood deck. The progress of the camp itself, built under such adverse conditions, was nothing short of remarkable.

Things are becoming more routine and Navy-base-like, and the place grows visibly. We all work harder than we have ever worked before because of deadlines we have to meet, and because there is nothing else to do. As exec, I've been largely busy with the construction of our own camp, which I'll try and describe to you. It's located in a gently sloping valley between two ridges which run down toward the harbor from the low mountains. Most of the camp area was once terraced into rice paddies, long abandoned, with coconut palm trees, bread fruit, mangoes and banana trees around the edges. Housing is entirely in heavy tentage, which we are now elevating with plywood decks. We found a good well, and have installed a water system for showers, galley, and drinking water only. Our permanent Quonset hut galley is almost finished –

it sports oil ranges and ovens, big reefers, flake icers and an ice cream machine. The mess halls are big tents with refectory type tables and benches. Officers' country is on the south ridge – 16 small double tents, decked and screened. And we have installed an electric power system – so we now have lights. The officers' country is high enough to get what little breeze there is – and affords a view of both harbor and open Pacific. Many of the trees were broken by shell fire, but we have saved all we can. Most of the terrain was honeycombed with shell holes and Jap caves, but both are getting filled in. We have installed a ship's store, where we dispense our meager supply of beer, cokes, candy, cigarettes and toilet goods; we have a barber shop, a tailor, a cobbler – but our present pride and joy is a laundry, just opened. The joy of clean clothes is something basic. We built a frame and canvas shed to house our 18 easy washes, 2 mangles, and 16 electric irons, hired 6 native women through civil affairs, and with our own 3 laundry experts are now in operation. The administration area is in a corner of the valley, where most of the palms were left. Fronting the road we have our transportation and shop area. Truck, crane and dozer service and repair shops, carpenter shop, paint shop, pipe shop, welding shop, and electric shop. In other words, a somewhat complete community – the materials for all of which had to be manhandled from the ship's hold to here. I forgot to mention the 60-bed hospital we built on the other ridge – Quonset hut surgical ward now under construction, and a dental laboratory. As to the camp generally, our chief worry is how many days the tents will last – the constant succession of heavy rains and blazing sun is very rough on canvas.

There were 15 Seabee battalions on Guam, building or rebuilding airstrips, radio stations, ammunition dumps, tank farms, roads, water and oil pipes, electric lines, hospitals, barracks, warehouses and supply dumps, piers, and seawalls. The principal responsibility of the 76th battalion was to build the Apra Harbor breakwater, an expansive rock "arm" extension from Orote Peninsula, which created one of the Navy's largest deep water ports in the Pacific. The breakwater would assure safe harbor, even in typhoons, for the largest Navy ships. Because the Japanese had destroyed Chamorro schools, the Seabees also helped to rebuild them.

The Chamorros, who are part Micronesian and part Spanish, were American nationals, though not citizens, which meant that they could not hold office or vote. They spoke English as well as a language of their own, and were very relieved the Americans had returned. Jack made friends with 12-year-old Jo Jo Salas and his little brother, whose school the 76th had rebuilt. When the battalion built their outdoor movie theater, Jo Jo and many of his fellow Chamorros from the nearby village of Piti came to the nightly movies, the parents, holding their babies, settling into the seats made from woven coconut fibers, the children with their snacks. Peggy sent Jo Jo and his brother presents from the U.S., and Jo Jo responded with two beautiful purses made from local shells – one for Peggy and one for the maid, Adelaide. Jack sent home another gift from Jo Jo – a carving of a carabao, a kind of water buffalo that was the local beast of burden on Guam.

There were still about 100 Japanese soldiers on the island, hidden in caves, who, festooned with hand grenades, foraged for food and were generally to be avoided. Jack wrote that no one ventured out of camp unarmed, but *our steel helmets do their best service as wash basins.*

Jack was receiving letters again from Peggy and Tommy, including some long delayed letters from the summer, and that cheered him. He was anxious to know more about his baby's first birthday and the comings and goings in the household. But some of the news confused and upset him. *I can never seem to get the whole picture – and it makes me frantic. This is what I do get, Tommy failed to make V-12 because of albumen. He graduated*

310

from Penn Charter okay, got a partial scholarship at Haverford, and entered for at least the summer term, intending to enlist in the Marines this fall. He has not done at all well, partially due to his own fault and partially due to the excessive time and energy spent in travelling plus lack of college contact and interest. He has again failed his physical. If he passes his makeup he will continue at H – otherwise what? It is natural and understandable that he should live at home. I can understand that while you live there, there is no alternative. Then the house business has me completely confused. If Tommy does go into the service, what then? What would you have done, or would you do? As to Sam W's letter, had you indicated to him that you wanted to sell the house? Another angle that adds to my confusion is a remark in a letter which I got, just before yours, from Alice Dunbaugh to the effect that she was so disappointed that Tom had talked you out of going to Florida. You had mentioned that idea to me only once in a letter, and then only briefly, in passing. What did you have in mind then – to sell, rent, or close the house? Disregarding other conditions my feelings about the house are very simple. It's our house, the one I left, and the one I'd like to come back to. That's sentimental, I know. But please know, darling, that I want you to do whatever you think is best, whatever you think is right, and whatever you have to do. I know the expense, and particularly in winter, the physical difficulties are the worst problems. And damn it, I can't even help to solve them from here. It hurts me most to know, to feel, that everything would be so much easier if I were only there.

Peggy really knew how to find Jack's most painful places. Sell the house he had thrown his soul into building? Had she cooked up some escape fantasy in which she would sell the house and move to Florida? Alice Dunbaugh, her best friend from boarding school, might have invited Peggy to move in with her for the duration of the war, which might have made some sense, now that Tommy was in college. In any case, she wasn't feeling any better in the fall of 1944. The following is the only war letter in her hand, written to her brother Tom in December 1944 as he was about to embark on a Navy ship that would take him from the east coast through the Panama Canal and into the Pacific war. Though Peggy didn't know it, Tom would have a much more hazardous assignment than Jack; he would be beach master, first off the boat for the invasion of Okinawa.

Tom dear,

Mother informs me Gladys has gone to Washington which means I guess Bon Voyage. I hope it's a shake down and you will be back in port.

This is a very hard letter for me to write. There are so many things to say. I feel badly I have never seen you to really talk to in the last year. And I feel so lost now that you are really going.

I know you have been as fair in every way as you could – but I think you should recognize my position as well as Gladys – she and mother are, I know, your first considerations – and should be – but I have always had to lean on you more than I should due to Jack's complete lack of responsibility – which I know you recognize without holding against him. I am sorry I have had to accept help with Tommy – but I do thank you for the $100 toward his tuition. I have been desperate to know what to do about him, and if the tables had been turned I feel that I would have done the same for you.

With your going off I am now in the position of being responsible for mother and the future of my two children and, if anything happens to Jack, $15,000 to bring them up on – and no one to turn to – anyplace in the world – also I am faced with a potential major operation which I sincerely hope I can postpone. I have an inadequate background – and I have not the strength for a full time job – whereas Gladys besides being amply provided for by you has a bulwark of strength and financial support in her *mother – all this is no one's fault, simply circumstances – but must be recognized.*

I shall miss you more than you can possibly know – thank you for all you have done to help me. God bless you and a speedy return...

Jack's "complete lack of responsibility?" I am comforted that Uncle Tom did not share her view. Only one page of Tom's response to this letter remains. While reassuring, he seemed surprised to hear about Peggy's need for major surgery. This subject never came up in any other context. I wonder if it was a bid for sympathy, and I think Uncle Tom did, too. In a later letter, Tom reassured Peggy that *Jack's work is necessary, much more so than mine, and if it weren't for men like him we would still be fighting in the South Pacific and not giving Japan the working over she is now getting from the South Pacific bases.*

Jack and the battalion strung up Christmas lights and put on a party for the children at Jo Jo's school, and they gave themselves the day off – their first – on Christmas day, but he was beginning to tire of the war and the troubles at home. He had received a letter from the Navy promising him a spot promotion to Lt. Commander, which hadn't come through, and he was homesick. Fresh rations were out, and they were living on canned vegetable stew, spam and Vienna sausage which, unaccountably, well-meaning friends had also included, to their despair, in Christmas packages, along with mountains of fruitcake. And Peggy and Tommy had taken a home movie and mailed it to him, but it seemed to be lost in transit. He wrote Peggy somewhat despairingly in a Christmas letter, *The baby and a Christmas tree – thinking of it is almost more than a person can bear. Your letter which came today carried an underlying note of bitterness. I don't blame you, you haven't had a happy lot compared to others you see and know – but still I'm hurt by it. ..I'm enclosing a check for $30 herewith, just for Christmas – I hope you'll go to a play and have decent seats. It isn't much, but* *that's all there is. I've scraped the bottom of the barrel. The hoped for promotion didn't come – so I guess it won't – and that's just another thing we'll have to accept.*

Jack cheered up considerably when he finally received the home movie in late January. *I spent the afternoon (Sunday afternoon off) rounding up our 16mm projector,* he reported, *clearing and darkening a Quonset hut, and seeing the film, time after time. I'm just crazy about it – it's a treasure – means more than anything you have ever sent me. Selby is just a darling and I about blew my top. Rounded up everybody within hailing distance to see it. And it was so wonderful to see you, Tommy, Adelaide, the dogs, the house, the yard. I just can't tell you, darling, what a bang it is to me. It is so good of all of you – and I got such a kick out of Selby's little blue ribbon on her top knot and the pinafore and the hula doll.*

After a semester at Haverford College, Tommy enlisted in the Navy and in January left for boot camp in Bainbridge, Maryland. Though Jack still wanted him to reapply for V-12, and wrote as much, Tommy decided to try for quartermaster school, with training on Long Island. It took him most of the spring to get through boot training, however, because of a series of illnesses picked up from his fellow sailors. The worst was a bout with mumps, which put Tommy in the hospital for a couple of weeks. Jack was surely disappointed but probably relieved that a decision had been made about Tommy's immediate future. Both Jack and Tom wrote Peggy that Tommy would be well taken care of by the Navy, and that she shouldn't worry needlessly about him. Peggy responded accusing Jack of "deliberate cruelty," sending Jack down for another count. Meanwhile, with Tommy away, his dog Sean adopted me, sleeping beside me and taking delicate nibbles of crackers I offered him through the slats of my crib.

As each week went by, the camp at Guam looked more and more "Pearl Harbor-like," Jack wrote, with paved roads, flush toilets, and table cloths, and an expanded 1500-seat movie theater they now called "Piti Palace" after the neighboring Chamorro village (and, of course, the Pitti Palace in Florence). One night, there was no movie to show. They showed a short film on skiing in Sun Valley (which set the Chamorro children to try strapping boards on their feet the next morning and "sliding" across the coral) and Jack, seizing a "golden opportunity," got out the home movie again and showed it full size on the big screen – *Selby's premiere, ably supported by Peggy, Tommy, Adelaide, and dogs. I loved it all over again – it was so wonderful.* Whether the other 1,499 people in the audience were equally thrilled is questionable, but I suspect they were happy to indulge their lovable Exec.

Jack was encouraged by the war news, too. With victory in the Philippines and the Russians marching on Berlin, it began to seem that the end might be near. But the reality of war was still depressing to him. Something Peggy wrote him caused him to respond with the following,

I cannot understand how anyone can remain untouched by the war. My God, how can any citizen of the United States be oblivious to the fact that the U.S. is in it up to its neck? That it must be over as quickly as possible – and as cheaply in lives and injuries as possible. What can be more important than that? I don't think I'm violating security in saying that now wounded Marines are being brought here in numbers. If those people you refer to could see just one stretcher being carried down a gangway, could see just one of those white, drawn bearded faces – could know the kind of a hell those kids walk into, hating it, but doing it because that's what they are in there to do, they would think and do more about helping. I don't mean being noble and heroic, but just to realize a little of what it's all about. I suppose, though, you can't blame people too much. People have a right to gripe about rationing and hardships – as long as they are actually enduring them. I don't know any man here that's satisfied – everyone, without exception, wants to be somewhere else – or doing something else – and groans and bitches about everything – mostly with fairly good reason. Right now every man in the battalion, with myself at the head of the list, is completely sunk by information we got yesterday, namely, there is no relief for us in prospect. Next month we will have served two years overseas. The men have counted on going back in April. I, trying to be conservative, had as you know, set it at midsummer. Now I don't know when it will be. There are no available battalions to relieve us. It's like running for a goal, almost realizing it, and having it snatched away. We feel that we have been tricked. The incentive is gone, and the sense of hopelessly serving time terribly intensified. Many – too many – of the men feel that their homes are breaking up because they are not there to "straighten things out." They bring in their so-called "Dear John" letters, with bewildered eyes. They begin, "Dear John, you might as well know that I want a divorce" – and usually come without any hint or warning. What the hell are those women thinking of?

It seems to me that there was a message in there for Peggy, but Jack would never have been more direct than that. I wonder if Peggy got the message.

By April 1945, Jack had been promised his long anticipated promotion once again, this time with a push from his brother Phil, trying to work magic back in Washington. Jack was grateful but not hopeful that it would come through. Meanwhile, for the first time he visited the Army Air Force's B-29 airfield on Guam, and became fascinated with the unit and their contribution to the war effort. B-29 Superfortress bombers had been introduced into wartime service in June 1944, and they were credited with helping turn around the war in the Pacific. It was a B-29 out of a base on Guam's neighboring island, Tinian, that carried one of the atom bombs that ended World War II in August 1945. *It did give me a chance to learn a little about the Army Air Force people – how they operate – how they live. They were all terribly nice and friendly; insisted on showing me and telling me everything. I sweated out the return from a mission over Japan with those who didn't go, and shared their anxiety as they counted each plane roaring in to the strip and tried quickly to spot battle damage. Then I sat in the interrogation of the crews, while they consumed coffee and doughnuts (Red Cross) and moved their hands in that graceful way flyers have to show how fighters made passes at them. They were like so many excited, dirty-faced boys after winning a football game. The commanding officer was a colonel, an old time flyer who went along for the hell of it – alleging it was the only way he can get any sleep, on that long monotonous hop.*

Jack's fellow officers, with whom he had lived in close contact these last two years, were beginning to get their orders to go home. He was dispirited by that (and envious), but he found two new friends, an Air Force colonel and a Lt. Commander from another Seabee battalion, who became regular companions. *Col Storrie is a flyer's flyer, a tall gaunt Texan with tremendous drive and energy – drops in at irregular intervals, to get me to go over to Lt. Comdr McCormick's with him. Purpose to bum a drink or get a boat ride, to forget for a moment his horribly enervating job. He carries a little book with a page for each of his combat air crews – 11 names to a page. The back section of the book are the crews who haven't come back, and each week that section grows a little thicker and the lines in Storrie's face get a little deeper. We're helping him fix up his camp a little, too.*

The other tremendous boost to Jack's morale was the arrival of Tom Talbot's ship, the U.S.S. Burleigh, in Apra Harbor. When Jack heard the ship was in sight, he rented a boat and coxswain and motored out to meet it. The brothers-in-law spent a long evening together, both onboard ship and ashore, catching up. Tom spent the night with Jack in his tent, regaling him with eyewitness accounts

317

of Peggy, Tommy, and me, not to mention the battle for Okinawa, which had just taken place.

At the end of April, the sad news came that President Roosevelt had died, and the good news that Germany was in defeat. There were rapid gains in the Pacific, thanks to the B-29s and their crews for whom Jack had such admiration. On May 8, Peggy's 42nd birthday, President Truman declared victory in Europe in a speech broadcast in the camp via short wave on the Armed Forces radio station. This came just a day after Jack had witnessed a horrifying scene in the harbor, when a Japanese kamikaze pilot crashed his plane into a hospital ship, using the red cross as a target and striking directly into a busy operating theatre. Doctors, nurses, corpsmen, and patients were buried on Guam in a mass funeral. It was time for the war to be over and for Jack to come home.

It was over, and soon, courtesy of the Enola Gay and the atomic bomb that was dropped on Hiroshima. With the second bomb on Nagasaki three days later, the Japanese gave up in defeat. Jack didn't know how he felt about the bomb, *The atomic bomb and the declaration of war against Japan by Russia are monopolizing our conversation. The first, to me, is simply terrifying, almost beyond comprehension. The second one was dropped on Nagasaki today. Perhaps if the war is ended quickly, it will be worth the awful responsibility of releasing such power. I don't know...*

Just as the war ended, on August 14 (in Guam, across the International Date Line), Jack received notice of his promotion to Lieutenant Commander. It was a qualified promotion, he would revert to his former rank as soon as he left his position as Executive Officer of the 76th Battalion. So it seemed a bit like a Pyrrhic victory to him, and he was beyond caring about it. But he would arrive home with an extra half stripe on his sleeve, and have a little extra money in his pocket.

Jack's last month on Guam was a flurry of activity. As Exec, he found himself buried in paperwork – points, discharges, releases to inactive duty, troop movements, overstuffed troop transports heading home, and decisions about what construction to carry on for a civilian base on Guam, and what was no longer a priority, now that the war was over. His relief finally arrived in mid-September, and in his last letter home, Jack indicated that he would try to leave aboard the S.S Asperion, embarking on September 15. He would be in San Francisco in two weeks, and would be able to come home for a month's leave soon after that. Navy records show that the 76th Construction Battalion was "inactivated" on the 29th of September.

1945 on...

Jack, Peggy, Tommy, and Selby

On the day I first met my father, I am sure I had a sense that something big was happening. I imagine that I, a two-year-old, sat expectantly next to my mother on the train's upholstered seat watching the bright sky and the farms and fields and trees whiz by outside the window, the train wheels clacking down the tracks. The train must have slowed as we crossed the Mississippi River, turning right to follow the river north a few hundred yards and chuffing into the station in Burlington, Iowa, my father's home town.

I think I must have spent the whole trip all the way from Philadelphia climbing over my mother's lap to press my face against the window glass and watch America go by. I wonder what I knew about my father. I wonder what, at two, my concept of "father" was. I wonder about the dress, surely a dress, that my mother had picked out for me to wear when I met my father.

I can picture my mother straightening my sash, picking me up, while someone helped her with the bags and, when the train came to a stop at the station, coming to the door of the car and climbing down the steps. I would have had my arms around her neck, feeling the October air on my cheeks, taking in the oily sooty smell of the train's engine, and smelling my mother's perfume.

Perhaps I scanned the faces for the one that belonged to Jack, standing tall, maybe still in his Navy uniform, nervous, curious, still hurt, apprehensive about this reunion with Peggy but anxious to meet his little war baby. After the Navy transport had delivered him home at the end of the war, he had traveled east by train from Port Hueneme, California while my mother and I traveled west from Philadelphia to meet him in Burlington, in the middle of the country.

I wonder what Peggy felt when she saw his face in the milling crowd of passengers and greeters on the platform. She must have felt a jolt of recognition, her enthusiasm tempered with resentment, her spirit still poisoned as they pushed towards each other, she carrying me, the little surprise.

I know, because my parents told me, that when I met my father I said, clearly, "Hello, Poppy," startling everyone with a name I had invented, as he took me into his arms at the train station. I'd like to remember the moment. I don't, but I feel sure that I reached unhesitatingly for my father, a large, handsome, burly man with a deep cleft in his chin and a wavy mane of prematurely gray hair.

How did they get back to normal? With the exception of a few letters, my primary sources dry up in 1945, and I rely on memories of childhood to tell the rest of Jack and Peggy's story. The remaining few letters from Jack to his mother, written in the fall of 1945 and winter of 1946, set the stage for the childhood I remember.

Tommy, who had been sent to Naval Station Great Lakes for further training, was denied a hoped-for leave for the long anticipated family reunion in Burlington, when I first met my father. Peggy and Jack and I came home from Burlington via

Chicago, where Emily, their old friend from Chicago days, met us for lunch, and then we rushed to get the Capitol Limited home to Philadelphia. Tommy was waiting for us at the front door of the house in Flourtown when we returned.

The Navy wanted Jack back at a Seabee base in Rhode Island by late November, but he was able to rearrange his next assignment after a trip to Washington, DC, and a visit to his brother Phil's contacts, using Phil's lavish office, car and chauffeur, so that after a leave, he would report instead to the Philadelphia Navy Yard.

Jack used his 45-day leave to attack neglected repairs to the house. He also reported to his mother that in the morning, while Peggy was at school, he had *"a particularly good opportunity to get further acquainted with Selby, who by this time is very possessive with me."* I bet I was.

Jack spent another nine months in the Navy, working as a transportation officer at the Public Works Office of the Philadelphia Navy Yard, and retaining the rank of lieutenant commander. Still wearing a uniform, he worked five days a week supervising the use of 1,600 vehicles, shipyard cranes and railroad facilities, commuted on the train from Flourtown, and arrived home for supper like a regular businessman.

Peggy continued to teach kindergarten at Pennybryn, her friend Mopsy Fox's nursery school, though she complained about having to work and thought she might stop at the end of the year. She did not. She was my kindergarten teacher three years later.

Tommy, still in the Navy for another year, was assigned to the Personnel Separation Center at Lido Beach, New York, a Long Island Navy base where, as paymaster, he closed out accounts with sailors returning to civilian life. Tommy was able to get liberties to go to New York City, where the USO on Park Avenue had free theatre tickets for soldiers and sailors, and he came home to Philadelphia most weekends. On an escapade from Lido Beach, dressed in his Navy whites, he crashed the debutante party of a wealthy young beauty, Phyllys (Fifi) Betts, who was from a prominent Long Island Catholic family. As fate would have it, he and Fifi would meet again and he would marry her several years later.

At Christmas, Tommy secured a five-day leave so that he could be part of the season of debutante parties that were packed into the Christmas holiday in Philadelphia. *His Philadelphia girl friends are all debutantes this year,* Jack wrote his mother, *and he has invitations which would book him for two weeks solid for dinner and dances at the Bellevue, the Barclay, and the Warwick* (the best Philadelphia hotels). *And such parties – I don't know where people get the money to throw around thus.*

By spring of 1946, Jack had decided not to go back to the Philadelphia Gas Company after his demobilization from the Navy, though they made it clear there was a job waiting for him. Instead, demonstrating newfound confidence, he decided to enter into partnership with his lawyer and start his own construction company. He described his plans to his mother in February.

It is still my intention to enter the construction business. My friend Sam Weinrott, who has had years of experience in both the legal and financial end of contracting and who has many connections with dealers, subcontractors, banks, and real estate people – feels as I do – and as I believe you do – that now is our opportunity. Others with whom I have discussed it feel the same, including (my uncle) *Tom Talbot, Henry Ringgold* (Jack's old friend), *and Tom Smith* (husband of Peggy's childhood friend Mary), *who can also be of great help because he is in the bonding business, and has many contacts with builders and contractors and – please keep this confidential – all three have evinced willingness to put up money to back their opinions. This may or may not be necessary. The way it stands now we intend to form a partnership – at least Sam and I, maybe more – with my share of a starting* *capital at about $6,000 to come from a G.I. loan. I will receive a fair salary for directing the enterprise, and in addition will share profits equally as a partner. We plan to go after small contracts – say $10,000 to $30,000, rather than do any speculative building. The present bugaboo is materials, which may be tied up to a large extent for low cost veteran's housing. In that case, we might go after concrete, excavations, or grading work – or even some of the housing. I'd start with an office without individual help – there are places where joint telephone and stenographic services are available. And most important, we want to have a job – a construction job – to start on the day I get out of the Navy so there'll be no dangerous lag in between. Such equipment as is needed I believe I can get from government surplus.*

This sounds like a more sensible, mature, grounded Jack. It was a brave decision, one that suggests he felt a new confidence in himself, and the energy to make a new start as a breadwinner for his family. Peggy may not have felt the same confidence and optimism, but she had to feel some sense of relief after the war years. Perhaps also Jack would have more status as a business owner and employer. Her decision to keep her teaching job may be an indication that she did not trust Jack to provide enough income from his new business, or that they made the decision together, as an anchor to windward.

They still didn't have money matters under control. In the same letter, Jack asked his mother to renew the loan on the house from Burlington Savings Bank, as they still did not have the means to repay it. It makes me sad that Jack got this far in his life, the Depression notwithstanding, without learning to live without debt, especially since his failure to do so made him so unhappy with himself.

Meanwhile, Tommy went back to Haverford in the fall.

Those were the circumstances of my childhood. Peggy was a kindergarten teacher, Jack had his own construction company, with his office in the basement room of our house in Flourtown, Tommy went to college, dropping in with friends on weekends, and Mary Vaughan and I were at home with the dogs – Phineas and Sean and later the dachshund Lena, and the irreplaceable Sean's successor, an Irish setter named Seamus. Eventually the household would also include my cat Murgatroyd.

In his letters to his mother during that first year home, Jack described me, at two, to his mother.

Selby Anne is getting along wonderfully, and is becoming such a conversationalist. A sunny little character, too – greets me every morning with a "GOOD morning, Poppy" in her most musical voice. She was very annoyed at losing the Wilson doll (which is enclosed in your box) but you will be glad to know I was able to get an exact duplicate, which she will get for Christmas. Selby is daily becoming more talkative; she is so sweet and pretty and yet has an iron determination, too. She has the oddest proclivity for books and magazines – takes them from anywhere and leafs through, calling your attention to pictures that interest her. Seems to prefer Life to Mother Goose – gets very mad when, to some torn pages, a book is taken away from her.

So there I am, finally, a character in the story. I like the little girl that Jack saw. She seemed to carry a strength of personality, a *brio* I felt then that I lost for a while. I think I was a happy and loved and confident little girl, and the house on Fleming Road was my realm, with four adults – my parents, Tommy, and Mary, and sometimes a fifth, the yard man Edward – attending to me.

The house that Jack built was my castle. From my room in the bedroom wing I could turn right and dart into Tommy's room where, when he was at home, he would lie in bed in the morning and lift me to soar as high as the reach of his arms and dive bomb into his pillows. Jack and Peggy's bedroom was at the other end of the hall, just at the top of the stairs. There Peggy set up her headquarters and the nerve center, really, of the household, the place to which Peggy and Jack and I retreated at some time during the day or evening, or when I was sick, or had a bath, sometimes at naptime, or to lie around and read a book. There were times when it was frightening to be outside the safety zone that room represented.

For me, the other nerve centers of the house were Mary's domain and Jack's office, hub for his secretary and his work men. The living room was mostly a transit area, and where parties took place. In the kitchen wing, with the dining room and Mary's bedroom, the three of us, Mary and Edward and I, drank lemonade in the summer while the dogs cooled themselves on the linoleum floor and the honeysuckle sent its sweet aroma through the kitchen door. Lena and Phineas were never far from each other, though Phineas was forced to wear bags over his droopy ears, because Lena, an intense little dachshund, had, in a fever of affection, chewed them to shreds.

Jack's office, down the big staircase to the garage level of the house, had a large desk with folders full of papers, a telephone, pens, paper clips and other props for my imaginary forays into the business world, swiveling in his office chair, writing important notes with the telephone's receiver at my ear. Often, as an adult, I have sat at my desk at work, thinking what an adventure it seemed to me as a child to be surrounded by papers and files and a telephone.

At the rear perimeter of the back yard, Tommy, who was not handy, one summer built me a rough but functional sandbox and a swing set. Back there, Jack had built Peggy a tiny swimming pool, where Tommy taught me how to swim, backing away as I paddled frantically from the steps, and Peggy planted a wooded wildflower garden with plants she stole from the roadside on summer trips to New England. Tommy was my teacher, my advocate, and my hero, with a big paw-like hand ready to lift me up and swing me into his safe embrace. My father was sweet and amiable, but passive, not the forces that my mother and brother were. Even at an early age, I think I had some sense that my father was a disappointment to my mother.

In the absence of neighborhood children, I created my own world in the yard, swinging on the swings Tommy built or playing in a playhouse Jack found and appropriated for me that stood near the steep bank down to a local spur of the Reading Railroad track. The trains would rumble and whistle as they passed behind the house, day and night. I had also conjured an imaginary friend, Sooty Cummings. I had to haul Sooty out of trouble as often as not (she didn't always make good behavior choices). Peggy began to take too much interest in Sooty, asking for nightly reports on her mishaps, and eventually the subject of Sooty bored me and I was forced to dispose of her; she fell down the large hole in the back yard, an excavation to create a cesspool for the house. It was a hole I'd been warned to stay away from, but Sooty didn't listen, and I had an opportunity to reassert control over my imaginary life.

At age three, I began to go to school with my mother every day, joining Miss Brown's three-year-old nursery class while Peggy worked with the five-year-olds a few doors away. Much to my mother's annoyance, I was reticent about my day while driving home in the car. Mary was my chosen confidante, and I ran through the swinging door to the kitchen to tell her everything. *"Brown say 'put your rubbers on!' and I did, all by myself!"* I would announce, standing on tiptoes at the edge of Mary's flour strewn worktable. Mary listened, white flour coating her dark arms while she rolled pieces of chicken, shaking her head and murmuring "Mm, mm, mm! ."

These memories are happy, uncomplicated, and I think they are a fair assessment of my experience as a beloved, probably spoiled child, a precocious little mini-grownup, living among adults. Jack was Poppy – he went to work at a job site in the morning, popped into his office at midday to make phone calls, and came home tired, perhaps even gritty and sweaty, distracted, combing his hand through his hair at the dinner table. I remember that he was worried about money, always. I remember making elaborate preparations for his birthday dinner one year, with pictures, streamers, and signs, and feeling disappointed that my efforts produced only an inauthentic attempt at good cheer. He was self-employed now, so all the burdens of running a business rested on his shoulders.

Peggy was Mommy, going to school, perhaps still in the wood paneled station wagon I dimly remember, with the Red Cross symbol painted on its side, or planting pansies in her garden in a cotton dress, a pretty, slim woman in her forties, preoccupied. Though she left no written record of a mother besotted with her baby, as she did with Tommy, I think she was a loving mother. Twirling my curls in her fingers, she would tell me my hair was made of spun gold. I remember rocking with her in an antique rocker, playing with the silver bracelets on her arm on a sunny afternoon, or crawling into her bed in the early morning. When I got a "bride" doll for Christmas, she went into a fever of industry, making a trousseau for the doll, complete with knitted Chanel-inspired suits, resort clothes and a wedding dress. She seemed pleased with my creative efforts and she was maddeningly curious about my inner life, my imagined world as well as real. She wanted to know everything. I think she found me somewhat puzzling. At nap time, I would hear her talk on the phone to a friend about my odd penchant for daydreaming, losing myself so utterly in my thoughts that I would, like Ferdinand under the cork tree, sit in my chair at a school performance, oblivious to the rest of the class, who got up on cue to sing a song during a class play. Later, she would complain that I was "remote."

What I don't remember is any vestige of the madcap gamine that my father met in 1923, the girl who defiantly smoked on the roof at boarding school, who donned a black silk frock to marry impulsively on a June afternoon, who used her sewing class to make slippery satin lingerie in anticipation of a honeymoon in a stateroom on the train to Chicago. Nor do I recognize the sweet timid doe-eyed girl, the one who kissed Jack's grimy oil stained hands after a tire change, who, self-effacing, feared that she was too unsophisticated and unread, who so intoxicated my father. Though she could be impish, a tease, I don't remember a laughing, lighthearted or even sweet mother. Instead, as time went by, she was more often angry and unhappy – weepy, tired, and unhappy.

By the time I was seven or so, I was accompanying my mother to her weekly appointments with a psychiatrist at a prominent Philadelphia psychiatric hospital. While I sat swinging my legs on a couch in a cavernous yellow hallway, Peggy would disappear behind a closed door. Perhaps the secretary at the desk outside the door was supposed to keep an eye on me. Often my mother came out weeping and we would drive home in snuffling silence. I know that she had bad luck with her psychiatrists. The first committed suicide, and the second left his practice and his wife and moved to Maine with his secretary. Neither of these unfortunate events had a salutary effect on my mother's mental health. For a couple of years, on summer trips to Maine, Peggy would beg Jack to drive down the street past the Maine love nest of her second psychiatrist. "I think you're in love with him," Jack would grumble. Unwilling to try again, Peggy was left without professional support for what troubled her, though she managed to cadge prescriptions for barbiturates from two different doctors, and she probably became addicted to them. Her ruse was eventually uncovered by one of the doctors. Her self-diagnosis was that she was neurotic, and that's a good place to start. Peggy was as terrified of living as she was angry at her life.

Perhaps Peggy's worst legacy to both her children was the generalized terror she carried around with her. She was afraid of many things – policemen, doctors, trucks, black people (though she happily employed them), long trips, exposure to shame or embarrassment in so many settings .Peggy worried, always, that I would be "disloyal," and tell "secrets" about her. Her insecurity was pervasive. I remember a scene on the main shopping street in Chestnut Hill, the suburban Philadelphia village in which we then lived. She had just bought me a dress at a nice children's store, Nana's. Suffused with gratitude as we walked out of the store I reached up, threw my arms around her neck and kissed her. Clearly mortified, Peggy pulled away, stammered "Well! Selby! My goodness..." and looked around to see who had witnessed this display, wondering, I guess, if it had made her look foolish. I knew right away that I had made an awkward gesture that embarrassed her, and I was mortified, too.

But Peggy's terror was most potent at home, especially after Mary Vaughan stopped working for us and we were alone in the house. It was unclear exactly what frightened her so, but I can only guess that it was what I learned to fear – the dark, intruders, silence, random noises, being alone. Just as she had barricaded herself and Tommy in her bedroom during the war, she did the same with me when my father was out at an evening meeting (he was by then on a couple of boards). After dinner we would gather up our belongings and retreat behind the locked door of Peggy's room with whatever dogs were in residence. The door to the hall and the door to a balcony off the bedroom were fixed with slide bolts, but still the dark windows giving on to the balcony held menace in their blackness. Peggy would listen for stray sounds, and I would, and so would the dogs, alert, ready to growl protectively on our behalf. If she heard something, some creaking floorboard, Peggy would cry, and my heart would leap, waiting for another sound. We were no comfort to one another, Peggy and I. We didn't hug each other or huddle together, but each hovered in our own private terror. I have a memory, or perhaps it's a memory of a nightmare, in which Peggy sent me out to check that all the doors were locked. I crept into the dark hall (why didn't I turn on the light?) and down the stairs into the impenetrable gloom of the living room. The stairwell down to Jack's office opened in front of me holding unknown evils in its black depths. The front door required a treacherous trip across the living room, past furniture behind which there might be danger lurking. There, I was horrified to find the top half of a French door open and the curtains moving in the night wind. I think I have never been more frightened than I was on those nights. In dreams I still find myself in that living room, a breeze coming from somewhere and the air alive with menace, wondering what dark terror lurks just beyond my view, just out of earshot.

In the summer, Peggy and I went to my grandmother's cottage in Spray Beach with Jackie Barnes and her daughter, Barbara. Our fathers would come down on weekends, and while Jack would join us in the house, Barbara's father would stay down the road at the Spray Beach Hotel, and we would climb splintery, cobwebby back staircases to wake him up in the morning. We spent our days at the beach, and in the evening Barbara and I would play, our skin dark and hot, while our mothers had cocktails on the porch. Then the four of us would go to the clam bar, a kind of open garage, and perch on high stools at the counter. While we ate soda crackers dipped in cocktail sauce, the bartender deftly wielded a knife to pry open the clams, one by one, severing the muscle so that the slippery flesh of the clam could slide into our mouths with a little stream of icy clam juice. On Sundays Barbara and I would pad barefoot down the street to a little store on the corner, an old fashioned place with a sandy floor and a screen door that creaked and slapped shut behind us, to get the Sunday papers. Jack would read us the funnies as a reward for our efforts. Dagwood's hapless encounters with Blondie and Mr. Dithers, his boss, always made my father laugh, so it made me laugh, too.

I don't know how many years we repeated this summer ritual, but it was to end when Peggy began to suspect a romance between Jack and Barbara's mother. Jackie was, so far as I know, the first of Peggy's intimates whose friendship she would ultimately reject, punishing them for perceived disloyalty to her in favor of Jack. Other friends, too loyal to Jack, would fall by the wayside as time went by. To this day, Barbara and I speculate about the possibility that our parents – her mother and my father – had an affair. I'm sure it was a tempting idea. Jackie was a pretty woman with an infectious laugh, a lot of fun to be with. But in the end I doubt it. Jack was never to give up the hope of winning back Peggy's admiration, and I don't think an affair would have been worth the risk to him.

Jack had matured in the Navy. He was less of a dreamer now, less inclined to promise Peggy the moon, more aware of his own self-worth. He had his own business now, and was in charge of his own success. I think he was modestly successful – he seemed to always have work, but the bills continued to accumulate, weighing on him when he came home at night and mixed himself a stiff scotch before dinner.

I ice skated and took ballet lessons and went to summer camp and my life was full of the activities of lucky children. Nevertheless, Peggy raged about money through my childhood, and Jack made another drink, and they bickered as they had through Tommy's. But now she was able to add another crime – that he had abandoned her to go to war. Her suspicions about Jackie – or later various secretaries – would flare up intermittently for the rest of their lives. But money was always the dominant theme.

What was Jack and Peggy's problem with money? The fear of poverty was to inflict itself on an entire generation of Americans who survived the Depression, but in the face of the facts of Peggy and Jack's life, the fear seems, if not groundless, at least commonly shared by a whole generation. They were not alone, and they were better off than many. They were never without food on the table or even the hired help to put it there. Jack was never without work, though he seemed from childhood constitutionally unable to live within his means. Their friends were more comfortable and their siblings more successful. They both had grand expectations of life and these only added to their yearnings. And surely Peggy's thwarted ambitions and her unrelenting resentment fed the myth that their life was wanting.

Tommy had a powerful ambition to achieve the success that had eluded Jack, and soon after college, he was a young phenomenon on the fast track, catapulting to success in the business world, commuting to the grand New York City office of a company in the metals industry, his promotions advertised with Bachrach portraits in the *New York Times*. He married Fifi, the debutante whose party he had crashed as a sailor stationed on Long Island. She was an elegant girl who was shy, sensitive and cerebral, bright, self-sufficient and hardworking, an ideal partner for Tommy on his ascent up the corporate ladder.

Their wedding was as grand and sophisticated as anything Peggy could have dreamed of. They were married under the gothic arches of St. James' Catholic Church in Manhattan, attended by many velvet clad bridesmaids and ushers in morning suits. My friend Gretchen and I, two seven-year-olds, trailed behind as flower girls in mustard velvet gowns with little gold ballet slippers, mustard satin hats with gold net crowns, carrying nosegays. Parties before and after the wedding were held in gilded New York City clubs, and Peggy was both thrilled and terrified. Jack pulled off the event with raffish Irish charm.

Tommy and Fifi lived in increasingly grand houses in the rural suburbs of Philadelphia and began having children. Their oldest son of four, Christopher, was born when I was eight years old. Because they were nearby, Tommy was accessible to my parents in a crisis. The crises were usually about money, but occasionally my father would reach the limit of his patience with Peggy's inventory of recriminations and would leave the house, slamming the door behind him. Tommy would be called in as a moderator. Though I don't know what bills Tommy paid, I know he provided more support than was good for any of them, and I suspect they were for the things that would make Jack and Peggy's life more glamorous. I know he picked up responsibility for unpaid bills, and perhaps he underwrote their trips, finally, to Europe. He and Fifi were listed in the Social Register which, because it lists maiden names, school and college affiliations and club memberships, is a useful tool for people looking for others' credentials and social connections. At Peggy's urging, Tommy called upon his well-placed friends and got us into it, too. His life was exactly what Peggy and Jack had wanted for themselves.

That Peggy had social ambitions was already well established by the time I came along. Even her earliest letters from boarding school reveal a girl who viewed herself as uncommon, a cut above the normal run of society. And even when fate turned against them, as it so often did, with the lost baby, with the dream-diminishing impact of the Depression, and through the War, Peggy doggedly held on to the idea that they were better than their circumstances, hiring servants they couldn't afford, joining clubs, and sending Tommy on scholarships to private school amongst the elite of the elite in a rigid Philadelphia society. Though in the end, wealth wasn't what mattered, money would have improved their circumstances, would have made it easier to pull off an improvement in their status. I think that was the source of her unrelenting anger at Jack's inability to make enough money, and especially of her cruel rejection of his own dream of dignity, realized in his wartime experience.

But she was fooled by Tommy's social success. An engaging, athletic boy who mingled easily with the boys in his class, he had been embraced as a member of the club. But Philadelphia society was never as interested in money as it was in breeding, in the provenance of a family, their history, which Peggy was to learn when it came to me. With their own money this time, my parents enrolled me at a little elite girls' school, Miss Zara's School, where I made friends among a group of little girls from "good" families. With my friends Gretchen and Gerda, and their mothers, Peggy and I went to Friday Afternoon Children's Concerts at the Philadelphia Orchestra, a ritual upper class event (designed to acculturate the next generation) that made my mother nervous as a cat in the company of the other mothers. One spring, something happened over lunch and *zabaglione* at the Italian restaurant that was our ritual luncheon spot before the concerts, something that left my mother feeling snubbed, and we stopped going to the concerts the next year.

Nevertheless, those two mothers introduced my name to the invitation list of Wednesday afternoon dancing classes at the Cricket Club in Chestnut Hill, and from age seven to 11, my friends and I came home from school and changed into party dresses with sashes, Mary Janes and little socks and white gloves (the boys wore clean pants, miniature blue blazers and ties, and they too wore white gloves). We braided or combed or curled our hair again to catch the vagrant wisps, climbed in the car and drove to the Philadelphia Cricket Club. There, in the ballroom, with the waning winter afternoon sun casting wan rays across the tennis courts and through the gracious windows to the dance floor, we learned the box step and the waltz and foxtrot – and, for a raucous break, the Mexican hat dance – while a desultory combo played "Glow Little Glow Worm" and the "Blue Danube Waltz," framed by potted palm trees on the ballroom stage. Our teachers were upper class ladies dressed in tasteful, slim black dresses, who were there to reinforce the good manners we were presumably learning at home. We would extend our hands and curtsey (or in the case of boys, bow) to each of them as we arrived and departed, and they would ensure that all boys crossed the room to pick a partner, and that no girl was left out.

Peggy's social ambitions would inadvertently deal me, at age thirteen, a vicious blow. Wednesday afternoon dancing class was in fact the first step in a carefully orchestrated vetting process, a series of increasingly narrow thoroughbred paddocks through which the select young of Philadelphia were destined to pass. On our side of the Schuylkill River, we went to the Wednesday afternoon classes through sixth grade. A similar series was held for eligible children across the river on the Main Line (a code term for Philadelphia's upper class western suburbs). In seventh grade we went through the first winnowing process to gain entry to Miss Lockwood's dances, held in the city for 7th and 8th grade children from upper class enclaves on both sides of the River. Next in the series were Friday Evening dances, for 9th and 10th graders, and Saturday Evening dances for the wellborn young in 11th and 12th grades.

In *The Perennial Philadelphians,* Nathaniel Burt describes the dancing classes.

For girls a far more bloodcurdling and elaborate tribal rite of passage has been devised – the debut and all the preliminary hurdles of the Dancing Classes. A boy's social life might conceivably be made or marred by his school-college-fraternity affiliations, but a girl has to go to dancing classes.

He goes on. *The transfer from one dancing class to the next represents each time a social hurdle, since each has a different committee, and attendance at one does not guarantee an invitation to the next, though it helps. A certain amount of pruning goes on during the process, and those girls who make the finish, or the Saturday Evening, about ninety of them at any time, are pretty well qualified as socially eligible.*

The dancing class committees were, Burt noted, *"Of all Philadelphia's boards,... unquestionably the most socially powerful."*

The gates began to close for me after Miss Lockwood's. After eighth grade, my friends' mothers managed to get me invited to two of five Friday evenings a season, a blow in itself, but after tenth grade it was understood that they had exhausted their influence and that I would not go to the Saturday evenings, or the ultimate paddock, the Assembly, where the daughters of the most social families would be invited as debutantes. However gently, I was winnowed out, and it was as gently handled as the mothers could manage, I knew what it meant and so did my friends. It was a humiliation both my mother and I felt keenly. My friends were always loyal and inclusive, and my social life did not suffer except for the fact that I could not be with them in the most exclusive settings. And in my adolescent mind, there was social stigma attached to that.

I think my father was wounded for me and angry, for once, at Peggy for starting down that path with me. Peggy had been naïve. She was chastened, wounded for herself, too.

Our social faux pas may have aggravated Peggy's relationship with me, but I think Peggy, given her own childhood history, was never going to find it easy being a mother to an adolescent daughter. She had suffered too many wars with her own mother to trust a relationship with me. Besides, I think as I got older my mother did not find in me a kindred spirit. I was more sober and serious than the defiant girl she had been. And I was wary of her. She became more pathologically needy as she grew older, requiring company to go everywhere from the grocery store to the hairdresser, complicating our lives with obsessive rituals. She wanted to know everything, listened in on phone calls, sat at the top of the stairs so she could eavesdrop on conversations in the kitchen. She clutched at my father and me to reassure herself of her control over us, endlessly delaying departures until she had packed her jewelry in her purse and a bucket of ice in case she got a headache in the car, breaking into tears when prodded to just put on her coat and go out the front door.

Though I resisted (and bitterly resented) her increasing demands for attention, I was not romantically rebellious, as she had been at fifteen. She loved my friends Gretchen and Barbara, both spirited girls who were willing to get into trouble. I was not, it's true – mischief frightened me. Peggy once wondered aloud why they were my friends. "They're so much fun," she said.

Jack, on the other hand, had less complicated feelings for me. We were kindred spirits, silently complicit, suffering from a reflexive fear of Peggy's anger, a fear that kept us from doing what needed to be done. On a long dreamed-for trip to Europe the summer before my senior year at school, Peggy broke her ankle in the cobbled courtyard of a Paris hotel. Because she was afraid of doctors, she refused to go to the hospital and instead of taking charge, instead of hiring a taxi and taking her to the hospital, Jack and I froze. For three days my father and I sat in our hotel room, paralyzed, as crazy as she was, really, reading our books while winged Victory stood waiting for us at the head of the stairs at the Louvre, the fabled stained glass windows of La Sainte Chapelle glittered like jewels in the French sun, and glass topped boats slid along the Seine in the shadow of Notre Dame. My mother, propped up in bed, railed at us for our silence, for not caring enough about her discomfort. She wanted us to do something, but what? So we did nothing until our hotel booking ran its course.

When I left for college Jack wept with grief.

Just before that trip to Europe, in the spring of 1960, the house on Fleming Road was gutted by fire, before Jack and Peggy had even finished paying off that 20-year mortgage from Western Savings Fund Society. On a May day when the three of us were in the city together getting our first passports, a routine furnace

339

cleaning in the tiny basement room off the garage sent a few sparks wafting into attic space containing old papers, clothes, toys, Jack's photographic equipment, and an accumulation of Tommy's childhood schoolwork. There they smoldered in the empty house, finally shooting through the roof with flames fifteen feet high. The walls were still standing, charred, when we came home, but the roof was gone. Books and photos and paintings had been saved by firemen and brave neighbors. Some of my old stuffed toys salvaged from the attic lay smoldering and discarded on the lawn, and though I was sixteen by then, almost ready to leave home, the sight of those old toys was haunting and sad. Furniture and curtains still inside reeked of smoke, and phonograph records were melted over the edges of the window seat as if in a Salvador Dali painting. Many of the letters now in my hands have blackened corners and smoke stains from flames that came very close to destroying this record of my family's story.

With insurance reimbursements, the house was rebuilt over the summer of 1960, but we would never live in it again. By that time, Jack and Peggy had bought and renovated a carriage house in Chestnut Hill, a tonier suburb of Philadelphia. Instead of selling or renting that house, as originally planned, we moved into it, and sold the house on Fleming Road. For me it was a positive move, nearer to school and my friends, more at the center of my social life in my senior year at school. Now it makes me sad to think of the loss to Jack and Peggy, but especially to Jack, of the house they built out of their own imaginations and hopes.

After I left for college, I never lived at home again except during vacations. I think their life was full, and I think, with Tommy's help, their money worries diminished. They still had many friends, with whom they had parties. Peggy held on to the increasingly run down shore house at Spray Beach, though they rarely stayed there. Tommy's boys, growing up around them, were a source of pride.

In 1968, I married a man who, like me, had a complicated relationship with aristocratic Philadelphia. His social position was better established than mine, in that his mother had married for the second time into an old Philadelphia family and he, as the stepson, had been swept into a secure position. He and I shared an attachment to, coupled with a resentment of, the whole system. Peggy got to plan a wedding with all the trimmings for me, and it was lovely, but she was, frankly, terrified of my in-laws.

In her sixties, Peggy retired from teaching and became increasingly reclusive, though she talked to her old friends on the phone. Like her mother, she spent most of her life in their bedroom, dominating the household with diminishing ferocity. Jack worked for the rest of his life, in later years advising and drawing up plans for Tommy's development projects. He was happy at work – Tommy gave him engineering design projects he was pleased to tackle, and supervision over their execution. The workmen fell in love with Jack, and Tommy, too, was happy to have his utterly reliable, trustworthy father, the one who had missed all those school football games, at his side.

At home, Jack retreated into a kind of frustrated meekness. He was still writing poetry. He didn't like aging, and he wrote this poem for his 70th birthday:

Cathode

Seventy.
Seventy years of age, I mean
Three score and ten
Man's allotted span
I don't like it.

Trouble is, I feel the same inside,
I think the same inside,
As ten – no, twenty years ago.
(I think)

White hair and seamed face
Did I win the meet and lose the race?
I find a not so subtle change
In manners toward me,
My children feel I shouldn't paddle.
Fiddle-faddle!
Dropped a quarter in a store
Girl scout of fifty beats me to the floor..
Humiliating!
I spot my buddies in the supermarket,
Plodding along with shopping carts
Behind their wives,
Poor bastards.
Why can't I rush to meetings,
And use words like "viable"
And "parameter"
And have my secretary hold California
While I get London on another line
And thus be, still, constructive?
Out to pasture – over the hill
Doctors don't get you, freeways will.
At least let me be creative
Like welding old iron into strange forms
Or writing nonsense
Or baking bread.
No potting in a garden, please
I'm no pot.
My critique on gardens – all gardens
Is, "yeah – nice."
At confirmation, took the name of Patrick
Gonna change it now to Jerry-atric.
Senior citizen, in the golden years,
Aimed for Sunset City, in the Vale of Tears.

You say I don't adjust
You say adjusting is a must
You say "It's later than you think."
Perhaps. Invisible's the brink.
Tomorrow's just a new today.
Why must I while the hours away?
Got the Social Security blues
Heads they win – tails you lose.
Interlode
Think again, fella.
You're walking aren't you?
You're wealthy – in experience – and love.
Not yet the slippered pantaloon
Nor yet that seventh age, sans everything.
Nor, (God postpone a little while)
Recycling with the earth.
Anode
Hello, Pollyanna!
I thought that second thought and must admit
It's good to be alive
To share, to talk, to see, to touch
To feel, to hear, to laugh
It's nice to be a grandfather
And I'm rather looking forward to
Greatgrandfatherdom.
My blessings? I just counted them.
Plenty blessings.
Ambivalent?
So's your old man.

Whatever disappointment Jack felt about his life he directed at himself. He was frustrated, befuddled by Peggy, but never bitter about her, never angry. When he was sick, it was Peggy he wanted at his bedside. When he read something funny in the *New Yorker*, he went upstairs to read it to Peggy, hoping to entertain her.

Peggy began to show symptoms of Parkinson's disease, which slowly took away her ability to manage the same motor skills she had so patiently worked on with all those children in her classrooms. And she slipped gradually into dementia. In her seventies, she broke both hips in separate incidents, and she became very thin and unsteady. Though we found daytime caretakers, Jack cared for her in the night, waking to take her to the bathroom, and sometimes they would both fall and Jack would arrive at Tommy's office the next day with a gash across his forehead. "They are a disaster waiting to happen," Tommy told me on the phone, and we persuaded Jack to let us install her directly in the nursing wing of a retirement community. It was, frankly, Peggy's worst nightmare. After years of combat with the people who loved her most, she feared she really would finally alienate us, and we would put her away in an institution, where she would keep her suitcase under her bed, waiting to die. The scene of her departure was almost that bad.

We sold the Chestnut Hill house soon after – that's where I found the box of letters – and Jack moved into an apartment in the same retirement facility.

They never stopped needing each other. Jack would go to work with Tommy in the morning, coming home to his apartment in the early afternoon for a nap. Two or three times each day he would go to the nursing floor to visit Peggy, and she would be ready to rail at him for not loving her enough, for warehousing her in this place. "Oh, Peggy," Jack would say, begging for forgiveness, holding her hand. It was crazy, really, his need for Peggy's approval, just as crazy as her need to punish him. It was exhausting to watch them, but I recognized that their connection, however crazy, was the one that most mattered in each of their lives.

I saw them out, each of them. I sat with Jack, then 84, in a hospital intensive care unit on the day he died, holding his hand while watching a concert on the television, in July 1985. I left too soon, though, and he died alone. I promised myself I would not make that mistake again. At Jack's funeral we read the poem he wrote for his own 80th birthday, less bitter and more plaintive than the one he'd written ten years before.

I don't want to be eighty
Please don't make me senile
Don't want to live in a rocker
Keep me young for awhile.
Let me see where I'm looking
Let me walk with no cane
May my laughter be easy
And my words not inane.
May I make contribution
To the world where I live
Let me still be productive
Not just take – but still give.
May my heart fill with kindness
May I help where I can
Let me love, and be loving
Let me stay still a man
Let me hear when I listen
Let me dance – let me run
When at last I'm a burden
Let me be a light one.

Peggy lived in the nursing unit for another four years. At first, she mustered her feisty self to make trouble as she had when she was a young girl. When Tommy and I came to tell her Jack had died, she sat up straight and, thinking of her former friend, then imagined rival for Jack's heart, said with clear malice, "So, was Jackie in the front pew at the funeral?" She would swing her arm at a passing cart loaded with pills, sending the cart over and scattering the pills, the result of some nurse's hard labors to sort patient dosages in individual paper cups. She invented a little white dog, who would sit beside her wheelchair, and we all pantomimed a circuit around the phantom dog. The nurses called her "Margaret" and she sneered at their ignorance, perversely pleased that they didn't know she was called Peggy.

Tommy always lifted her spirits – he always had. Unlike Tommy, I was still timid and fearful of her, reluctant to get into confrontations, resentful of her voracious neediness, all qualities she disdained in me. I didn't like going to see her – it depressed me – so I didn't go enough.

I wasn't aware that I missed her absence as a mother to me, now that I was a mother myself. One day, though, as I hoisted her out of the car on an outing, she looked at me appraisingly and said, "You are stronger than you look." I felt bathed in maternal recognition and approval, and I could have wept with joy.

With Parkinson's disease, Peggy lost the ability to talk which, frankly, made her easier to be with, but she still knew how to deliver a message. The last time I took her out, I drove her onto the pretty campus of a private school she knew well, and we sat in the car while I offered her a chocolate milkshake – a favorite treat of hers – with a straw. I held the cold sweating cup and put the straw in her mouth, but she wouldn't suck, instead staring at me impassively, with what I could not help but recognize as a last trace of defiance. Sometimes Peggy confused me with my childhood friend Sophie, and her face would be transformed by a charming smile. To me as Sophie, she would become winsome and hospitable.

On the day that Peggy died, my sister-in-law, Fifi, and I sat on either side of her emaciated form, holding her hands until she took her last breath. She hated doing things alone and I felt that she had waited for us. I felt proud that she entrusted me with that moment.

2011

Coda

Twenty years later, Tommy died. He was the hardest to let go of. My brother, my ally, my advocate. So here I am, on my own, figuring out the lessons of the past. One thing I know is that the apple doesn't fall far from the tree.

The dancing class experience made me an awful snob, by which I mean that whether I embrace them or not, I am acutely well trained in the values of Philadelphia's upper class. I know good names and good clubs and good schools and I know the difference between wealth and breeding. Though it hurt, and I resented it, I knew when my mother tried too hard or wore the wrong clothes, or when her anxiety betrayed her. I knew that my father's self-effacing charm won him friends but not status. I spent a career working with private schools, schools founded to sustain the very class system that had set me aside. I became an insider, an expert in the tiniest details and most intimate gossip surrounding these institutions devoted to training privileged children for leadership. Private schools are now more democratic, but the sense

347

of privilege lingers and in my career I put myself right in the center of it. As interesting as it was to be working with schools, which are mostly noble institutions, driven by idealistic missions, there was a kind of masochism to my choices that I think I have finally shed.

Tommy managed to thrive in "old" Philadelphia, though I suspect under some suspicion. I remember an in-law of mine mouthing "dirty money" to his wife as she met Tommy at a cocktail party. An imposing physical presence, tall, overweight, bursting out of his pink shirts and Brooks Brothers ties, he was bright and intense with a big personality, but not without rough edges. The old rules notwithstanding, Tommy relied on money to assure himself of status, just as he used his money to take care of all of us. Tommy's drive to make even more money, and faster, ultimately led him to invest in increasingly risky business ventures that drove him into perilous financial straits. To the end of his life, he lived well, but in the background remained on a treadmill, just ahead of the bill collectors, and just short of the deal that would make millionaires of his sons.

He and I were both ambitious for our children. They were to be educated in the best available private schools, and Tommy's, he hoped, would be financially care-free, unlike himself as a child. He imagined all of them riding high as financial wizards, cutting crafty deals, just as he was trying to do himself. Just as social acceptance was my brass ring, wealth was his.

A yearning for money has haunted me, too. In my first marriage, I did a perfect imitation of Peggy, spending a couple of decades seething with anger at my husband, a good person who grew up with privilege, but who had trouble keeping a job and generating a sufficient income stream. Like my mother, I built a career of my own – and I tip my hat to her for finding paid work that she was good at – but still the money was never enough. I have been careless with money, like Jack, and my reach has exceeded my grasp. Like my mother, I am capable of using conflict to reassure myself of the intensity of my relationships.

Those truths notwithstanding, life has been good to me in a successful second marriage to someone who loves me in spite of myself, and daughters who are good mothers and busy, productive women of their age.

I understand now that in reading the letters I also wanted to come to terms with my mother. I wanted to love Peggy – she was my *mother*. One of the things that happens to a child of a family dominated by dysfunction is that we learn not to trust our own perceptions of reality. I needed to figure it out, *Was* my mother crazy or was the fault mine - was I an insensitive, ungrateful, passive, remote daughter, as she thought? *Did* I treat her cruelly, misuse her, fail to love her enough? I'm clear now about my father, having read their correspondence, he never abandoned his attachment to her, and he never deserved the recriminations she showered on him.

I'm also clearer about myself now. I do, of course, love my mother, but I feel released from the guilt I have carried, the weight of disloyalty because I was not capable of unquestioning filial love for her. My mother may have suffered from a borderline personality disorder. She experienced some of the classic causes, including rejection as a child, the traumatic loss of her baby, and some of the classic symptoms – fearfulness, terror of abandonment, debilitating self-absorption, delusions of grandeur, a need to strike at and then cling to the people closest to her. I understand her better. I don't think she ever had a chance to be at peace with herself or the world. She had a terrible start, and she had some very bad luck. But she was not easy to love, she was cruel to my father, and our family life was too much about her. I don't have to love all of that.

But of all the legacies that we inherited from Peggy and Jack, especially an ability to communicate that sets us free, I think our biggest legacy was this ferocious capacity for love.

I wish I had known that bad girl and romantic boy who had so many hopes, who fought so hard for the American dream, a dream that eluded them. I wish I could reassure them that in the end, with all the heartache and with all the hard work, they did a good job raising a family that knows how to carry on. I think they did. I think they did.

THE END

BIBLIOGRAPHY

To put Jack and Peggy's letters in the context of their times and circumstances, I found the following books very helpful:

Allen, Frederic Lewis, *Only Yesterday: An Informal History of the 1920's,*
  © 1931, Harper Collins Perennial Classic

Baltzell, E. Digby, *Philadelphia Gentlemen: The Making of a National Upper Class*
  © 1971, 1989, Transaction Publishers

Barry, John M, *Rising Tide, The Great Mississippi Flood of 1927 and How it Changed America*
  © 1997, Simon and Schuster

Burt, Nathaniel, *The Perennial Philadelphians: The Anatomy of an American Aristocracy*
  © 1963, 1999, University of Pennsylvania Press

Camburn, Robert S., *The Story of Greater Glenside,* © 1977, Montgomery Publications,
  for the Glenside Free Library

Eisenhower, John S.D., with Eisenhower, Joanne T., *Yanks, The Epic Story of the American Army in World War I,* © 2001, The Free Press

Fass, Paula S., *The Damned and the Beautiful, American Youth in the 1920s*
  © 1977 Oxford University Press

Huie, William Bradford, *Can Do! The Story of the Seabees,* © 1944, E.P. Dutton & Co.

Huie, William Bradford, *From Omaha to Okinawa, The Story of the Seabees,*
  © 1945, Naval Institute Press

Jordan, Philip D., *Catfish Bend – River Town and County Seat: An Informal History of*
  Burlington, Iowa 1836-1900, © 1975, Craftsman Press Inc., Burlington, Iowa

Kreisman, Jerold J., M.D., and Straus, Hal, *I Hate You – don't leave me: Understanding the*
  Borderline Personality, © 1989, Avon Books

Kyvig, David E., *Daily Life in the United States 1920 to 1940: How Americans Lived Through*
  the 'Roaring Twenties' and the Great Depression, © 2002, Ivan R. Dee, Publisher

Lawson, Christine Ann, *Understanding* the *Borderline Mother*
  © 2000, Roman & Littlefield Publishers, Inc.

Marks, Percy, *The Plastic Age,* Bibliobazaar Reproduction Series

McElvaine, Robert S., *The Great Depression, America, 1929-1941*
  © 1984, 2009, Three Rivers Press

McPhee, John, *The Control of Nature,* © 1989, Farrar, Straus, Giroux

McLachlan, James, *American Boarding Schools, A Historical Study,*
  © 1970, Charles Scribner's Sons

Morley, Christopher, *Travels in Philadelphia,* © 1920, David McKay Company

Ochs, Stephen J., *Academy on the Patowmack, Georgetown Preparatory School 1789-1927,*
   1989, Georgetown Preparatory School

Twain, Mark, *Life on the Mississippi,* © 1848, Viking Penguin Edition, 1984

The UGI Circle, 1927, 1928, company newsletter of UGI Utilities, King of Prussia, PA

Yearbook, 76th Construction Battalion, U.S. Navy, 1946

Yearbook, *The Nineteen Twenty Three Cornellian, The Annual of Cornell University and Class*
   Book of the Senior Class, Cornell University, 1923

Zeitz, Joshua, *Flapper, A Madcap Story of Sex, Style, Celebrity, and the Women Who Made*
   America Modern, © 2006, Three Rivers Press

ABOUT THE AUTHOR

Selby McPhee was a staff writer and editor at schools, universities, and other educational institutions including Tufts University and the National Association of Independent Schools (NAIS), where she was marketing vice president. In addition to her administrative work, she was the editor of numerous institutional newsletters, magazines, and e-publications, and she served as chapter author of an NAIS book on school marketing.

As a freelance writer, McPhee has published articles in a variety of magazines and newspapers, including *Vermont Life, HighFidelity/Musical America, Independent School, Burlington (VT) Free Press,* and *IB World* (the International Baccalaureate magazine). While living in Vermont from 1970 to 1980, McPhee was innkeeper at a small ski lodge, manager of an attached condominium development, and producing director at the Stowe (VT) Playhouse.

Love Crazy, McPhee's first book, began to germinate in 1984, when she found a box of letters, marked with the admonition "to be destroyed unopened," in a closet at her parents' house.

McPhee, a graduate of Vassar College, grew up in Philadelphia, Pennsylvania. She lives with her husband in Maryland.

9 781625 530097